Law and Legalization in Transnational Relations

This volume addresses the emergence of multiple legal and law-like arrangements that alter the interaction between states, their delegated agencies, international organizations and non-state actors in international and transnational politics.

Political scientists and legal scholars have been addressing the 'legalization' of international regimes and international politics, and engaging in interdisciplinary research on the nature, the causes and the effects of the norm-driven controls over different areas and dimensions of global governance. However, the perspectives on the essence of legalization still diverge.

This book claims that the emergence and spread of legal and law-like arrangements contributes to the transformation of world politics. It argues that 'legalization' does not only mean that states co-operate in more or less precise, binding and independent regimes, but also that different types of non-state actors can engage in the framing, definition, implementation and enforcement of legal and law-like norms and rules, e.g. in terms of private standard setting or certification schemes. To capture these diverse observations, the volume provides an interpretative framework that includes the increase in international law-making, the variation of legal and legalized regimes and the differentiation of legal and law-like arrangements. This book will be of interest to students and researchers of international politics, international relations and law.

Christian Brütsch is Senior Research Fellow at the Centre for Comparative and International Studies at the University of Zurich, Switzerland. **Dirk Lehmkuhl** is Assistant Professor at the Centre for Comparative and International Studies at the University of Zurich, Switzerland.

Routledge advances in international relations and global politics

Law and Legalization in Transnational Relations

Edited by Christian Brütsch
and Dirk Lehmkuhl

Routledge
Taylor & Francis Group

LONDON AND NEW YORK

First published 2007
by Routledge
2 Park Square, Milton Park, Abingdon, Oxon OX14 4RN

Simultaneously published in the USA and Canada
by Routledge
605 Third Avenue, New York, NY 10017

Routledge is an imprint of the Taylor & Francis Group, an informa business

© 2007 Selection and editorial matter, Christian Brütsch and
Dirk Lehmkuhl; individual chapters, the contributors

Typeset in Times by Wearset Ltd, Boldon, Tyne and Wear

British Library Cataloguing in Publication Data
A catalogue record for this book is available from the British Library

Library of Congress Cataloging in Publication Data
A catalog record for this book has been requested

ISBN13: 978-0-415-42328-1 (hbk)
ISBN13: 978-0-203-96442-2 (ebk)

Contents

Illustrations

Figures

Tables

Contributors

Mathias Albert is Professor of Political Science at the University of Bielefeld (Germany).

Bas Arts is Professor at the Forest and Nature Conservation Policy Group at Wageningen University (The Netherlands).

Dorothée Baumann is Ph.D. candidate at the University of Zürich and is currently working for the European office of the Fair Labor Association in Geneva (Switzerland).

Christian Brütsch is Senior Research Fellow at the Center for Comparative and International Studies at the University of Zürich (Switzerland).

Edward S. Cohen is Associate Professor of Political Science and Chair of the Department of Political Science and Sociology at Westminster College in New Wilmington, Pennsylvania (USA).

William D. Coleman holds the Canada Research Chair in Global Governance and Public Policy and is Director of the Institute on Globalization and the Human Condition at McMaster University (Canada).

Dieter Kerwer is Assistant Professor of International Politics at the Technical University in Munich (Germany).

Sonja Kierzek is Research Fellow at the Chair for Accounting and Auditing at the University of Mannheim (Germany).

Dirk Lehmkuhl is Assistant Professor at the Center for Comparative and International Studies at the University of Zürich (Switzerland).

Errol Meidinger is Professor and Vice Dean of Law for Research, Adjunct Professor of Sociology at the State University of New York at Buffalo (USA), and Honorary Professor of Forestry and Environmental Science at the University of Freiburg (Germany).

Mark Pieth is Professor of Criminal Law and Criminology at the University of Basel (Switzerland).

Austina J. Reed is Ph.D. candidate at the Department of Political Science, McMaster University (Canada).

Erich Schanze is Professor of Private and Business Law, and Director, Institute for Comparative Law at the Philipps-Universität Marburg (Germany), Professor II at the Faculty of Law at the University of Bergen (Norway) and Senior Lecturer in Law and Economics at the University of St Gallen (Switzerland).

Andreas Georg Scherer is head of Institute for Organization and Theories of the Firm and holds the Chair for Foundations of Business Administration and Theories of the Firm at the University of Zürich (Switzerland).

Jens Wüstemann is Professor of Accounting and Auditing at the University of Mannheim and Executive Dean of the MBA Programme at the Mannheim Business School (Germany).

Acknowledgements

On the long and winding road to this volume, we were happy to receive support from a number of people and institutions. We first of all wish to express our appreciation to all of the contributors for their efforts to explore patterns of complex legalization and for their willingness to be with us all the long time of the making of the volume. We also thank the original participants at the 2002 workshop on Legalization in Zürich who are no longer involved in the final product but who provided substantial input to our debate. We thank the Center for Comparative and International Studies (CIS) at the University of Zürich, and the Swiss Federal Institute of Technology, Zürich for its financial support for the workshop in 2002. Dieter Ruloff as head of the Institute of Political Science at the University of Zürich gave us all the support and leeway we needed to pursue our idea of the conference and the edited volume. Yvonne Rosteck as the former executive secretary of the CIS was of the utmost importance in the organization of the conference and in the early days of the book project. Finally, we are grateful to Staempfli Publishers for permission to reprint the contribution by Erich Schanze. Schanze's contribution appeared in P. Nobel (ed.) (2005) *International Standards and The Law*, Stämpfli Publishers Ltd, Berne, 83–103.

1 Introduction

Christian Brütsch and Dirk Lehmkuhl

For much of the last century, the 'realists' among the political scientists argued that international politics is determined by the struggle for power and peace. They acknowledged that international law could be instrumental to the exercise or the preservation of power. But they claimed it had no significant impact on the politics among nations in what they considered an essentially anarchical world. However, already in the late 1960s, critics observed that international relations were changing. Institutionalists argued that states were likely to pool or surrender parts of their sovereignty if they believed that transferring authority to more or less formalized regimes would reduce the costs for the management of increasingly complex cross-border interdependencies. The English School linked the emergence of normative structures and institutions to the historic development of the international society that conditioned interactions within the international states system. Constructivists showed that norms and rules shaped the behaviour and the identity of political actors.

The economic, social and political globalization of the past few decades has accentuated the role of international norms and rules. Today, legal controls may still be weak with regards to interventions against potential threats to international security. But on the whole, the politics among nations are no longer measured against the principles and provisions of the UN Charter alone. Trade policies are subject to the norms and rules laid out in the GATT/WTO Agreements, labour standards are set by the ILO Declaration on Fundamental Principles and Rights at Work, 'the most serious crimes of international concern' can be prosecuted according to the Rome Statute for an International Criminal Court.

At the same time, the fragmentation of political agency and the diffusion of legal or law-like arrangements at different levels and across different dimensions of global governance have blurred the boundaries between the international states system, the international community and transnational society. Thus, the international community agreed upon a new generation of treaties and conventions framed and wanted by civil society rather than states, such as the Kyoto Protocol against global warming and the Ottawa Convention for a Comprehensive Landmine Ban. Besides, many of the more traditional regimes that were established to solve collective action problems have assumed legal or law-like characteristics that affect not just the behaviour of states, but also that of sub-state or non-state actors. Moreover, non-state actors are increasingly engaged in the creation, implementation and monitoring of more or less binding norms and rules. Thus, even though the terms of engagement vary, the WTO, the ILO and the ICC rely on the contributions of the entrepreneurs, activists, advocacy groups, professional associations and experts that constitute 'civil society'. Lastly, a growing number of non-state actors have engaged in the creation, implementation, monitoring and enforcement of autonomous law-like arrangements ranging from accounting standards to forest certification schemes or codes of conduct to fight corruption.

Political scientists and legal scholars have addressed these moves to law both in terms of a 'legalization' of international regimes and in terms of a 'juridification' of international politics.[1] They have engaged in interdisciplinary research on the nature, the causes and the effects of the norm-driven controls over different areas and dimensions of global governance. However, the perspectives on the essence of legalization still diverge.

A prominent group of – mainly US American-based – political scientists and lawyers suggest extending the rationalist institutionalist research agenda and to interpret the 'legalization of world politics' in terms of the degrees of precision, obligation and delegation of international regimes (Abbott and Snidal 2001; Abbott and Snidal 2002; Goldstein et al. 2001). In Europe, Zangl and Zürn argue that legalization should be considered a 'building block of global governance' that facilitates the shift from interest- and consensus-oriented bargaining to norm-oriented legal procedures that help structuring and resolving disputes about the interpretation and implementation of different elements of governance 'by, with and without governments' in a more rational manner (Zangl and Zürn 2004). Others are less optimistic. Hurrell acknowledges that 'the rhetoric of interests, of regimes, of governance mechanisms' has been 'crucial to increased dialogue between international relations and international law', but denounces its tendency to obscure the 'the equally important links between law and power' (Hurrell 2000: 329).

Not surprisingly, the debate about the epistemic relevance of legalization has not been resolved. Rationalist institutionalists argue that legalization can explain the transition to co-operation, and suggest analyzing when either 'soft' or 'hard' forms of legalization can be expected to better resolve collective action problems (Abbott and Snidal 2002). Zangl and Zürn suggest examining whether the legalization of procedural elements – adjudication, enforcement, law-making – and the socialization of norms contribute to the constitutionalization of the complex architecture of global governance (Zangl and Zürn 2004).

In this volume, we do not attempt to pre-empt the debate by opting for one rather than the other proposal. Indeed, we believe that despite the extensive coverage of the different areas and aspects of legalization, the overt assumptions and the relatively narrow analytical focus that characterize many of the most prominent approaches provide an inadequate picture of the impact legalization has on world politics. Research on the legalization of international regimes captures the emergence of an increasingly 'objective' system of norms and rules, but ignores the emergence of transnational legalities, and struggles to acknowledge the asymmetries of power and the distortions produced by the more or less clouded shadow of hegemony. And while the analysis of the spreading of legal or law-like procedures helps us to interpret the transformations of political agency 'beyond' the state, the assumption that the legalization of international affairs and the socialization of norms and rules (should) lead to a constitutionalization of global governance tends to underestimate both the murkiness of legalization and the relevance of the capability of specific actors to influence outcomes and to determine which norms and rules eventually succeed in shaping different areas and dimensions of global governance.

The main aim of this volume is to re-frame the debate on legalization and to extend research on the different dimensions that characterize the 'complex legalization' of international affairs. Its ambition is to provide an interpretative framework that enables us to capture different moves to law and to map the paths different actors take to advance or detour legalization. Thus, rather than suggesting that research on complex legalization should either confirm the realist claim that power relations determine the reach, scope and role of international norms and rules, extend the rationalist institutionalist focus on the transition to co-operation, or develop constructivist research on the socializing factors of norms, we suggest that, each and any of these claims may provide bits and pieces to explain different dimensions of complex legalization. The puzzle we try to resolve is how and to what extent international affairs are transformed by overlapping, often competing and potentially conflicting legalities that emerge in distinct settings, have different law-like properties, and have different policy implications

The contributions in this volume document that many of the legal or law-like arrangements that have emerged in the past few decades cannot be explained in terms of a changing order of preferences of the usual suspects involved in creating regimes. Legalization has transformed – and/or benefited from the transformation of – the institutions of global governance and the broader frameworks of agency that enable different actors to participate and operate in world politics. To a certain extent, the process may even modify the power relations and structures on which these frameworks are built.

On an analytical level, the case studies in this volume seek to interpret the manifold legalities that shape international affairs in terms of the increase, variation and differentiation of international law making and implementation in the broader context of 'complex' legalization by:

- identifying legal and law-like arrangements that address specific problems in different areas of international/transnational affairs;
- reconstructing the dynamics leading to the emergence of such arrangements, in particular with regards to the actors and policies that contribute to the framing, implementation and monitoring of these arrangements;
- addressing the co-evolution and the interaction among different legal or law-like arrangements.

The contributions to this volume are organized as follows:

In the next chapter, Brütsch and Lehmkuhl introduce the notion of 'complex legalization', arguing that research on legalization should not only explain when more or less precise, binding and independent regimes facilitate international co-operation or look for legal law-like arrangements that may, eventually, contribute to a 'constitutionalization' of global governance. Challenging state-centred interpretations of the role of law in world politics, they propose to extend research on 'complex legalization' to capture a broader range of legal and law-like arrangements affecting both international and transnational relations: research should acknowledge that 'complex legalization' includes different moves to law that lead to an increase of international law-making, a variation of legal regimes and a differentiation of legal and law-like arrangements. On the analytical level, Brütsch and Lehmkuhl suggest abandoning theoretical parsimony for a pluralistic framework of interpretation, and propose to direct research on complex legalization to capture how legal and law-like arrangements contribute to the framing and management of the increasingly complex and thick interdependencies that link states, their delegated agencies and private actors at different levels of governance and across different geographical locations.

In their discussion of the development, endorsement and enforcement of international accounting and disclosure standards for publicly traded companies, Wüstemann and Kierzek document a first controversial dimension of transnational legalization. They show that the International Accounting Standards Board's efforts to define a common core of globally valid accounting and disclosure standards are clearly conditioned by the competition between the world's two major trading blocs: the European Union and the United States of America. They also show that 'private' forms of legalization are not necessarily independent from public authority, but may well be a tool in policymaking. But they also highlight a dilemma: to be credible in the business community, private standard setters have to balance the demands of their two most important interlocutors – although the bundled weight of the US capital markets puts US regulators in a favourable position. Wüstemann and Kierzek conclude that the transatlantic divide does not only prevent the emergence of global accounting standards. It exacerbates differences in national regulatory philosophies and implementation patterns and thereby contributes to legal uncertainty within the EU.

In his account of the harmonization of secured transactions, Cohen explores the dynamics of legalization with regards to the transformation of private international commercial law. He illustrates the complex patterns of interaction that enable legal experts to cross the boundaries between domestic and international markets and thereby blur the distinction between public and private legal authority. In fact, according to Cohen, legalization is the result of the exchange between legal experts and national and international institutions aimed at settling divergences about the meaning and effectiveness of individual principles and norms. Cohen also notes that in these exchanges, power relations and power differentials play a significant role – a point in case being the different gravity of

US, European or Asian financial markets or the willingness and capability of national regulators to export their own regulatory frameworks.

According to Pieth, the 'Wolfsberg Anti-Money Laundering Principles' and the 'Partnering against Corruption Initiative' reveal both the potential and the drawbacks of private alternatives to international law. The Wolfsberg Principles emerged after a series of scandals struck the European banking sector and the prospect of a hardening of the traditionally rather soft mixture of legal instruments regulating money laundering became more probable at both the national and the international level. In this context, the major banks agreed that a self-imposed arrangement would minimize the risk of excessive regulatory costs. However, stained by competition, they struggled to agree on a common strategy to fight against transnational economic crime. This changed when two non-profit organizations became involved as intermediaries and helped to establish an atmosphere of trust amongst competitors. At an early stage, an exclusive strategy helped to establish a set of coherent principles that increasingly extended its reach and by now is incorporated into many national provisions.

Although the development of anti-corruption principles also adopted a multi-stakeholder approach with intermediaries displaying similar entrepreneurial capacities, the cross-sectoral nature of the problem made a more inclusive strategy necessary right from the beginning. Given the absences of the direct threat of hard public regulation, however, initial obstacles to co-operation among competitors were much harder to overcome. Both initiatives may serve as examples of how in sectors with existing significant public intervention, private parties provide genuine contributions that reach beyond public rules.

Coleman and Reed's discussion of the certification of organic agriculture offers a complimentary perspective on the linkages between public and private initiatives for legalization. Initiated by farmers to provide alternative agricultural products on local and domestic markets, organic agriculture has experienced a significant growth both in consumer demand and producer supply since the 1990s. With rising stakes, the internationalization of the markets for organic agriculture has undermined the legal framework controlling that organic agriculture be organic. According to Coleman and Reed, the initial pattern of private norm production, in which producer co-operatives established national networks that eventually defined international norms, has been complemented by government interventions at different levels. The parallelism of the extraterritorial extension of domestic arrangements and 'global' initiatives for legalization has created a range of overlapping and conflicting norms and rules. Different standards of organic agriculture, requirements for the accreditation of certification organizations and approaches to the certification of organic agriculture support and compete with each other. A series of contradicting provisions documents that global legalization does not necessarily imply a rationalization. Indeed, despite far reaching and often complimentary efforts, the core principles of governance for organic agriculture remain contested.

The co-ordination of and competition between different rules systems is also at the centre of Meidinger's account of the efforts of different transnational coalitions attempting to establish norms and principles for sustainable forest management. In what he describes as an example of 'competitive legalization', NGO-driven, industry-sponsored and government-supported initiatives have lead to the emergence of a 'set of multi-centered, competitive regulatory systems that are increasingly rule-permeated and changeable at the same time.' Meidinger finds similar developments in other areas in which certification matters, such as organic agriculture, mining, apparel and fisheries. In each of these cases, certification is part and parcel of an institutional environment in which private actors have succeeded in defining functioning systems of rule-making, adjudication and enforcement. However, in all cases, the co-existence of multiple legal and law-like arrangements also creates problems of coherence and coordination. Although Meidinger identifies a dialogue between these different legal or law-like systems, he shares Coleman and Reed's scepticism about a convergence at higher levels of rationalization.

In their comparison of 'how standards work' with regards to sustainable forest management on the one hand, and capital reserves of banks on the other hand, Arts and Kerwer discuss the operational side of global regulatory approaches and challenge the view that standardization should be considered a form of legalization. They make two substantial statements: first, they argue that the relative success of transnational standards essentially depends on the expertise that relevant stakeholders attribute to the standard setters, even though they acknowledge the fact that other explanatory factors, such as the problem structure of the respective sector do matter. Second, they identify standards as a specific instrument for the governance of transnational issues, corroborating the scepticism of other contributors in this volume and elsewhere (e.g. Brütsch and Lehmkuhl; Cohen; Finnamore and Toope 2001) to rely on the rational institutionalist interpretation of legalization. However, they challenge the analytical usefulness of 'complex legalization', arguing that distinct categories and approaches should be used to capture different aspects of transnational rule making.

In explicitly addressing the role of standards in processes of legalization from a practitioner's perspective, Schanze opens the volume's discussion section. Schanze suggests adopting a 'drafting perspective' to resolve some of the problems economic realism, international governance and New Institutional Economics face in accommodating 'law' and 'extra-legal' norms. Focusing on the question of when the drafter of a contract will opt for a legal rather than a non-legal norm, he first discusses the linkages between legal and 'extra-legal' norms, concluding that while domestic legal systems are usually designed to accommodate non-legal norms (including transnational standards) they also set limits to the inclusion of such norms. Stressing that these limits are usually set to guarantee substantial and incentive compatibility with domestic law, Schanze then shifts his analysis to the role they play in regimes, recalling that 'the most salient international transactional regimes such as franchise systems, international finance consortia or systems of production networks are composed of legal and extra-legal components'. In this context, the drafter of a commercial contract has to be able 1. to identify incentive compatibility and be sure to accommodate different interests with regards to substance, 2. to integrate (institutional) modules such as standards or model provisions in order to assure the functionality of a contract and, finally, 3. to facilitate the monitoring of compliance by stating the compatibility of the contract with relevant domestic or international law.

Albert's system-theoretical account suggests that while multi-dimensional and multi-faceted, complex legalization should be interpreted in terms of a single legal order, arguing that it takes place within *one* social system (the legal system) of world society. In Albert's view, legalization refers to both 'changing forms of the internal differentiation of the legal system of world society and, closely connected, new structures emerging within this system' and its structural coupling with other social systems. Thus, even though legalization takes place within a unique legal order, it does not have to be interpreted in terms of a uniform or hierarchically structured process. On the contrary:

> much of the vibrancy of the evolution of the global legal system takes place as a more or less 'spontaneous' law formation without the involvement of the political system at the interstices of the legal system and various function systems which exhibit an ever-increasing demand for legal regulations in an – in their perception – ever more complex globalized environment. It is in this sense that 'legalization', in relation to the political or other function systems of world society ... happens as a chaotic process of systems co-evolution (which is not even necessarily synchronized).

The main analytical benefit of translating the increase, variation and differentiation of law and law-like arrangements into a system-theoretical account is that it provides a robust and coherent conceptual framework in which a broad range of different but linked social phenomena can be integrated.

Scherer and Baumann start out with the assumption that the traditional understanding of the state as a unique source of norms is adequate neither in descriptive nor in normative terms. Focusing on the significance of the corporate social responsibility role for transnational companies, they challenge the dominant claim that firms should limit their responsibility to profit maximizing. Instead they suggest that the purposes and objectives of economic activities include the promotion of corporate citizenship, and infer that corporate efforts to create law-like arrangements to structure business in the global economy should be more than self-serving window dressing. However, after an extensive review of the current debates on traditional economic theories, stakeholder approaches and business and society research, Scherer and Baumann conclude that only a few of the more recent approaches vest transnational companies with a political responsibility to contribute to the global governance.

Note

1 In principle, we agree that '[s]emantically, "legalization" is the process of making legal, as in the phrase "the legalization of soft drugs", and would therefore seem to be more appropriate for the legislative process of law-making. The term "judicial" and its derivations is more apt to refer to the court-like procedures'. For the sake of terminological simplicity, however, we generally use legalization even when referring to developments which more strictly would qualify as juridification (de Bièvre 2003: 6). For similar reasons, we avoid a strict distinction between legalization and regulation. For discussion of the concept of regulation and its different interpretations see Black 2001.

Bibliography

Abbott, K. and Snidal, D. 2001 'Hard and Soft law in International Governance', in J. Goldstein, M. Kahler, R. O. Keohane and A.-M. Slaughter (eds) *Legalization and World Politics*, Cambridge, MA: The MIT Press.

Abbott, K. and Snidal, D. 2002 'Values and Interests: International Legalization in the Fight Aginst Corruption', *Journal of Legal Studies* XXXI: 141–178.

de Bièvre, D. 2003 'International Institutions and Domestic Coalitions: The Impact of the WTO in the EU' *European Consortium for Political Research (ECPR) Joint Sessions of Workshops, Edinburgh, 29 March–2 April 2003*.

Black, J. 2001 'Decentring Regulation: the Role of Regulation and Self-Regulation in a "Post Regulatory" World', *Current Legal Problems* 54: 103–146.

Finnamore, M. and Toope, S. J. 2001 'Alternatives to "Legalization": Richer Views of Law and Politics', *International Organization* 55(3): 743–758.

Goldstein, J., Kahler, M., Keohane, R. O. and Slaughter, A.-M. (eds) 2001 *Legalization and World Politics*, Cambridge, MA/London: The MIT Press.

Hurrell, A. 2000 'Conclusion: International Law and the Changing Constitution of International Society', in M. Byers (ed.) *The Role of Law in International Politics. Essays in International Relations and International Law*, Oxford: Oxford University Press.

Zangl, B. and Zürn, M. 2004 'Make Law, Not War: Internationale Verrechtlichung als Baustein für Global Governance', in B. Zangl and M. Zürn (eds) *Verrechtlichung – Ein Baustein für Global Governance?* Bonn: Dietz, 12–45.

2 Complex legalization and the many moves to law

Christian Brütsch and Dirk Lehmkuhl

The conceptual vantage point of this volume is to explore the 'legalization' of world politics in terms of a complex set of transformations creating a multitude of overlapping, at times complementary, at times contradictory legal realms, or 'legalities'. Its basic assumption is that the emergence and co-existence of multiple legalities alter patterns and features of international co-operation, modify the interactions between states and non-state actors, and contribute to the redefinition of agency and identity in world politics. In this chapter, we review different analytical approaches addressing different dimensions of international legalization, and integrate their findings in a common frame of reference that is broad enough to capture the increase in international law making, the variation of legal regimes, and the differentiation of legal and law-like arrangements, and, at the same time, focused enough to identify the politics of the many moves to law that characterize the 'complex legalization' of transnational relations.[1] We argue that only by combining these dimensions, can we fully appreciate the transformations of law and politics in the context of globalization.

The approach and scope of this volume differ from the research agenda proposed by Goldstein *et al.* (2001), which considers the investigation of the legalization of world politics as an extension of the rationalist–institutionalist research on the institutionalization of international co-operation. We agree that the 'legalization of world politics' can be interpreted in terms of the modification of specific properties of international regimes, their obligation, the precision of their rules and procedures, and the delegation of their interpretation, implementation and monitoring to third parties (Abbott *et al.* 2001: 17f). We share the authors' view that the degrees of obligation, precision and delegation of any regime may vary independently, and agree that international regimes can be classified in the 'multidimensional continuum' extending between the two 'ideal types' of institutionalized co-operation by identifying elements typically associated with the 'hard law' of fully legalized regimes such as the EU or the WTO, and elements typical of the 'soft law' that governs by and large informal regimes such as the Group of Seven (G7). The authors are right to contest that only '[h]ighly legalized arrangements ... will typically fall within the standard international lawyer's definition of international law', and convincingly argue that legal scholars and political scientists should be aware that soft law does affect state behaviour, and that opting for different types of legalization should be thought of in terms of the different strategies states adopt to tackle collective action problems (Abbott *et al.* 2001, Abbott and Snidal 2002). However, we do not think this is where the story ends.

The rationalist–institutionalist interpretation of legalization explains why states opt for soft rather than hard types of legalization. It assumes that the legal design of regimes can vary, but that the choice to create more or less obliging, precise and independent regimes ultimately depends on the (perceived) costs and benefits derived from using legalization as a means to facilitate co-operation or to enforce specific norms, rules, and procedures (Abbott and Snidal 2001). Yet, by limiting its focus on the idea that bargaining outcomes determining the degree of legalization of a regime depend on the capabilities and resources of the individual actors involved in its formation, the institutionalist interpretation gives an incomplete picture of the complex linkages between power and law that shape the role of law in international politics (Hurrell 2000). Indeed, the rationalist–institutionalist interpretation of legalization does not provide enough analytical leverage to identify when different strategies of legalization serve partisan interests or when legalization codifies or mystifies the working of structural power and hegemony. The frequent combination of soft and hard legal arrangements 'suggests that both form and content are relevant to the sense of legal obligation' (Shelton 2000: 4) that is necessary for legalization to modify state behaviour and patterns of international co-operation. The relationship between legalization and national interests remains obscure. Indeed, some critics claim that the systemic tension between norm-oriented and interest-based politics undermines the very hypothesis of a 'move to law'. They point out that under the veil of 'legalization', long standing principles of international law have been abandoned to make the structures of international conflict and co-operation more responsive to the interests of the powerful, 'multilateral' agreements that are accused of advancing a hegemonic order (Trachtman 1997; Wiener 1999).

Recent debates about the rules of war, the conditions of trade and the scope of international criminal jurisdiction have left little doubt that (national) interests, political power and brute force remain crucial to understanding the role of law in international affairs. However, despite scepticism about the relevance of legalization, the very debate as to whether or not pre-emptive warfare is compatible with international law suggests that legalization goes beyond what rationalists expect: it made clear that even powerful actors have to engage in legal arguments and reasoning to justify their actions. Indeed, one could argue that Carr's prediction that '[p]olitical power must be based on a co-ordination of morality and power' (Carr 1969: 97) should be amended: even in a constellation of unipolarity, the use of political power must be explained and defended in legal or law-like terms. If powerful actors – implicitly or explicitly – accept that 'certain "political" types of behaviour are foreclosed and other "legal" types are licensed and empowered' (Reus-Smit 2004b: 37), constructivists are certainly on track when they claim that a diffuse form of legalization – advanced through legal reasoning – is reshaping the nature of power politics.[2]

The dialectics between interests and norm-oriented and procedural incentives designed to modify state behaviour through international institutions and legal arrangements gain further analytical relevance if we consider the constructivist emphasis of the constitutive role that norms and institutions play in shaping political identity and agency. From a constructivist perspective, it is doubtful as to whether legalization can be explained in terms of the degree of obligation, precision and delegation through which regimes affect state behaviour without taking into account that legal arrangements mould political agency and identity 'beyond' the interactions within a regime or the bargaining processes that lead to its establishment. As Finnemore and Toope (2001) point out, it makes little sense to 'measure' legalization by the (formal) characteristics of the treaties and agreements that govern regimes without taking into account that legalization depends upon 'deeply embedded practices, beliefs and traditions of societies' that have 'shaped interactions among societies' for quite some time now (ibid.: 743). According to Reus-Smit (2004), any concept of legalization should there-fore embrace these social phenomena and articulate how they affect inter-national politics, and at least consider international customary law in explaining how the socialization of norms and law-like procedures affects international politics.

If the interests and the behaviour of states are shaped by norms and ideas, the strategic choices they make to resolve collective action problems through legal-ization are influenced by the social fabric in which they are embedded. In fact, extending the concept of legalization to include constructivist concerns about the definition of values and ideas provides additional analytical leverage to capture the dynamics that make norm-creation and implementation viable. However, we believe that even a combination of rationalist and constructivist explanations of state behaviour falls short of capturing how legal and law-like arrangements condition political agency by transforming political arenas, actors and inter-actions.

A first lead to understand the actual workings of legalization with respect to the implementation of international norms and rules emerges in recent research on compliance suggesting that legalization works best where the involved parties have had the opportunity to deliberate and agree upon norms, rules and procedures (Zürn and Joerges 2005; Neyer *et al.* 1999; Wolf and Zürn 1993). But even though the analysis of different patterns of compliance refines our understanding of the conditions for the implementation of international norms and rules, it provides little more than a glimpse on the role legalization plays in the transformation of international affairs. In particular, it lacks a coherent perspective on the role of non-state actors.

For a broader perspective, we have to turn to another proposal by Zangl and Zürn (2004), who interpret legalization in terms of the socialization of norm-oriented behaviour and distinguish different patterns of legalization according to their procedures for adjudication, enforcement and law-making, as well as their contribution to the constitutionalization of world politics.[3] Arguing that legaliza-tion cannot be interpreted without taking into account that traditional forms of governance by governments are making room for more complex modes of governance *by*, *with* and *without* governments, Zangl and Zürn follow constructivists in challenging the (narrow) rationalist assumption that legalization can be explained in terms of state preferences in the resolution of collective action problems (see also Zürn 1998: 166–180). However, rather than attempting to explain the conditions for the social construction of the preferences of states or the legal arrangements designed to condition their behaviour, Zangl and Zürn focus on the linkages between national, international, and transnational processes of norm-setting, implementation, and sanctioning, arguing that the socialization of norms and efforts aiming at the 'constitutionalization' of global governance both contribute to the emergence of a global order (Zangl and Zürn 2004).

We share many of Zangl and Zürn's key assumptions. Their analysis supports our view that the rational choices of states are neither the only nor the most important variables explaining the legalization of world politics. They, too, stress the relevance of private initiatives aimed at the creation and implementation of norms and rules affecting both state and non-state actors. However, despite these similarities, we have opted for a different approach to explore the legal and law-like arrangements that are emerging from the politics 'beyond' state – both descriptively and analytically. Rather than creating a single set of hypotheses to interpret different legal and law-like arrangements, we propose to deconstruct the different dimensions of legalization to account for the profound transformation of the linkages between law, politics and society. Instead of trying to identify a uniform pattern common to the different moves to law, we propose the use of different sets of criteria to explore and assess how distinct dimensions of 'complex' legalization affect different areas of global governance. And rather than associating legalization with the constitutionalization of global governance, we suggest thinking of the outcomes of complex legislation in terms of multiple, potentially overlapping, and possibly conflicting legal realms or 'legalities'.

In the following, we propose to explore the legalization of international affairs in terms of the increase of international law-making, of the variation of legal regimes, and of the differentiation of legal and law-like arrangements. For each of these three dimensions, we identify distinct analytical categories and considerations. However, we do not claim to re-invent the wheel. Our approach to complex legislation incorporates many of the key findings of established work on regimes and the transformations of legal order and policy networks to gain a more comprehensive understanding of the many moves to law that characterize the 'legalization' of international relations and affairs. We propose to interpret the legalization of world politics not just in terms of the choices states make to manage co-operation in an increasingly complex and 'thick' web of interdependencies, but to direct research to explore how legalization transforms international relations: why legal arguments traditionally associated with domestic politics have become frequent features in international affairs, how the emergence of legal and law-like arrangements relates to the disaggregation of governance at the domestic level, how it responds to the multiplication of non-state actors in the international arena, and how it redefines the terms of engagement of non-state actors in international affairs.

The increase of international legalization

The first dimension of the concept of complex legalization covers the increasing breadth and depth of international law. The breadth is the result of the international community's growing reliance on legal instruments to frame, regulate or resolve international affairs. Its most obvious indicator is the number of bi- or multilateral treaties which, according to the World Treaty Index Programme, has risen from *c.*2,000 in 1946 to more than 55,000 in 1997.[4] A second indicator is the scope of international contracts and conventions[5]. They address not only human rights, the rules of war or the terms of international trade, but also accounting standards, consumer protection, rules for cross-border investments and money laundering, environmental protection, and labour conditions.

The depth of international legalization reflects the increase of international treaties and conventions designed to enhance compliance and to effectively restrict the margins of state sovereignty. In many respects, compliance is the result of the rapid growth of international courts, tribunals and dispute settlement bodies. In 2005, we count 22 permanent, independent courts; if we add the quasi-judicial tribunals, panels or commissions charged with similar function, the total amounts to more than 40 institutions. If we add the 'quasi-judicial, implementation control and dispute settlement bodies', we count at least 125 institutions (Romano 1999: 923–928; Keohane *et al.* 2001: 73; PICT 2004).[6]

Despite occasional concerns about the potentially detrimental effect of uncontrolled proliferation of international norms, rules, and standards, and the risk of an undue interference of international courts and tribunals in domestic politics, most observers agree that the increase of legalization has contributed to the stabilization of international relations. International treaties and courts have played a crucial role in the 'rationalization' of interstate relations by enforcing the principle of legal equality 'like cases are treated alike'. However, as neo-liberal institutionalists have shown, it would be misleading to assume that the recourse to international law and the creation of international courts implies that international politics falls under the rule of law, or that international dispute settlements function like domestic courts. Abbot and Snidal (2001) remind us that the legalization of international regimes is not an act in the (general) will of a sovereign and cannot rely on a legitimate threat of coercion. The institutions of international law are the result of strategic choices of rational actors opting for – rather than against – institutionalized forms of co-operation to resolve collective action problems. In other words, states may accept precise and obliging rules and agree to delegate their implementation to third parties if they expect this to reduce transaction and opportunity costs – but they may do so only as long as this is the case (Abbott and Snidal 2001: 71). The essentially positivistic interpretation of legalization allows rationalists to reframe the question as to why states support international law making, and leads us beyond the traditional concern about the impossibility of legalizing international politics without a 'global' sovereign. At the same time, their refusal to discuss the 'nature of law' in order to guarantee that research on legalization remains 'empiricist in origin' (Abbott and Snidal 2001: 19) implies that the outcomes of legalization – the hard or soft laws of regimes that shape international co-operation – are expected to simply reproduce the traditional hierarchy of legal sources. Thus, even though rationalists recognize soft legalization as a promising tool to promote co-operation among states that are reluctant to risk their sovereignty to resolve collective action problems, the rationalist approach ignores the fact that legalization is not just a matter of states opting for more or less formalized regimes and dispute settlement systems. More to the point, it lacks the instruments to capture the variations of the moves to law through which states, their delegated agencies and international organizations attempt to shape international affairs by moving beyond traditional regimes. In other words, exclusively rationalist approaches ignore the fact that legalization is a complex and multifaceted process that restructures the relations between established and emerging members of international society, and thereby redefines patterns of political agency and identity within the international states system.

Variation

While the rationalist neo-liberal institutionalist interpretation of legalization explains why states choose to institutionalize co-operation through more or less binding and precise norms and rules, and why they accept to delegate their implementation and monitoring to more or less independent third parties, we believe its limitations lie *inter alia* in its narrow focus, its inadequate account of how international law transforms – and not just the re-orients – state behaviour, as well as in its failure to account for the emergence of new members of international society and their role in legalization. Thus, while we recognize that rationalist interpretations of international legalization offer a plausible explanation for the increasing importance of legalized regimes in the absence of a global sovereign, we think that they underestimate the significance of the variation among international legal arrangements and their role in international affairs. In the following section, we discuss research that documents significant variations of the legalization in international relations, including the transformation of the role of law and legal reasoning, a norm-based momentum likely to further advance legalization, as well as the diffuse expectation that different actors should comply with legal or law-like provisions, concerns about the legitimacy of legalization, and the significance of the reconfiguration of actors engaging in the 'complex' legalization of international affairs. We show that research on each of these developments has a considerable impact on the explanatory power of the concept of complex legalization, and that constructivist accounts provide the necessary leverage to capture its significance for the transformation of world politics.

The two-step transformation of international law

Traditionally, international law has been interpreted as an instrument to regulate the interactions of sovereign and equal states defined by their territorial unity.[7] In the 'Westphalian' model of international politics, international (public) law operates on the assumption that states interact under a condition of anarchy. In this setting, the primary objective of international law is to preserve peace and security. Besides, it is expected to provide an interface for different jurisdictions operating in a decentralized and horizontal legal system. Recently, however, this picture has been shaken by a two-step transformation: first, international law has evolved from a mere law of coexistence into a law of co-operation and, second, it emancipated itself from simply serving states as its prime source and targets.

The first step of this transformation can still be explained along the lines of the traditional interpretation of international law, according to which sovereign states set the limits of the legal framework they recognize 'beyond' the nation state. However, the assumption that the move towards a law of co-operation is driven by utilitarian cost–benefits considerations (Wolfrum 1986; Dicke 2001) rather than being a consequence of the increasing economic and technical interdependence of states, implies a shift from the earlier focus on the functionalist causes of the institutionalization of co-operation (Friedmann 1964) to a concern about the politics of international law-making. But although it acknowledges inequalities of legal subjects with regards to size and power, it confines rationalism by maintaining that the obligation of international law derives from the consensus of the sovereign units which addresses it. The assumption recognizes that sovereign actors may be exposed to political pressure, a traditional interpretation of the law of co-operation, but expects states to face no legal restrictions in their choice to adhere to international treaties. Assuming that the legalization of any arrangement vested with the authority to restrict state sovereignty requires the formal consensus of the state concerned, one could therefore argue that the emergence of trans- or supranational elements of international law and the establishment of relatively independent supra- or transnational legal institutions is the result of states willing to pool or delegate competences.[8]

In recent years, legal scholars observed a second transformation that has the potential to alter the traditional hierarchy of legal sources. While international treaties typically prevail over custom, and custom prevails over general principles of law, scholars argue that the shift from a sovereignty- and consensus-based law of coexistence to a law of co-operation has lead to the emergence of what some call an 'objective' legal order founded on norms the international community recognizes as valid even if they are not explicitly agreed upon by all states (Delbrück 2002: 416).[9] One key to this second transformation of international lies in the revival of the notion of natural law, according to which positive law can be considered void if its provisions contradict generally accepted principles of morality or the fundamental principles of reason. Although the scope of such principles is highly contested, their validity in terms of the *ius cogens* has been affirmed for the 'peremptory norms of general international law' (Malanczuk 1997: 57).[10] So far, peremptory norms have been called upon to enforce norms addressing crimes against humanity and severe human rights violations, such as genocide, slavery, trafficking, torture, or systematic racial discrimination. However, the logic of a *ius cogens* can also be traced in instruments such as the ILO Declaration on Fundamental Principles and Rights at Work and its follow-up, which states 'that in freely joining the ILO', states had not only recognized the content of its funding documents, but also agreed to work 'towards attaining the overall objectives of the Organization', and concludes that the 'very fact of membership' thus obliges each member 'to respect, to promote and to realize' principles and rights that have been 'recognized as fundamental both inside and outside the Organization' even if it has not ratified the relevant conventions (ILO 1998).

Addressing the developments separately, the shift from a law of coexistence to a law of cooperation remains within the rationalistic frame of reasoning, while the recognition of non-derogable norms relies on the growing recognition and acceptance of the idea that members of the international community should accept that certain legal obligations are enforceable *erga omnes* because their violation 'is deemed to be an offence not only against the state directly affected by the breach, but also against all members of the international community' (Malunczuk 1997: 59). Taken together, the two developments suggest that, even though the international community does not stand as a sovereign, it can assume some of the characteristics typically associated of a 'constituent' power by claiming to be capable of establishing, enforcing, and legitimizing 'non-derogable' norms. One could argue that the binding character of *ius cogens* for non-consenting states derives from an international public interest expressed by the members of the international community (Delbrück 2002: 430). Yet, we believe it is more reasonable to assume that, if a majority of states cutting across the major cultural and ideological divides accepts the validity of a norm (Malanczuk 1997: 58), its legitimacy derives from the opportunity each state has to participate in the (public) discourse about its scope.

To summarize, the first variation of legalization acknowledges that international legal and law-like arrangements matter not only if they create incentives for co-operation. World politics are also affected by the existence of regimes claiming universal validity for norms without requiring the actual consent of each individual single state – and, we believe, without having to assume to represent the will of a global polity. To capture the politics of the variation of legalization, research should therefore be able to capture the effects of the decoupling of norms and rules form the interstate bargaining processes. Rather than relying on the formal legitimacy of norms and rules established through the international states system, it should explain how debates about the legitimacy of (substantial) norms affect world politics.

Legitimacy and compliance

If the first variation of legalization, referring to the shift from utility- or interest-driven to norm-oriented institutions of legal and law-like arrangements, raises the problem of the legitimacy of *jus cogens* norms considered to be valid *erga omnes*, the second variation is linked to international efforts to guarantee the legitimacy of legalization. Consequently, it addresses a series of problems usually ignored by the positivist concern for the incentives created by the degree of obligation, precision and delegation of an international regime. While empirically minded institutionalists may claim that the legalization of a regime implies that its principles, norms, rules, and procedures are considered legitimate by its addressees, most legal scholars agree that legitimacy cannot simply be presumed, and that it increases if legalization is an inclusive process, ideally framed by a broad public discourse about the issues at stake. Indeed, the tenor of many recent studies is that legal and law-like arrangements are most pervasive – and that adherence and compliance are most likely – when they are established in an open process involving a wide range of stakeholders mutually recognizing their status and the legitimacy of their claims (Koh 1997; Neyer *et al.* 1999).

The observation that the perception of legitimacy matters has lead constructivists to analyse the politics of the deliberations that result in the legalization of international affairs (Reus-Smit 2004). The role of the deliberative process has also been at the core of the current research on compliance assessing the conditions under which states are most likely to recognize the legitimacy and internalize international norms and rules. Compliance research does not focus on how international legal or law-like arrangements are implemented at the domestic level, nor does it argue in terms of the mere efficacy of specific forms of regulation (Neyer and Zürn 2001: 4). Its primary concern is to identify the broader set of conditions that make addressees of specific norms and rules 'adhere to the provision of the accord and to the implementing measures that they have instituted' (Jacobson and Weiss 1998: 4, quoted in Neyer and Zürn 2001: 4). It assumes that the extent of juridification depends on the extent to which legalization delegates the authority to resolve disputes to third parties. It suggests that if disputes can be settled through legal reasoning rather than political bargaining, and if the members of a dispute settlement body are shielded from political interference, the degree of juridification is high. To measure the internalization of norms and rules, compliance research further distinguishes between the 'legal' internalization, according to which inter- or supranational norms are accepted by national courts without national governments having a chance to veto them; and civil internalization, which enables those who have a (direct or indirect) claim on those norms to access inter- or supranational courts. While the European Court of Justice can be seen as an example for the realization of both forms of internalization, the dispute settlement procedure of the WTO lacks civil internalization (ibid.).

Thus, at the analytical level, compliance research interprets international legalization in terms of the juridification and internalization of norms and rules in legal systems. It contributes to the research of the variations of legalization because it shows that the conditions under which states comply with positively-set rules, i.e. with rules written into formal international agreements, do not necessarily depend on their utility, but that they can depend on their very degree of legalization: 'the more an international institution is legalized, the more likely compliance with the rule becomes' (ibid.: 11).

New realms and actors

The third development we suggest addressing in terms of a variation of the traditional patterns of international legalization concerns the transformation of the frameworks of agency that define the arenas where international legal and law-like arrangements are created, the reach and scope of their rules and regulation, and the actors involved in the spreading of legalization at the international and at the domestic level.

The increase of legalization would have been impossible without transgovernmental networks capable both of framing issues suitable for legalization and of spreading the know-how to interpret and implement the legal and law-like arrangements. As Anne-Marie Slaughter (1995, 2004) has shown, transgovernmental networks play a crucial role in the complex system of governance that emerged from the fragmentation of liberal states and the analytical disaggregation of government in the component institutions – regulatory agencies, legislators, chief executives, courts, central bankers etc. – dealing with increasingly complex cross-border interactions. Research on transgovernmental networks shows that complex interdependence and the increase of cross-border interactions has been accompanied by an increase of transgovernmental contacts, and suggests that the policies to manage cross-border co-operation are designed within horizontal networks. It adds an important element to the variations of legalization because it documents that legalization does not simply concern matters of state, but also, and we suspect primarily, sectoral issues affecting different governmental departments in a different way. It expands the scope of research on legalization to focus not only on the sources and defining features of legal and law-like arrangements, but also on the constitutional framework that enables government agencies at the domestic level to define patterns of interaction with other public or private actors in an increasingly transnational world.

Indeed, Slaughter reminds us that transgovernmental networks should not be confused with regimes. Contacts and meetings among members of international organizations and domestic officials make it possible to exchange information, to learn from each other's experience, or to review common programmes that can be functional to the drafting of international treaties, contribute to their success by co-ordinating their implementation and enforcement in signatory states, and more generally, support legalization by contributing to the development of a common interpretation of specific legal or law-like arrangements. Besides being the backbone for policy transfers, transgovernmental networks are also one of the main venues for the transfer of legal and law-like arrangements – the export from major powers to weaker states being a frequent, but not the only or inevitable pattern that has been observed (Raustiala 2002: 7). Lastly, by enabling government officials to define best practices for public regulations of cross-border activities, they also provide room to discuss to what degree public arrangements can be avoided to favour self-regulation or private law-like arrangements.

With regards to the variations of legalization, research on transnational governmental networks suggests that the multiplication of actors engaged in the management of globalization and the variation of the tools at their disposal does affect the working of legal and law-like arrangements. It also provides an insight into the importance of the growing number of legal and law-like arrangements that have a direct impact on domestic policies. The fact that international legalization penetrates domestic boundaries when it addresses behind-the-border issues implies that research on legalization cannot simply assume to be dealing with the transformation of legal institutions designed to stabilize interactions between distinct territorial units (Kahler 1995: 2). It has to address the politics of the transposition of international legal and law-like arrangements into the domestic context (Zürn 2003: 9).

Lastly, an important – but still relatively under-theorized – aspect of the transformation of international law is related to the impact international norms and rules have on societal actors. Instruments such as the Rome Statute for the ICC and the ILO Declaration on Fundamental Principles and Rights at Work address not only states, but also individuals and TNCs. As subjects of international law, they are endowed with rights and duties, and make themselves liable to sanctions, thereby challenging the traditional interpretations of international law and international legalization. Indeed, although the discovery of non-state actors on the international scene is no new phenomenon (e.g. Friedmann 1964; Mansbach, Ferguson and Lampert 1976), the recognition of their importance for international legalization is rather recent. Non-state actors such as professional associations, firms, or civil society actors actively influence the international policy agenda, contribute to the framing and design of international agreements, shape the broader public debate and, finally, participate to a significant degree in the implementation and monitoring of legal or law-like obligations (Fischer-Lescano 2002; Keck and Sikking 1998; Risse *et al.* 1999; Risse 2001). Research on the variations of legalization would be incomplete without considering the involvement and the terms of engagement of domestic and transnational non-state actors, and without acknowledging that legalization is a complex process, rather than an outcome, that involves the framing and the socialization of practices, norms, and ideas concerning not only the efficiency, but also the legitimacy of international legal arrangements.

Differentiation

By examining the variations of legal and law-like arrangements, we extend the framework for interpreting complex legalization to address not only the quantitative and qualitative increase in international legalization, but also the changing role of law in international affairs. While there are few doubts about the importance of authorities capable of settling disputes through principled legal reasoning rather than intra-state bargaining, research on the variations of legalization moves beyond the traditional concerns with utilitarian considerations. First, it provides elements to analyse how a changing hierarchy of legal sources and the emergence of universally valid norms affect the behaviour of state and non-state actors, and to challenge the assumption that the agreement of sovereign states remains the ultimate condition for legalization. Second, it emphasizes the relevance of norm-driven dimensions of legalization, and thereby challenges the merely interest-based accounts of a more or less binding, precise and autonomous institutionalization of co-operation. Third, it addresses concerns about the legitimacy of legal and law-like arrangements, and challenges the presumed neutrality of explicitly rationalist or implicitly functionalist interpretations of legalization. Finally, it recognizes that the legitimacy and enforcement of legal and law-like arrangements is not just a matter of state politics and that it affects a wide range of public and private actors, including firms, professional associations, and civil society organizations.

The recognition of these variations has significant repercussions on research into the politics of complex legalization. The different logics of legal and law-like arrangements that refer to an 'objective' legal order, that raise the question of their legitimacy, or that emerge from transgovernmental networks shows that legalization cannot be explained in terms of the utility considerations of more or less resourceful states eager to institutionalize co-operation. The politics of legalization involve a wide range of actors dealing not only in power but also in virtue, and banking not only on efficiency but also on legitimacy. Yet, addressing the variations of legalization does not exhaust complex legalization. Research on the variations of legalization does recognize that international organizations and non-state actors contribute to the framing, implementation and monitoring of international legal and law-like arrangements, but assumes that their contributions can be explained within the limits of an essentially state-centred approach to international relations because they affect international norms and rules that still identify states as their key addressees. This applies even to constructivist approaches, which explicitly recognize the influence that non-state actors have in the framing of international legalization and state behaviour. Constructivist approaches cover some mileage in explaining the conditions for compliance or to explore the role of legitimacy because it recognizes the importance of social norms and ideas for political deliberation. On the other hand, most constructivists seem to accept that, while norms and ideas are constitutive of the identity of political actors, international legalization ultimately is – to paraphrase Wendt (1992) – what states make of it (see also: Kratochwil 2000; Toope 2000).

Despite the considerable analytical leverage of different theoretical approaches addressing the variation of legalization, they leave much uncharted territory. On the one side, frequent references to a 'constitutionalization' of legal and law-like arrangements reveal a constructivist fascination with the eventual emergence of a global hierarchy of norms (Frowein 1999; Zangl and Zürn 2004), which leaves little room for contradictory or murky trends in legalization – or assigns such developments a merely transitory status. On the other side, research on transgovernmental networks struggles to come to terms with the role of transnational legalities involving public and private initiatives to frame, implement and monitor legal or law-like arrangements governing transnational exchanges.

Considering ample evidence showing that private legalization does take place, and suggesting that the constitutionalization of world politics will remain elusive for quite some time to come, we propose to further extend the analytical scope of complex legalization. Indeed, we believe that besides addressing the increase and variation of international legal and law-like arrangements, research on legalization gains substantial empirical ground if it is capable of accounting for the differentiation of legal and law-like arrangements documented by the emergence of transnational legalization. At the same time, the studies in this volume show that the lush expense of empirical cases further undermines any attempt to interpret the politics of complex legalization in a theoretically parsimonious approach.

The emergence of transnational legal and law-like arrangements – such as standards, guidelines, codes of conduct, and multi-stakeholder initiatives – documents that legalization is not necessarily driven by states, their delegated agencies or international organizations. It involves a wide range of private actors, including firms, professional associations, and civil society organizations. Currently, there is little evidence to suggest that the emergence of transnational legalities follows a coherent trend, and less to suggest that private initiatives are converging towards a global legal order or simply serving hegemonic interests. Whether company codes of conduct subvert or enforce domestic or international norms or guidelines, or whether they serve producers, consumers, workers, investors or communities at large seems to depend primarily on the context in which they are applied – and only partially on their design. Accordingly, we do not see a clear-cut line separating two distinct 'worlds of world politics' (Rosenau 1997) – one run by sovereign states, the other populated by non-sovereign actors. As we have argued so far, it appears more productive to distinguish between states advancing legalization to create a stable framework for interaction on the one side, and on the other side, the transformation of legal and law-like arrangements that redefine the terms of engagement for both states and non-state actors, in order to explore when and how transnational actors succeed in transcending or replacing the boundaries set by the international states system. Thus, rather than considering the international and the transnational society as distinct spheres, we propose to examine their interactions, and to analyse transnational initiatives to establish or implement legal or law-like arrangements in terms of a differentiation of legalization.

Defining the emergence of transnational legal and law-like arrangements as a distinct dimension of complex legalization allows us to focus on their inherent decentralization and to identify the conditions of their evolution within specific functional, sectoral or territorial boundaries. It further allows us to question the methodological nationalism that conditions most of the theoretical concepts used in international relations and international law (Zürn 2001), to challenge the dogmatic distinction between public and private law, and to move beyond the positivistic interpretation according to which international law remains a means to condition state behaviour even when it provides room for non-state actors (Noortmann 2001). All of this is a prelude to our proposal, outlined in the next section, to explore the differentiation within complex legalization in terms of the presence of a plurality of legal orders, of the hybridization of legal arrangements, and, most radically, of the emergence of a legal order 'without a state'.

Plurality of legal orders

Traditionally, legal order has been conceptualized as a hierarchically structured and systematic whole, with legal doctrine transforming legal order into a legal system (Wilhemsson 1995: 127). This monistic perspective on legal ordering derives from the orthodox interpretation of the working of law at the domestic level. However, it is also deeply entrenched in the interpretation of legal ordering beyond the domestic level. Legal integration within the European Union is usually presented as a process in which the fragmentation of distinct national laws is overcome in a supranational legal order that does not simply promote a harmonization of national law, but restores the unity of law at a higher level. Legal integration at the international level has been interpreted along the same lines, when lawyers and legal scholars envisage the emergence of a 'world domestic law' (*Weltinnenrecht*) that constitutes a body of law that incorporates both international public law and the legal and law-like arrangements non-state actors are assumed to develop in the common interest of mankind (Delbrück 2002). Adhering to Kelsen's vision of a global constitutionalism, scholars have characterized this 'world domestic law' by a hierarchy of norms, rules and rule systems founded on the non-derogable *ius cogens* norms we have already referred to.

Besides the scepticism of most political scientists about the feasibility of a global constitutionalism, there are good arguments to assume that the paradigm of law as a unified system is both misleading and fictitious (Wilhemsson 1995: 127; Macdonald 1998: 75ff.). At the domestic level, legal anthropologists and pluralists have challenged the usefulness of the concept of a unified legal order, having identified the simultaneous presence of different legal orders in most societies (e.g. Benda-Beckmann 2002; Falk Moore 1983; Galanter 1981; Griffith 1986; Merry 1988; Moore 1973). Traditionally, pluralists have focused on the solution of disputes that were subject to different settlements according to different legal systems co-existing within a single polity. However, under the influence of post-modern conceptualizations of law, recent approaches have extended pluralist research to explore the broader implications of 'interlegality', i.e. situations in which 'different legal spaces' are 'superimposed, interpenetrated and mixed in our minds as much as in our actions'. Their assumption is that '[i]nter-legality is a highly dynamic process because different legal spaces are non-syn-chronic' (de Sousa Santos 1995: 473).

We believe pluralist research on interlegality can contribute to our under-standing of the differentiation of legalization because it allows us explicitly to address the simultaneous presence and interaction of legal spaces defined at a local, national and global level (Wilhelmsson 1995: 129). By challenging the assumption of the unity of law and the necessary prevalence of one particular legal order, legal pluralism provides the analytical instruments to capture the complex and dynamic patterns of legal ordering in different legal or law-like arrangements operating within specific and often overlapping sectoral, func-tional and territorial spaces. It enables us to deal with the fact that jurisdiction is already globalized to the extent that there is growing competition among differ-ent territorial and functional institutions offering their laws and services to frame, adjudicate, or settle disputes (Schiff Berman 2002: 318).

Hybridization

The second development that documents a differentiation of legalization con-cerns hybrid schemes leading to the establishment or maintenance of legal and law-like arrangements. We believe the notion of hybridization adds an important element to our discussion of the differentiation of complex legalization because it emphasizes the importance of the involvement of 'private' actors in the making, implementation and monitoring of legal and law-like arrangements. In the area of economic regulation, the phenomenon is not new (Braithwaite and Drahos 2000). In the continental European countries, many of the policies of the co-operative state (*verhandelnde Staat*) have been shaped by public–private interactions (Benz 1994; Ritter 1979); in the US context, regulatory agencies interact with their target groups (Breger 1988; Selznick 1966). However, traditionally, the involvement of private actors has been functional to policy-making, and administrative laws defined the relation between those within the administration and those outside it (Shapiro 2001: 369).

This started to change when administrative law itself changed in response to a series of challenges. With the shift from government to governance, the boundaries between those inside administrative agencies and those outside has been blurred. The growing complexity of regulation has increased the need – and the willingness – of administrative agencies to incorporate 'outside' exper-tise in the framing, preparation and implementation of public policies or – more importantly for our concerns – legal and law-lake arrangements. While the pop-ularity of concepts like 'network governance' (Kohler-Koch 1999) or 'mixed administration' (Freeman 2000) document the success of these new arrange-ments, critics observe that an 'unbounded' administrative law accentuates con-cerns about the generally weak political control of agency discretion and the concomitant threats to democratic accountability (Shapiro 2001).

At the international level, political processes are generally elitist, frequently lack transparency and usually follow only the most basic procedural rules, making it difficult to identify insiders and outsiders. Taking into account the complexity and the lack of transparency of transnational politics, research on hybridization is likely to confirm that the politics 'behind' the framing and the implementation of legal or law-like arrangements are 'far more complex and unbounded than the typical processes defined by conventional constitutional and administrative law' suggest (ibid.: 375).

Global law(s) without the state

The importance of the transformations of international relations that has lead to a multiplication of the venues of governance along sectoral, functional and geographical lines is most obvious when private actors are vested with prescriptive capacities, i.e. when private (market) actors are not just trying to lobby governments or their delegated agencies, but capable of using their 'epistemic authority' to challenge state-promoted laws or law-like arrangements (Sinclair 1999: 159f.). The 'move' to private authority has stimulated a broad reflection on the analytical tools needed to capture the logic of situations where public authority plays only a marginal role. Political scientists have revisited the core concepts of the discipline, focusing on the diffusion and transformation(s) of power and authority (see e.g. Strange 1996; Arts 2003; Bruce Hall and Biersteker 2002). However, a systematic debate on the implications that the shift from public to private authority has on the politics of legalization is still missing (but see Cutler 2003; Arts *et al.* 2001).

In a radical departure from a conventional state-centric interpretation of legalization, legal scholars have proposed to abandon the notion that law emerges within a rule hierarchy 'with a constitutionally legitimated political legislation at its top' in favour of a notion of 'heterarchy', and to extend research on 'global law' to include the role of independent rule-making systems (Teubner 1997: xiv; Gerstenberg 1997). Assuming that legalization ('global norm-production') does not have to be confined to the traditional 'centres' of law-making, they reframe legal pluralism (and move beyond hybridization) to embrace the basic validity of decentralized definitions of contractual relationships that are open to both public and private actors. The differentiation of legalization in terms of the emergence of law(s) 'without the state' is further documented by the intra-organizational production of norms (Muchlinski 1997) and standardization processes (Mattli 2001). According to Teubner, the driving force behind the emergence of a decentralized definition of contractual relations, codes of conduct or standards of behaviour is the difference between the more or less advanced functional differentiation of the economic, social, and political systems at the global level.

While research on transgovernmental networks covers some aspects of this 'differentiation' of international law-making when it analyses how territorially bound political actors cope with increasingly 'thick' arrays of globalized issues, research on global 'laws without the state' focuses on private legal and law-like arrangements that address regulatory needs in specific functional fields that are not necessarily constrained by territorial boundaries. As such, private legalities analyse how stable relationships can produce order without state intervention when, for example, co-operating agents design, implement and enforce specific norms and rules in a condition of 'stretched' reciprocity (Ellickson 1991). Such patterns have been observed in many 'modern forms of firm-to-firm co-operation in the advanced industrial and service context' (Schanze 1994: 119). It has also been observed that they can have a considerable impact on 'public' or hybrid legalization (Cutler *et al.* 1999; Haufler 1991; Ronit and Schneider 1999).

Exploring the heterarchy of legal and law-like arrangements, research on the politics of private legalization should address at least three controversial points, the answers to which we expect to depend on the individual case.

First, it should take into account that the notion of decentralized norm-production does not imply that private legalization is the result of spontaneous and unco-ordinated interactions. Studies suggest that, usually, private legalization is promoted by 'formulating agencies' (Stein 1995) Thus, research on the politics of private legalization should examine whether a particular arrangement is the product of intentional design, or whether it is the result of an evolution over time – rather than presupposing either to be the case (e.g. Knight 1992: 85).

Second, while private legalities can operate without the involvement of government, they may still operate their shadows. Studies on the 'social regulation of the market' (Haufler 2001) provide a wide range of examples that document the self-maintaining character of the design, implementation, and enforcement of private legal and law-like arrangements. Yet, markets are usually regulated, and government agencies may advocate, accept or oppose 'private' standards, codes of conduct or certification programmes. Research on private legalities should therefore consider how the positions of (different) governmental agencies affect markets and market regulation.

Third, the 'social' production of legalities raises concerns about the legal quality and legitimacy of private legalization. As constructivists point out, it is necessary to identify the 'distinctively legal' in order to settle the question whether 'legal norms, as a type, operate differently from any other kinds of norms in world politics' (Finnemore 2000: 701; cf. also Kratochwil 1989: 42f.). Research should therefore address normative issues that may challenge the notion that transnational arrangements can have distinctively legal features – or reclaim legitimacy.

The politics of complex legalization: an analytical framework

Our first aim in reviewing different analytical approaches that document the increase, variation and differentiation of complex legalization has been to broaden the perspectives for research on the multitude of legal or law-like arrangements that shape international affairs. However, while we believe it is important to acknowledge that legalization is a 'complex' process involving different moves to law that affect international affairs to varying degrees, we believe that the main challenge in addressing the increasing breadth and depth of legalization, the emergence of 'objective' norms, changing patterns of compliance and legitimacy, or the linkages between multiple legal orders, their hybridization, and the emergence of legal and law-like arrangements 'without' the state is to capture the politics of legalization. Private and public actors framing, implementing, or enforcing transnational legal and law-like arrangements do not simply promote international co-operation. They advance particular interests, strengthen particular groups, sectors or classes, and consolidate or contest an existing order through legalization. At the same time, the structures, institutions and dynamics of contention (and co-operation) are modified by the impact of 'complex' legalization.

In this chapter, we have proposed to address the politics of globalization by exploring the growing importance of legal and law-like arrangements, the changing role of international law, and the diffuse expectation that actors engaged in current affairs should comply with legal or law-like arrangements. We have shown that research should be concerned with the legitimacy of 'objective' norms, the existence of a plurality of legal orders, hybrid arrangements and laws created 'without' the state. We therefore suggest interpreting the politics of legalization not just in terms of the 'costs' of more or less binding, precise and independently administered regimes. Indeed, we believe that in order to understand the politics of legalization, we have to ask who gets – or expects to get – what from any particular legal or law-like arrangement, independently as to whether the arrangement appears too soft rather than hard, and whether it is promoted by governments, international organizations, professional associations, firms or civil society organizations.

Our review of the research on the different dimensions of legalization shows that legal and law-like arrangements can emerge at the centre or at the periphery of the international states system, that they can be public, private, or a combination of both. It also shows that there is no single factor driving legalization and no single variable capable of explaining its impact. Because legalization produces multiple legalities with different scopes and aims that may or may not converge, we believe it is necessary to operate with a broad analytical framework rather than a parsimonious theoretical model to analyse individual legalities or their interactions in specific policy or problem areas. This may seem eclectic. However, we think that only a more detailed map of the different dimensions of legalization may capture the transformation of law and politics in contemporary international affairs.

The major challenge ahead is how to evaluate these findings with regards to the key concepts of (international) law and (international) politics. Our interpretation of legalization as a complex multidimensional process evokes many of the recent challenges to the traditional theories of international law and international relations: it questions the boundaries between disciplines and sub-disciplines, e.g. between politics, law and economics or between domestic and international politics; a decay of some of the pillars of the Westphalian temple, e.g. internal and external sovereignty (Zacher 1992); and fading explanatory value of some of the most fundamental distinctions, e.g. between public and private, between law and regulation, or between states and markets.

Notes

1 We follow Keohane and Nye's (1971) definitions, according to which transnational relations include 'contacts, coalitions, and interactions across state boundaries that are not controlled by the central foreign policy organs of governments' as well as describing 'the movement of tangible or intangible items across state boundaries when at least one actor is not an agent of a government or of an intergovernmental agency' (xii).
2 Although counter-developments do occur, most research suggests that 'de-legalization' affects a relatively small share of day-to-day interactions (Watts 2000: 9).
3 Zangl and Zürn further distinguish between the access to procedures, the obligation to adjudicate, and independence of the judiciary (adjudication), authorization (enforcement), transparency, participation (law-making) and substantial values, consistency (constitutionalization).
4 See World Treaty Index Research Programme: db.lib.washington.edu/wti/ wtdb.htm [accessed 16 April 2003].
5 Frequently, the difference between the two forms of international relationships is explained by (over-) emphasizing the utility and opportunity calculations of states choosing (not) to enter sovereignty restricting contracts or the normative commitment to universal principles that make states sign up to conventions (see Abbott and Snidal 2001: 40).
6 The significant increase of international judicial bodies is not without consequences as overlapping jurisdictions may lead to forum shopping and multiple proceedings (Shany 2003).
7 'Sovereign equality' is the term used in article 2 (1) UN Charter.
8 See Moravcsik (1998: 67) for the distinction between pooled sovereignty, i.e. states' effort to reach a decision within an international organization, and delegated sovereignty, i.e. the delegation of state authority to an international body.
9 We do want to engage in a discussion on the changing importance of informal sources of law, especially of customary law. Price provides an interesting contribution to this discussion with his study on anti-personnel landmines (Price 2004).
10 Cf. The Vienna Convention on the Law of Treaties of 1969, Art 53.

Bibliography

Abbott, K. 1989. Modern International Relations Theory: A Prospectus for International Lawyers. *Yale Law Journal* 14: 333–441.
Abbott, K. and D. Snidal. 2001. Hard and Soft law in International Governance. In *Legalization and World Politics*, edited by J. Goldstein, M. Kahler, R. O. Keohane and A.-M. Slaughter. Cambridge: The MIT Press. 37–72.
Abbott, K., and D. Snidal. 2002. Values and Interests: International Legalization in the Fight Aginst Corruption. *Journal of Legal Studies* XXXI: 141–178.
Albert, M. 2002. *Zur Politik der Weltgesellschaft. Identität und Recht im Kontext Internationaler Vergesellschaftung*. Weilerswist: Velbrück.
Arts, B. 2003. 'Non-State Actors in Global Governance: Three Faces of Power'. Preprints aus der Max-Planck-Projektgruppe Recht der Gemeinschaftsgüter, Bonn (www. mpp-rdg.mpg.de/pdf_dat/2003_4.pdf, last visited 09/07/2003).

Arts, B., M. Noortmann, and B. Reinalda, eds. 2001. *Non-State Actors in International Relations*. Aldershot: Ashgate.

Beck, R. J. 1996. International Law and International Relations: The Prospects for Inter-disciplinary Collaboration. In *International Rules: Approaches from International Law and International Relations*, edited by R. J. Beck, A. C. Arend and R. D. V. Lugt. New York/Oxford: Oxford University Press. 3–33.

Benda-Beckmann, K. 2002. Globalization and legal pluralism. *International Law/Forum du Droit International* 4 (1): 19–25.

Benz, A. 1994. *Kooperative Verwaltung. Funktionen, Voraussetzungen und Folgen.* Baden-Baden: Nomos.

Braithwaite, J., and P. Drahos. 2000. *Global Business Regulation.* Cambridge: Cambridge University Press.

Breger, M. 1988. Negotiated Rulemaking by Government Agencies. Washington D.C.: Washington Legal Foundation.

Bruce Hall, R. and T. J. Biersteker, eds. 2002. *The Emergence of Private Authority in Global Governance.* Cambridge: Cambridge University Press.

Byers, M. 1999. *Custom, Power and the Power of Rules.* Cambridge: Cambridge University Press.

Byers, M., ed. 2000. *The Role of Law in International Politics. Essays in International Relations and International Law.* Oxford: Oxford University Press.

Carr, E. H. 1969. *Twenty Years Crisis, 1919–1939: An Introduction to the Study of International Relations.* 3rd edn. London: Palgrave Macmillan.

Clapp, J. 2003. Transnational Corporate Interests and Global Environmental Governance: Negotiating Rules for Agricultural Biotechnology and Chemicals. *Environmental Politics* 12 (4): 1–23.

Cutler, A. C. 2003. *Private Power and Global Authority: Transnational Merchant Law and the Global Political Economy.* Cambridge: Cambridge University Press.

Cutler, A. C., V. Haufler and T. Porter, eds. 1999. *Private Authority and International Affairs.* New York: State University of New York.

Delbrück, J. 2002. Prospects for a 'World (Internal) Law'? Legal Developments in a Changing International System. *Indiana Journal of Global Legal Studies* 9 (2): 401–431.

Dicke, K. 2001. Erscheinungsformen und Wirkungen von Globalisierung in Struktur und Recht des Internationalen Systems auf Universaler und Regionaler Ebene sowie Gegenläufige Tendenzen. In *Völkerrecht und Internationales Privatrecht in einem sich Globalizerenden System – Auswirkungen der Entstaatlichung Transnationaler Rechtsbeziehungen*, edited by K. Dicke, W. Hummer, D. Girsberger, K. Boele-Woelki, C. Engel and J. Frowein. Heidelberg: C. F. Müller. 12–44.

Ellickson, R. C. 1991. *Order Without Law. How Neighbours Settle Disputes.* Cambridge, MA and London: Harvard University Press.

Falk Moore, S. 1983. *Law as a process: An Anthropological Approach.* London: Routledge and Kegan Paul.

Finnemore, M. 2000. Are Legal Norms Distinctive? *New York University Journal of International Law and Politics* 32 (2): 699–706.

Finnemore, M., and S. J. Toope. 2001. Alternatives to 'Legalization': Richer Views of Law and Politics. *International Organization* 55 (3): 743–758.

Fischer-Lescano, A. 2002. Globalverfassung: Los Desaparecidos und das Paradox der Menschenrechte. Zeitschrift für Rechtssoziologie 23 (2): 2.

Freeman, J. 2000. The Private Role in Public Governance. *New York University Law Review* 75 (3): 543–675.

Friedmann, W. G. 1964. *The Changing Structure of International Law.* New York: Columbia University Press.

Frowein, J. 1999. Konstitutionalisierung des Völkerrechts. In *Völkerrecht und Internationales Privatrecht in Einem sich Globalizerenden System – Auswirkungen der Entstaatlichung Transnationaler Rechtsbeziehungen,* edited by K. Dicke, W. Hummer, D. Girsberger, K. Boele-Woelki, C. Engel and J. Frowein. Heidelberg: C. F. Müller. 427–445.

Galanter, M. 1981. Justice in Many Rooms: Private Ordering, and Indigenous Law. *Journal of Legal Pluralism* 19: 1–47.

Gerstenberg, O. 1997. Law's Polyarchy: A Comment on Cohen and Sabel. *European Law Journal* 3 (4):343–358.

Goldstein, J., M. Kahler, R. O. Keohane and A.-M. Slaughter, eds. 2001. Legalization and World Politics. Cambridge, MA/London: The MIT Press.

Griffith, J. 1986. What is Legal Pluralism? *Journal of Legal Pluralism* 24: 1–55.

Haine, J. Y. 2003. The Imperial Moment: A European View. *Cambridge Review of International Affairs* 16 (3): 483–510.

Haufler, V. A. 1991. *Risk and reaction: State and Market in the International Risk Insurance Regime.* (Vol. Published as 'Dangerous Commerce', Ithaca: Cornell University Press, 1997.) Ann Arbor: UMI.

Haufler, V. 2001. *A Public Role for the Private Sector: Industry Self-regulation in Global Economy.* Washington D.C.: Carnegie Endowment for International Peace.

Hurrell, A. 2000. Conclusion: International Law and the Changing Constitution of International Society. In *The Role of Law in International Politics: Essays in International Relations and International Law,* edited by Michael Byers. Oxford: Oxford University Press. 327–348.

International Labour Organization (ILO). 1998. *ILO Declaration of Fundamental Principles and Rights at Work.* Adapted at the 86th Session, Geneva, 19 June 1998.

Kahler, M. 1995. *International Institutions and the Political Economy of Integration.* Washington D.C.: Brookings Institution.

Keck, M. E., and K. Sikkink. 1998. *Activists Beyond Borders: Advocacy Networks in International Politics.* Ithaca: Cornell University Press.

Keohane, R. O. and J. S. J. Nye, eds. 1971. *Transational Relations and World Politics.* Cambridge, MA: Harvard University Press.

Keohane, R. O., A. Moravcsik and A.-M. Slaughter. 2001. Legalized Dispute Resolution: Interstate and Transnational, edited by J. Goldstein, M. Kahler, R. O. Keohane and A.-M. Slaughter. Cambridge, MA: The MIT Press. 73–104.

Knight, J. 1992. *Institutions and Social Conflict.* Cambridge: Cambridge University Press.

Koh, H. H. 1997. Why Do Nations Obey International Law? *The Yale Law Journal* 106: 2599–2659.

Kohler-Koch, B. 1999. The Evolution and Transformation of European Governance. In *The Transformation of Governance in the European Union,* edited by B. Kohler-Koch and R. Eising. London: Routledge.

Kratochwil, F. V. 1989. *Rules, Norms, and Decisions.* Cambridge: Cambridge University Press.

Kratochwil, F. V. 2000. How do Norms Matter? In *The Role of Law in International Politics. Essays in International Relations and International Law,* edited by M. Byers. Oxford: Oxford University Press. 35–68.

Macdonald, R. A. 1998. Metaphors of Multiplicity: Civil Society, Regimes and Legal Pluralism. *Arizona Journal of Comparative and International Law* 15 (1): 69–91.

Malanczuk, P. 1997. *Modern Introduction to International Law*. 7th revized edn. London/New York: Routledge.

Mansbach, R. M., Y. H. Ferguson and D. E. Lampert. 1976. *The Web of World Politics. Nonstate Actors in the Global System*. Englewood Cliffs, NJ: Prentice-Hall.

Mattli, Walter. 2001. The Politics and Economics of International Institutional Standard Setting: An Introduction. *Journal of European Public Policy* 8 (3): 328–344.

Merry, S. E. 1988. Legal Pluralism. *Law & Society Review* 22 (5): 869–896.

Moore, S. E. 1973. Law and Social Change: The Semi-Autonomous Social Field as an Appropriate Subject of Study. *Law & Society Review* 7: 719–746.

Moravcsik, A. 1998. *The Choice for Europe: Social Purpose and State Power From Messina to Maastricht*. Ithaca, NY: Cornell University Press.

Muchlinski, P. T. 1997. 'Global Bukowina' Examined: Viewing the Multinational Enterprise as a Transnational-Law-Making Community. In *Global Law Without a State*, edited by G. Teubner. Aldershot: Dartmouth. 45–77.

Neyer, J. and M. Zürn. 2001. Compliance in Comparative Perspective. The EU and Other International Institutions. *InIIS-Arbeitspapier* 23 (1).

Neyer, J., D. Wolf and M. Zürn. 1999. Recht jenseits des Staates. Bremen: Zentrum für Europäische Rechtspolitik and der Universität Bremen (ZERP).

Noortman, M. 2001. Non-State Actors in International Law. In *Non-State Actors in International Relations*, edited by B. Arts, M. Noortmann and B. Reinalda. Aldershot: Ashgate. 59–76.

PICT (Project on International Courts and Tribunal) 2004. Synoptic Chart Version 3.0 (November 2004) [last visited August 2005].

Price, R. 2004. Emerging Customary Norms and Anti-Personnel Landmines. In *The Politics of International Law*, edited by C. Reus-Smit. Cambridge: Cambridge University Press. 106–130.

Rajagopal, B. 2003. *International Law from Below: Development, Social Movement and Third World Resistance*. Cambridge: Cambridge University Press.

Raustiala, K. 2002. The Archietcure of International Cooperation: Transgovernmental Networks and the Future of International Law. *Virginia Journal of International Law (UCLA, School of Law Research Paper No. 02-26; Princeton Law & Public Affairs Working Paper No. 02-5)* 43: forthcoming.

Reus-Smit, C. ed. 2004. *The Politics of International Law*. Cambridge: Cambridge University Press.

Reus-Smit, C. 2004b. Introduction. In *The Politics of International Law*, edited by C. Reus-Smit. Cambridge: Cambridge University Press. 1–44.

Risse, T. 2001. Transnational Actors and World Politics. In *Handbook of International Relations*, edited by W. Carlsnaes, T. Risse and B. A. Simmons. London: Sage. 255–274.

Risse, T., Stephen C. Ropp and Kathryn Sikkink, eds. 1999. *The Power of Human Rights. International Norms and Domestic Change*. Cambridge: Cambridge University Press.

Ritter, Ernst-Hasso. 1979. *Der Kooperative Staat. Bemerkungen zum Verhältnis von Staat und Wirtschaft*. 389–413.

Romano, C. 1999. The Proliferation of International Judicial Bodies: The Pieces of the Puzzle. *New York University Journal of International Law and Politics* 31 (4): 709–751.

Rosenau, J. N. 1997. *Along the Domestic–Foreign Frontier: Exploring Governance in a Turbulent World*. Cambridge: Cambridge University Press.

Ronit, K. and V. Schneider. 1999. Global Governance through Private Organizations. *Governance* 12 (3): 243–266.

de Sousa Santos, B. 1995. *Toward a New Common Sense. Law, Science and Politics in Paradigmatic Transition*. New York/London: Routledge.

Schanze, E. 1994. Toward a Realistic Science of Institutional Design. *Journal of Institutional and Theoretical Economics* 150: 117–122.

Schiff Berman, P. 2002. The Globalization of Jurisdiction. *University of Pennsylvania Law Review* 151 (2): 311–529.

Selznick, P. 1966. *TVA and the Grass Roots*: Harper Torchbook Edition/California Reprint (1980); California Paperback (1984).

Selznick, P., P. Nonet and H. M. Vollmer. 1969. *Law, Society, and Industrial Justice*. New Brunswick, N.J.: Transaction Books.

Shany, Y. 2003. *The Competing Jurisdictions of International Courts and Tribunals*. Oxford: Oxford University Press.

Shapiro, M. 2001. Administrative Law Unbounded: Reflections on Government and Governance. *Indiana Journal of Global Legal Studies* 8 (2): 369–377.

Shapiro, M., and A. Stone Sweet. 2002. *On Law, Politics, and Judicialization*. Oxford: Oxford University Press.

Shelton, D. 2000. Law, Non-Law and the Problem of 'Soft Law'. In *Commitment and Compliance. The Role of Non-Binding Norms in the International Legal System*, edited by D. Shelton. Oxford: Oxford University Press. 1–18.

Sinclair, T. J. 1999. Bond-Rating Agencies and Coordination in the Global Political Economy. In *Private Authority in International Affairs*, edited by A. C. Cutler, V. Haufler and T. Porter. Albany: State University of New York. 153–168.

Slaughter, A.-M. 1995. International Law in a World of Liberal States. *European Journal of International Law* 6 (1995): 503–538.

Slaughter, A.-M. 2000. Governing the Global Economy through Government Networks. In *The Role of Law in International Politics. Essays in International Relations and International Law*, edited by M. Byers. Oxford: Oxford University Press. 177–206.

Slaughter, A.-M. 2002. Breaking Out: The Proliferation of Actors in the International System. In *Global Prescriptions. The Production, Expoprtation, and Importation of a New Legal Orthodoxy*, edited by Y. Dezalay and B. Garth. Ann Arbor: The University of Michigan Press. 12–36.

Slaughter, A.-M. 2004. *A New World Order*. Princeton: Princeton University Press.

Stein, U. 1995. *Lex Mercatoria: Realität und Theorie*. Frankfurt/M.: Klostermann.

Stiftung-Entwicklung-und-Frieden, ed. 2001. *2001: Globale Trends 2002*. Bonn: Dietz.

Strange, S. 1996. *The Retreat of the State. The Diffusion of Power in the World Economy*. Cambridge: Cambridge University Press.

Teubner, G. ed. 1997. *Global Law Without a State*. Aldershot: Dartmouth.

Teubner, G. 2004. Global Private Regimes: Neo-Spontaneous Law and Dual Constitution of Autonomous Sectors in World Society? In *Public Governance in the Age of Globalization*, edited by K.-H. Ladeur. Aldershot: Ashgate. 71–87.

Toope, Stephen J. 2000. Emerging Patterns of Governance and International Law. In *The Role of Law in International Politics. Essays in International Relations and International Law*, edited by M. Byers. Oxford: Oxford University Press. 91–108.

Trachtman, J. P. 1997. Externalities and Extraterritoriality: The Law and Economics of Prescriptive Jurisdiction. In Economic Dimensions in International Law: Comparative and Empirical Perspectives, edited by J. S. Bhandari and A. O. Sykes. Cambridge: Cambridge University Press.

Watts, A. 2000. The Importance of International Law. In *The Role of Law in International Politics. Essays in International Relations and International Law*, edited by M. Byers. Oxford: Oxford University Press. 5–16.

Wendt, A. 1992. Anarchy Is What States Make of It: The Social Construction of Power Politics. *International Organization* 88 (2): 384–396.

Wiener, J. 1999. Globalization and the Harmonization of Law. London/New York: Pinter.

Wilhemsson, T. 1995. Legal Integration as Disintegration of National Law. In *Legal Polycentricity: Consequences of Pluralism in Law*, edited by H. Petersen and H. Zahle. Aldershot: Dartmouth. 127–148.

Wolf, K. D. and M. Zürn. 1993. Macht Recht einen Unterschied? Implikationnen und Bedingungen Internationaler Verrechtlichung im Gegensatz zu Weniger Bindenen Formen Internationaler Verregelung. In *Internationale Verrechtlichung*, edited by W. K. Dieter. Pfaffenweiler: Centaurus-Verlagsgesellschaft. 11–28.

Wolfrum, R. 1986. International Law of Cooperation. In *Encyclopedia of Public International Law (EPIL, 9)*, edited by R. Bernhardt. New York: Elsevier Science. 193–198.

Zacher, M. W. 1992. The Decaying Pillars of the Westphalian Temple: Implications for International Order and Governance. *Governance Without Government.* J. N. Rosenau. Cambridge: Cambridge University Press. 58–101.

Zangl, B. and M. Zürn. 2004. Make Law, Not War: Internationale Verrechtlichung als Baustein für Global Governance. *Verrechtlichung – Einb Baustein für Global Governance?* B. Zangl and M. Zürn. Bonn: Dietz. 12–45.

Zürn, M. 1998. *Regieren Jenseits des National Staates. Globalisierung und Denationalisierung als Chance.*

Zürn, M. 2001. Politik in der Postnationalen Konstellation. Èber das Elend des Methodologischen Nationalismus. In *Politik in Einer Entgrenzten Welt. 21. Wissenschaftlicher Kongress der Deutschen Vereinigung für Politische Wissenschaft*, edited by C. Landfried. Köln: Verlag Wissenschaft und Politik. 181–204.

Zürn, M. 2003. Global Governance under Legitimacy Pressure. In *European Consortium for Political Research (ECPR) Joint Sessions of Workshops*, Edinburgh, 29 March–2 April 2003.

Zürn, M. and C. Joerges, eds. (2005). *Law and Governance in Postnational Europe. Compliance Beyond the Nation-State.* Cambridge: Cambridge University Press.

Zürn, M. and D. Wolf. 1999. European Law and International Regimes: The Features of Law Beyond the Nation-State. *European Law Journal* 5 (3): 272–292.

3 Transnational legalization of accounting

The case of international financial reporting standards*

Jens Wüstemann and Sonja Kierzek

Introduction

It was a question of time that expanding capital markets and increasing economic internationalization pushed the quest for internationally accepted accounting rules for companies to the top of the agenda of economic and political actors. For capital market-oriented companies, the existence of globally accepted accounting rules would be an opportunity to offer listings at different foreign stock exchanges with the same set of financial statements. International standards would further facilitate the accounting in international groups and, ideally, for international investors, uniform accounting rules would provide worldwide comparable financial information allowing for an efficient choice between investments (van Helleman and Slomp 2002).[1]

At the same time, it would be naive to believe that any system of internationally accepted accounting rules would emerge without frictions and conflicts. On the one side, complex technicalities make the design of such a system a quite demanding task. On the other side, and more importantly, the making of accounting rules involves different actors with specific interests in and ideas about international standards. Indeed, accounting practices are shaped by private rule-setters as well as national and supranational regulators from both sides of the Atlantic. The combination of technicalities and the complexity of the actor constellation make transnational accounting a fascinating case to study the way in which the legalization of contemporary international affairs takes place.

In a nutshell, we are dealing with a case in which, first, norms are generated transnationally by a private body; second, these norms are endorsed with supranational public authority via a process of incorporation into EU law (a process in which again a private association plays an important role); third, the enforcement of the rules takes place in the complex multi-level and multi-arena polity of the EU; fourth, the processes of endorsement and enforcement reveal incompatibilities between regulatory approaches both between public and private actors and between the Member States of the EU; and fifth, the entire process must be read on the background of an international co-ordination, co-operation and competition and between regulatory approaches of the European Union and the US in their efforts to influence the international system of accounting.

As a consequence, transnational legalization in the area of accounting is much more than the outcome of states negotiating an international agreement that increases the efficacy of public regulation on a global scale. Indeed, it would miss the point to describe the transnational legalization of accounting merely with respect to the dimension of obligation, precision and delegation as developed by Abbott *et al.* (2000). Rather, the case is informative with respect to both the growing complexity and variation of transnational legalization. In particular, it informs us that the emergence of globally accepted rules results from the interplay between power-based, interested-based and functional factors that help to understand the way in which legalization takes place.

The remainder is organized as follows: part two presents the standard-setter and the process of standard-setting. Part three addresses the process by which the privately developed norms are endorsed, and thereby vested with public legitimacy, in the context of the European Union. The fourth part is dedicated to the process of enforcement and related problems.

Standard-setter and the process of standard-setting

The way of rule-making in the field of financial reporting and the legal quality of accounting rules vary significantly in different legal traditions. For whatever reasons, in countries with a Common Law system, private professional accountancy bodies are usually responsible for the setting of accounting standards, whereas in countries with a Civil Law tradition, accounting rules are set predominantly by the national legislator. Private standard-setters do not have the authority to make their standards compulsory. The International Accounting Standards Board (IASB) does not make an exemption from this rule. Rather, the worldwide application of International Financial Reporting Standards (IFRS) depends on their acceptance by the relevant actors, especially securities regulators, governments, national standard-setters, preparers and users. Consequentially the IASB has established close contact and collaborations with the relevant parties, in particular in the EU and the US. In the following, we analyse the organization of the standard-setting body, the IASB, under the special interest of the political dimension and then present the international accounting standard-setting process ('due process').

The International Accounting Standards Board

The predecessor of the IASB, the International Accounting Standards Committee (IASC), was established in 1973 in London as a voluntary association of professional accountancy bodies from North America, Europe and Asia. Sponsored by the British government at the time of the British accession to the European Economic Community, the idea of a privately organized international standard-setter was to establish an alternative to the highly legalized, state-controlled Continental European accounting approach in the harmonization process of European accounting (Hopwood 1994).

After some years of restructuring, the IASB replaced the IASC in 2001.[2] The IASB now consists of 12 full-time and two part-time members. The main selection criterion of the Board members is their technical expertise, comprising both technical competence and experience in international business. However, a fair mix of perspectives and experiences is attempted through the formal integration of diverse professional backgrounds (at least five auditors, three preparers, three users and an academic) and different regional interests. In addition, seven Board members serve as contact persons with national standard-setters. Whereas the IASB is responsible for the development of the Standards, the International Financial Reporting Interpretations Committee (IFRIC) is in charge of the interpretation of the Standards and of providing timely guidance on accounting issues that are not dealt with in any IFRS.[3]

The members of the IASB are appointed by the IASC Foundation (IASCF). The IASCF, a not-for-profit association incorporated in Delaware, has been the parent entity of the IASB since 2001. The Foundation's overall objective is to develop a coherent set of global accounting standards[4] and, moreover, to promote the convergence between national accounting standards and IFRS. The IASCF is principally composed of a Board of Trustees and the IASB.[5] The members of the Foundation's Board of Trustees come from various geographic (mainly North America, Europe and Asia) and functional (auditors, preparers, users and

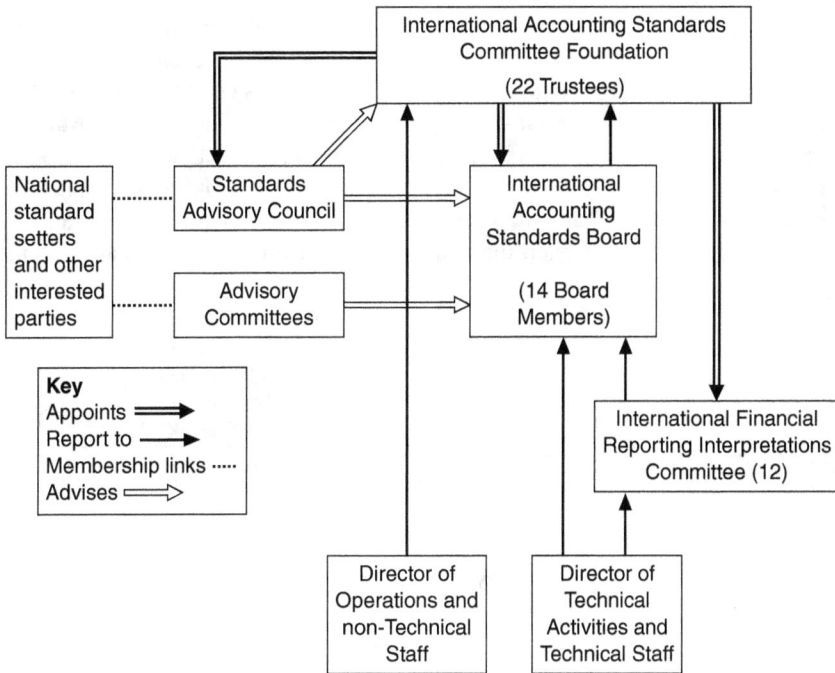

Figure 1 Structure of the IASC Foundation (source: www.iasb.org/About+US/ About+US.htm).

academics) backgrounds. The 19 trustees' main function consists of fundraising. In the past, the IASCF has mainly been funded by a relatively small number of private companies, accounting firms, international organizations and central banks.[6]

The separation of governance and funding from technical matters is an important element supporting the IASB's emphasis on its independence in the standard-setting process. However, since the Trustees select and appoint the IASB members, not only the Trustees themselves but also the sponsoring parties may exert an indirect influence on the IASB. For example, US companies were threatening to withdraw their funding from the IASB, as a reaction to the IASB's release of Exposure Draft No. 2 proposing the treatment of stock options as expenses (*Accountancy Age* 2003). Another case is the threat of Novartis, a major Swiss pharmaceutical company, to switch from IFRS to US Generally Accepted Accounting Principles (US GAAP) in 2001 if the IASB were not to follow the US Financial Accounting Standards Board's approach to goodwill accounting (Zeff 2002).

The main influence on the IASB is executed by the European Commission and the US Securities and Exchange Commission (SEC), respectively the US Financial Accounting Standards Board (FASB). The European Commission has a high influence on the work of the IASB, because the EU has been requiring publicly traded EU companies to apply IFRS in their consolidated accounts since 2005. The important role of US actors in the regulation of international accounting can be attributed to the attraction of US capital markets for both foreign investors and an increasing number of non-US companies. At present, the SEC requires the use of US GAAP for listings at the US capital market, or at least, reconciliation from national GAAP or IFRS to US GAAP. A precondition for the acceptance of financial statements prepared according to IFRS at the US capital market without reconciliation is a 'close alignment' of IFRS and US GAAP requirements and disclosures.[7] It becomes obvious that a collaboration of the IASB with the SEC and the FASB is significant for the global acceptance of IFRS. Traditionally, however, the FASB was reluctant to engage in any outside

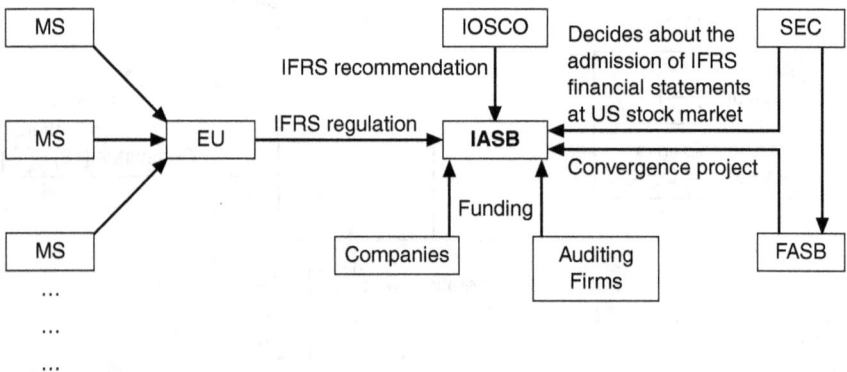

Figure 2 Collaboration of the IASB with national/international authorities.

collaboration in the field of financial reporting (Kostelitz 2002). Rather, it claimed that only US GAAP could be the basis for a convergence of global accounting standards. Yet, the US corporate accounting scandals around Enron and subsequent disputes about the supremacy of the rules-based US GAAP have been changing the situation. As a consequence, IFRS got more hearing in the US and have been increasingly discussed as an alternative to US GAAP (*Investor Relations Business News* 2002). In 2002, the FASB and the IASB concluded a memorandum of understanding ('The Norwalk Agreement'[8]). In this memorandum the Boards agreed to converge IFRS and US GAAP by eliminating existing differences between the two sets of standards and to coordinate their working agendas in order to maintain the level of compatibility once achieved.

The 'due process' in standard-setting

The expression 'due process' generally 'describe[s] the steps taken to ensure that an administrative matter is given the careful consideration needed to adequately protect the interests of those involved' (Miller *et al.* 1998). Since the IASB as a non-governmental standard-setter cannot require the application of IFRS, it seeks acceptance of IFRS by a 'democratization' of its standard-setting process, i.e. by giving the concerned parties, such as national standard-setters, securities regulators, users and preparers, the opportunity to participate in the development of IFRS (Whittington 2005).

The standard-setting process involves a set of procedures, consistently refining and enhancing the proposed accounting rules on each stage (Flower and Ebbers 2002). After the admission of a new topic, that can be put forward by organizations, individuals or the IASB staff to the IASB's working agenda, the IASB usually publishes a discussion document describing preferred and refused alternative accounting rules, followed by an exposure draft – a proposed IFRS – and, in the end, by the final Standard. The total cycle time of the standard-setting process depends on the project and varies from one year up to three or more years. According to the IASB's strategy to converge IFRS and national accounting standards, the IASB pursues a close co-ordination with the rule-making process of national standard-setters.

Endorsement

Initially, the European Commission designed accounting rules through Directives, the Fourth Company Law Directive on annual accounts and the Seventh Company Law Directive on consolidated accounts. Given the limited success of the two Accounting Directives to harmonize European accounting regulation, the Council shifted its policy and approved an EU regulation that requires the use of IFRS in the consolidated accounts of all listed companies in the European Union ('IFRS Regulation') in 2002.[9] With the decision to incorporate the private accounting standards IFRS into Community Law via a European regulation, the Council opted for an approach that implied the set up of a quite demanding mechanism of endorsement, comprising the aspects of incorporation, oversight and control. In the following, we introduce the way in which privately set international accounting standards are endorsed with public authority in the European context. We will then address the potential for conflicts resulting from the EU's aim to ensure compatibility of IFRS with the EU's economic and legal framework on the one hand and to promote the world-wide acceptance of IFRS on the other hand.

The objective of the adoption of IFRS in the European Union

Since the EU Accounting Directives contain by nature quite a few principles that are open to different interpretations and options that may be exerted differently in the Member States, the Directives only established minimum equivalent requirements in the Member States (European Commission 1995, 2000 and 2001). With regard to the EU's objective to realize a fully integrated European capital and financial service market[10] the level of harmonization of financial reporting achieved by the two Accounting Directives was not considered to be sufficient (European Commission 2000 and 2001). In order to enhance the comparability of financial statements of publicly traded EU companies, thereby enabling them to compete under equal conditions for financial resources in the Community capital markets, the EU saw the need to completely standardize the financial reporting framework applicable to those companies. With the aim to disburden EU companies being listed in international capital markets, for example in the US capital market, from the requirement to prepare two sets of financial statements, the EU also considered it necessary to establish a set of accounting standards that is globally accepted (European Commission 1995, 2000 and 2001; Rationale 4 IFRS Regulation). Due to this reason, the EU chose to adopt IFRS for application by listed EU companies, instead of setting a distinct European body of accounting standards (European Commission 2001).

Endorsement of IFRS into the European legal framework

Purpose of the endorsement mechanism

In order to 'achieve full legal certainty and consistent application of [IFRS] by all listed EU companies' the EU chose to integrate the professional standards IFRS into the EU legislative framework by means of a Regulation (European Commission 2001), which is 'binding in its entirety and directly applicable in all Member States' (Art. 249(2) Treaty Establishing the European Union). Since '[t]he European Union cannot delegate responsibility for setting financial reporting requirements for listed EU companies to a non-governmental third party', such as the IASB,[11] the EU set up a mechanism in which the democratically authorized EU bodies provide IFRS with the status of Community Law and thereby exercise the necessary regulatory oversight over the adoption of IFRS into the EU legal framework (European Commission 2000).

The function of the so-called endorsement mechanism is to confirm that IFRS 'provide a suitable basis for financial reporting by listed EU companies' (European Commission 2001). IFRS should only be rejected if they 'contain material deficiencies or have failed to cater for features specific to the EU economic or legal environment' (ibid.). In order to avoid the creation of an EU-specific version of IFRS, the Standards and Interpretations should neither be reformulated nor replaced in the endorsement process (ibid.).

In order to 'maintain a base level of comparability for all limited liability companies across the EU' (ibid.) and to 'preserve its own achievements in the direction of harmonisation' (European Commission 1995), the EU decided that the Accounting Directives should remain applicable for all limited liability EU companies and that only the legal framework applicable to publicly traded EU companies should be supplemented by IFRS (European Commission 2001; Rationale 3 IFRS Regulation). Due to the required internal coherence between norms within Community Law (Canor 1998), the adoption of IFRS for application in the EU requires the Standards and Interpretations to be compatible with the Accounting Directives (European Commission 1995, 2000 and 2001; Rationale 9 IFRS Regulation).

However, the endorsement of IFRS does not require a strict conformity of the Standards and Interpretations with each single provision of the Accounting Directives (Rationale 9 IFRS Regulation); rather IFRS qualify for endorsement and thus for application in the EU if they are not contrary to the true and fair view principle, this principle being considered in the light of the Fourth and Seventh Company Law Directive (Art. 3(2) IFRS Regulation). The European Court of Justice clarified in a specific case that the '[a]pplication of [...] [the true and fair view] principle must, as far as possible, be guided by the general principles contained in Article 31 of the Fourth Directive', such as the prudence principle, the realization principle and the accrual principle.[12] Apart from this requirement, IFRS should be conducive to the European public good, and they should deliver a basis for users of financial statements in the EU to make sound economic decisions by meeting the fundamental criteria of understandability, relevance, reliability and comparability (Art. 3(2) IFRS Regulation).[13]

Instead of rejecting an IFRS that is not regarded to be compatible with the true and fair view principle, the EU may also amend the Accounting Directives (European Commission 2000 and 2001). This was actually done in 2003, when the Council and the European Parliament adopted a Directive ('Modernization Directive') in order to update the Fourth and Seventh Company Law Directives towards the so-perceived state of the art of international accounting. However, amendments of the Accounting Directives should be limited to exceptional cases since the issuance of new Directives and their transposition into national law by the Member States is a long-winded process (European Commission 1995) that might reverse the advantages of the IFRS Regulation.

Endorsement procedure

While the Council chose to confer the responsibility of the endorsement of IFRS to the Commission, it established a comitology committee, the Accounting Regulatory Committee (ARC)[14] that controls and assists the Commission in carrying out the endorsement of IFRS. The system of comitology represents a form of decision-making process that the EU has already implemented in other areas, such as agriculture, trade, custom policies, research and development, environmental affairs and telecommunications (Eriksen and Fossum 2002). The ARC's power of vetoing a Commission's opinion about the adoption of an IFRS with a qualified majority provides the Council with a strong say in the endorsement process (Ballmann *et al.* 2002): If the ARC rejects the Commission's endorsement proposal and the Commission does not withdraw it for redrafting, the proposal needs to be submitted to the Council which may then decide on the adoption or rejection of the respective IFRS[15]. Additionally, the European Commission has to inform the European Parliament which, in turn, may decide whether the Commission has exceeded its authority. Since the ARC is composed of representatives of all EU Member States mainly coming from national ministries, it serves the Member States as a means to gain influence in the decision-making process on the EU level, compensating the growing shift of national authorities to EU bodies (Wessels 1998). From a practical point of view, the inclusion of national civil servants enhances the political legitimacy of IFRS and is supposed to facilitate their implementation in the EU Member States (Eriksen and Fossum 2002).

The Commission is provided with support and technical expertise in the assessment of IFRS by the European Financial Reporting Advisory Group (EFRAG). In contrast to the ARC, the EFRAG is not part of the EU's committee

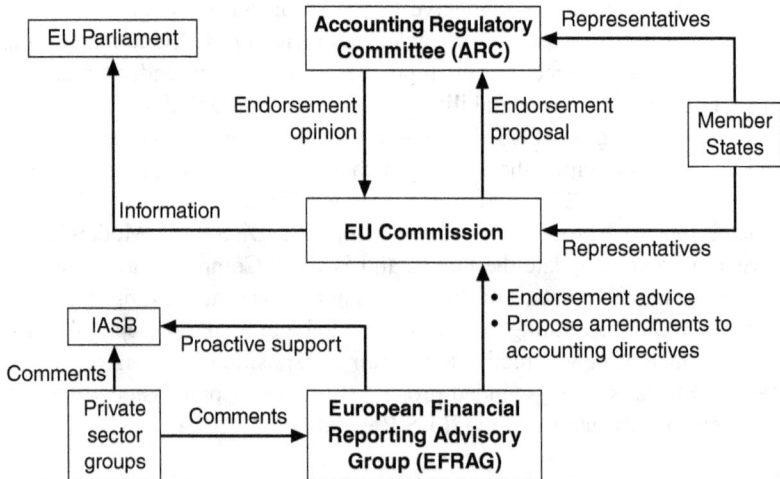

Figure 3 EU endorsement mechanism of IFRS.

structure. Rather, it has been established by private sector groups, such as stock exchanges, small and medium size entities, financial analysts, accountancy professions and national standard-setters. Apart from providing the Commission with advice concerning the endorsement of IFRS, it is the EFRAG's role to proactively contribute to the IASB's work. Mainly through comments during the standard-setting process, the EFRAG is supposed to ensure that European interests are regarded by the IASB, and to prevent conflicts between IFRS and the EU Accounting Directives at an early stage. Finally, the EFRAG shall initiate amendments of the EU Accounting Directives to adjust them to IFRS if this is considered to be necessary.

Conflicts in the endorsement of IFRS

Conflicts between the EU's objective to make applicable globally accepted IFRS and the required compatibility of IFRS with the EU economic and legal environment

It follows from the objectives of the IFRS Regulation that IFRS need to be compatible with the EU economic and legal environment, especially with the EU Accounting Directives, in order to be applicable in the Community on the one hand and that IFRS should be globally accepted so that EU companies can offer listings on capital markets inside and outside the EU with one single set of financial statements on the other hand. In order to achieve a world-wide acceptance of IFRS, the IASB needs to consider the interests of all relevant actors on a global level. However, parties outside the EU are presumably not interested in the compatibility of IFRS with the EU-specific economic and legal circumstances. For example, the FASB places heavy emphasis on the convergence of IFRS with US GAAP, but it should rather not have an interest in ensuring the conformity of IFRS with the EU Accounting Directives. Since it is the IASB's aim to develop global accounting standards, it rather seems impossible for the IASB to always ensure the compatibility of IFRS with the EU economic and legal environment, especially with the EU Accounting Directives. In the endorsement process, the EU accordingly has to trade off the objective to endorse the full set of IFRS, enabling EU companies to offer listings with their financial statements prepared according to IFRS on capital markets outside the EU, and the necessity to reject any IFRS that does not fit into the European economic and legal environment.

The case of financial instruments

Already in the first endorsement procedure in 2003, in which the whole set of IFRS was supposed to be adopted for application in the EU, the Commission faced the conflict of having to trade off the objective to make applicable the entire set of IFRS in the EU on the one side and to preserve the specific European interests on the other side. While the EFRAG proposed the endorsement of all IFRS, the Commission rejected IAS 32 *Financial Instruments: Disclosure and Presentation* and IAS 39 *Financial Instruments: Recognition and Measurement*, because it regarded the Standards not to give consideration to the particular circumstances of European banks. An important factor in the decision to reject the two Standards was the political pressure exercised especially by French banks and the French Prime Minister Chirac (Whittington 2005). On the other hand, the SEC warned the EU 'not to water down' IAS 39, as this would derogate the aimed convergence of IFRS and US GAAP (Evans 2004) and the IASB's Chairman appealed to the Commission's objective to avoid competitive disadvantages of EU companies on the global capital market and considered the rejection of IAS 32 and 39 to be a counteraction to the recognition of financial statements of EU companies at the US capital market (Reynolds 2003). As a reaction to the IASB's revision of the two Standards in 2004, in the same year, the EU endorsed IAS 32 entirely, IAS 39, however, was only partly endorsed; the Commission rejected the provisions relating to the 'full fair value option' and 'hedge accounting'. After another revision of IAS 39, the EU endorsed the provisions relating to the 'full fair value option', but the critical provisions relating to 'hedge accounting' have still not been integrated into Community Law.[16]

The long winded approach to finding a consensus on the accounting of financial instruments reveals that both the IASB and the EU have to make difficult trade offs in the standard-setting process, respectively the endorsement process. While the IASB puts emphasis on the need to find a consensus of the interests of all concerned parties in the standard-setting process and thus to design financial reporting standards that can be globally applied, the EU stresses the need for IFRS to be compatible with the EU economic and legal environment (Whittington 2005).

The case of goodwill accounting

As the EU Accounting Directives continue to exist beside endorsed IFRS, conformity of endorsed IFRS with the Accounting Directives is required. After the promulgation of the Modernization Directive in 2003, the EU Commission claimed that all conflicts between the Fourth and Seventh Company Law Directives and IFRS had been removed (Rationale 15 Modernization Directive).

In the first endorsement process in 2003, the Commission endorsed IAS 22 *Business Combinations*. IAS 22 requires acquired goodwill to be systematically amortized over its estimated useful life, which should normally not exceed 20 years (IAS 22.44, 22.49). The Accounting Directives follow the same approach. According to Art. 37(2) in relation with Art. 34(1a) Fourth Company Law Directive and Art. 30(1) Seventh Company Law Directive goodwill should be written off within a maximum time of five years, whereby Member States can allow companies to systematically amortize goodwill over a longer period.

As a consequence of the FASB's adoption of SFAS 141 *Business Combinations* and SFAS 142 *Goodwill and Other Intangible Assets* in 2001, the IASB issued IFRS 3 *Business Combinations*, which superseded IAS 22 in 2004. In contrast to IAS 22 and the Accounting Directives, the new Standard IFRS 3 prohibits the amortization of goodwill (IFRS 3.55). Instead, goodwill should be annually tested on impairment (IFRS 3.55) and depreciated if a loss in value is recognized (IAS 36.88).

Since the EU Accounting Directives unambiguously require the amortization of acquired goodwill, whereas IFRS 3 clearly prohibits it, IFRS 3 seems to be contrary to the true and fair view principle as referred to in the IFRS Regulation.[17] Nevertheless, the European Commission endorsed the Standard in 2004. One may conclude from this decision that the Commission preferred to adopt a Standard, which does not fit into the European legal environment, instead of creating EU-specific IFRS with its rejection.

In its comment letter on the Exposure Draft 3 *Business Combinations* the EFRAG considered the impairment test to be 'conceptually imperfect' and demanded for a systematic amortization of goodwill as a standard rule, only allowing the use of the 'impairment-only approach' in the rare cases when goodwill has an indefinite life (European Financial Reporting Advisory Group 2003). The IASB's adoption of the 'impairment-only approach' in IFRS 3 with only slight changes to the Exposure Draft reveals that the EFRAG's influence in the IASB's standard-setting process is not yet strong enough to enforce the European interests and to prevent conflicts between IFRS and the EU Accounting Directives at an early stage.

The legal consequences of the endorsement of IFRS 3 are, however, not clear. According to the jurisprudence of the European Court of Justice, a contradiction between a Council Regulation (the basic regulation) and the Commission Regulation (the implementing regulation) renders the latter void.[18] Hennrichs (2005) follows from the perceived incompatibility of IFRS 3 with the true and fair view principle as referred to in the IFRS Regulation, that the Commission Regulation, which endorsed IFRS 3, contradicts the IFRS Regulation. He concludes that the Commission Regulation is void and that the provisions in IFRS 3, which relate to the 'impairment-only-approach', are therefore not applicable in the EU (Hennrichs 2005).

Enforcement

Enforcement means 'the act of putting something such as a law into effect' (Black 1996). With regard to financial reporting enforcement means 'monitoring compliance of the financial information with the applicable financial reporting framework' and 'taking appropriate measures in case of infringements discovered in the course of enforcement' (CESR Standard No. 1, principle 2). With globalizing capital markets and the need for comparable financial information, a uniform application of IFRS is regarded to be just as desirable as a uniform endorsement of the Standards themselves. An important requirement to achieve this objective is the harmonization of the national enforcement mechanisms (Brown and Tarca 2005). In the following, we first introduce the EU's efforts referring to the co-ordination of the enforcement mechanisms in the Member

States and then focus on interdependencies with US enforcement mechanisms. Finally, we discuss the role of courts, particularly of the European Court of Justice, in the interpretation of IFRS and point out the related problems.

Corporate governance and market regulation as complementary means of enforcement

Enforcement is accomplished by the corporate governance system or market regulation (Leuz and Wüstemann 2004). Enforcement via corporate governance comprises the proper application of the relevant accounting regulations by management when preparing financial statements (self-enforcement), the approval of financial statements by the shareholders or the board of directors, a closer examination by the supervisory board or an audit committee (depending on the national corporate governance system) and the statutory audit (Wüstemann 2003, 2004). The main functions of the statutory audit in relation to enforcement are to ensure compliance with the underlying accounting rules by exercising control, and to underpin investors' confidence in financial reporting by giving an opinion on the compliance of accounting practices with legal requirements (Gehring 2001).

Enforcement via market regulation encompasses the monitoring of financial reporting by an independent supervisory body and reactions of the press and the public (Wüstemann 2002). In market-orientated financial systems, being characterized by a dispersed share ownership, enforcement is mainly based on market control by regulatory institutions. As the concrete organization and legal status of such bodies depend on the national institutional framework and corporate governance system, it strongly varies between different countries (Schipper 2005).

The case for a uniform enforcement of IFRS in the European Union

Apart from cases of fraud and error, enforcement actions are often taken in the event of accounting issues that are not specifically addressed by any Standard or Interpretation. If a transaction or event is not dealt with in any IFRS, it is up to the management to develop and apply appropriate accounting policies under consideration of the requirements in Standards and Interpretations relating to similar issues and the general concepts and principles in the IASB Framework (IAS 8.10, 8.11). In this context 'management may also consider the most recent pronouncements of other standard-setting bodies that use a similar conceptual framework to develop accounting standards, other accounting literature and accepted industry practices' if they do not conflict with the IASB Framework, the Standards and the Interpretations (IAS 8.12). In order to be able to judge whether the accounting policies developed by management comply with IFRS, enforcers have to interpret the general concepts and principles laid down in the IASB Framework as well as other IFRS dealing with similar issues (Schön 2004a). Since enforcers are likely to interpret IFRS similarly in comparable cases, preparers are expected to consider the publicly available enforcement decisions in their application of IFRS and particularly in case of the choice of accounting policies for 'unregulated' issues in order to avoid violations of IFRS.

Due to the impact of enforcement decisions on the interpretation and application of IFRS, the achievement of the objective of the IFRS Regulation to ensure a high degree of comparability of financial statements in the EU does not only require the mandatory use of the same set of accounting rules, but also a uniform enforcement mechanism (Brown and Tarca 2005). Accordingly, along with the introduction of IFRS in the European Union, the IFRS Regulation requires the co-ordination of enforcement of IFRS on the European level (Rationale 16 IFRS Regulation).

Collaboration of the national supervisory bodies on the European level

As significant differences in the corporate governance systems and the legal and economic environments in the EU Member States currently render the establishment of a centralized European regulatory authority impossible (Committee of Wise Men 2000; Fédération des Experts Comptables Européens 2002), the securing of compliance with IFRS is supposed to remain in the Member States' authority (Rationale 16 IFRS Regulation). Nonetheless, there is a call for convergence of enforcement mechanisms through collaboration between the independent supervisory bodies of the EU Member States in order to foster market confidence, to avoid regulatory arbitrage and to ensure consistent enforcement practice on the European level (e.g. Fédération des Experts Comptables Européens 2002). Based on the proposal of the Committee of Wise Men[19], in 2001, the European Commission established the Committee of European Securities Regulators (CESR), consisting of securities experts representing national public authorities. With regard to the enforcement of IFRS it is the CESR's role to encourage and administrate co-ordination between the national supervisory bodies by developing common rules in the form of guidelines, recommendations and standards and by supervising the regulatory practices in the EU Member States (Committee of European Securities Regulators 2002).

The CESR has been issuing two standards relating to the enforcement of IFRS so far. The national supervisory bodies are expected to stick to these rules even if they do not have legal status. CESR Standard No. 1 *On Financial Information – Enforcement of Standards on Financial Information in Europe* lays down certain minimum requirements as regards the organization, competence and functioning of the supervisory bodies in the EU Member States. The Standard requires the existence of a 'competent independent administrative authority' being responsible for the enforcement of IFRS in financial statements of publicly traded companies in each EU Member State.[20] As to the significantly varying forms of such authorities in the EU Member States, CESR Standard No. 1 only requires 'consistency of the scope and reliability of those enforcement systems'. For example, in the UK the enforcement authority, the Financial

Reporting Review Panel (FRRP), takes the form of a privately organized supervisory body, whereas in France, the body being responsible for the enforcement of accounting regulation, the 'Autorité des Marchés Financiers' (AMF), operates in the form of a public independent regulatory authority.

The Standard furthermore identifies common enforcement methods and actions. According to principle 16 of CESR Standard No. 1 'enforcers should take appropriate actions to achieve an appropriate disclosure and where relevant, public disclosure of misstatement', when they have detected material misstatements in financial information. Characteristically for the approach in the UK is that in cases of assumed violation of the accounting requirements, the FRRP seeks to persuade management to take remedial actions on a voluntary basis. If the issuer is not willing to take the corrective actions demanded by the FRRP, the latter can pass the case to the Court in order to require management to revise the accounts by means of legal action (Financial Reporting Review Panel 2006).[21] By contrast, in France the AMF is empowered to require management to take corrective actions and even to impose sanctions. Moreover, the AMF can demand the district court to enforce the rectification of the detected misstatement and it can pass the case to a civil, criminal or administrative court (Richard 2001).[22]

In CESR Standard No. 2 *On Financial Information – Co-ordination of Enforcement Activities*, the CESR proposes measures to achieve the required co-ordination of the national independent supervisory bodies in the EU. A convergence of the national enforcers' decisions on the compliance of accounting practices with IFRS should be reached by the creation of a database, containing all positive and negative enforcement decisions and being accessible to all members. In the sense of a case law system, these precedents should be considered in future cases and in identical or similar transactions and events similar decisions should be reached all over Europe. Additionally, European Enforcers Co-ordination Sessions (EECS) should be organized on a regular basis, giving the national regulatory authorities the opportunity to discuss previous enforcement decisions and to exchange experiences. It is strongly emphasized that the responsibility for the interpretation of IFRS is strictly reserved to the IFRIC and that neither on a national nor on the EU level should a distinct interpretation of IFRS be developed by the supervisory bodies.

Although a harmonized enforcement and consistent application of IFRS in the EU on the one hand and the avoidance of the development of EU-specific interpretations and applications of IFRS on the other hand is highly desirable, the achievement of these objectives does not appear to be feasible with the measures proposed by the CESR. That is because the interpretation of IFRS under consideration of the specific national economic and legal environments will presumably in many cases lead to different enforcement decisions in the Member States. Beyond this, the database only serves as a 'source of information' and 'a useful tool for the enforcers' decision-making process' (CESR Standard No. 2), but national supervisory bodies are not legally bound to stick to previous decisions of other enforcers in identical or similar transactions and events. Second, it is highly questionable whether the interpretation and enforcement of accounting standards can clearly be separated. We have shown above that enforcement decisions often require the interpretation of the underlying accounting rules and thereby lead to the creation of a sort of virtually binding body of accounting case law.[23] These interpretations might compete with decisions taken by other enforcers and courts, or even with Interpretations subsequently issued by the IFRIC. The CESR's intention to withdraw previously published enforcement decisions from the database if the IFRIC issues a contradicting Interpretation may avoid the emergence of conflicting interpretations of IFRS (CESR Standard No. 2), but, it affects the legal certainty as regards the application of IFRS, because preparers cannot rely on the 'legal validity' of the enforcers' interpretations of IFRS.[24]

Interdependencies with US enforcement

As stated above, one of the objectives that the EU pursued with the adoption of the IFRS Regulation was to facilitate EU companies to offer listings on capital markets inside and also outside the EU with the same set of financial statements. The world-wide acceptance of financial statements prepared according to IFRS by EU companies preconditions the consistent application of IFRS on a global level. Therefore, it is not only desirable to harmonize the enforcement of IFRS within the Community; rather the EU also needs to co-ordinate the enforcement of IFRS with the relevant actors outside the EU.

Since the acceptance of IFRS for cross-border listings at the US stock market without reconciliation to US GAAP is planned to be achieved until 2009[25], the SEC will have a major impact on the enforcement of IFRS. Its extensive enforcement powers grant the SEC a strong influence on accounting practice in the US, either by legally binding court decisions or by virtually obliging publications. This argument is supported by the much higher number of legal procedures initiated and conducted by the SEC[26] compared to the respective European supervisory bodies. In order to avoid the creation of a US-specific interpretation of IFRS and thus the requirement for multinational companies, being listed in the US, to have to adjust financial statements to the US-specific application of IFRS, the SEC and the CESR agreed to make a joint effort in the enforcement of IFRS.[27]

Interpretation of IFRS by courts

National courts

Since IFRS are provided with the status of Community Law in the endorsement process, they are expected to become subject to interpretation by courts in litigations relating to presumed non-compliances of financial statements with endorsed IFRS (Kirchner 2005; Schön 2004a; Schulze-Osterloh 2004). The impact of court rulings on the interpretation of accounting rules depends on various factors, such as the quality of accounting rules (legal norms vs. professional standards) and the relation of financial accounting and tax accounting.

In Germany, courts have interpreted the rather general accounting principles codified in statutes 'in literally thousands of court rulings' and thereby 'established a system of sound accounting principles and detailed standards' (Leuz and Wüstemann 2004). These cases have predominantly been submitted to the courts for clarification of accounting issues for taxation purposes; rulings on the compliance of financial statements with the requirement to provide 'true and fair' information have not been taken so far.

In the Netherlands, a legally determined group of interested parties can directly address a complaint about misleading financial statements to the Enterprise Chamber ('Ondernemingskamer'), a forum of the Court of Justice in Amsterdam. The fact that, out of 50 decisions concerning complaints about financial statements from 1974 to 2001, only 10 per cent were taken in the last ten years, can be regarded as an indicator for decreasing interest in individual complaints in the domain of accounting[28]. Beside the little frequency, these verdicts usually referred to very specific cases and therefore can hardly be considered as having created generally accepted accounting principles (Klaassen 2001).

As we have seen above, oversight institutions operating under the form of a privately organized review panel like the FRRP in the UK are not legally empowered to enforce corrective actions or to sanction non-compliance. Although they may enforce compliance by transmitting the respective cases to the Court, since now, none of the reviewed cases has been brought to the Court. The possibility to complain about criminal acts like fraud of managers in the preparation of financial statements has so far been only rarely exercised.

In France, our findings lead to a similar conclusion. Beside the infrequent transmission of accounting cases to courts by the AMF, similar to British legislation, aggrieved individuals can file a law-suit against the company's governing bodies if the provided information in the annual accounts is misleading, i.e. if it does not present a 'true and fair view' ('image fidèle') of the company's situation (Art. 425, 437 and 460 French Commercial Law) or if fictive dividends were distributed (Art. 347 French Commercial Law). Anyhow, only one court ruling concerning the application of accounting regulation has been taken in the French jurisprudence so far (Raffegeau *et al.* 2001).

From our findings we draw that as long as the application of IFRS is only required for information purposes in the EU, national court rulings may rather not have a significant influence on the interpretation of IFRS. However, the trend is that EU Member States increasingly permit or mandate the application of IFRS for purposes of the determination of distributable and taxable profits,[29, 30] so that national courts are expected to gain influence in the interpretation of IFRS in the future.

The European Court of Justice

In general, according to the EU principle of subsidiarity, the interpretation of Community Law is dedicated to the national courts of the Member States. In order to ensure the uniform application of Community Law in all EU Member States, the European Court of Justice possesses jurisdiction to give preliminary rulings on the interpretation of Community Law (Art. 234 Treaty). As IFRS become part of Community Law with their adoption by the European Commission in the endorsement process, national courts can call the European Court of Justice for interpretation of questions concerning endorsed IFRS if they consider the European Court of Justice's interpretation to be necessary for their final judgement (Art. 234 EC Treaty). The possibility to appeal to the European Court of Justice is reserved to national courts of the EU Member States; individuals cannot directly file a law-suit at the European Court of Justice when the application of Community Law is concerned.

So far, the European Court of Justice has interpreted accounting principles of the Fourth Company Law Directive only in three cases that all related to the determination of distributable or taxable profit[31]; the principles set out in the Seventh Company Law Directive have not yet been subject to interpretation by the European Court of Justice. As for the influence of national court rulings on the interpretation of IFRS, actions by the European Court of Justice should only rarely occur as long as the application of IFRS is only required in accounts,

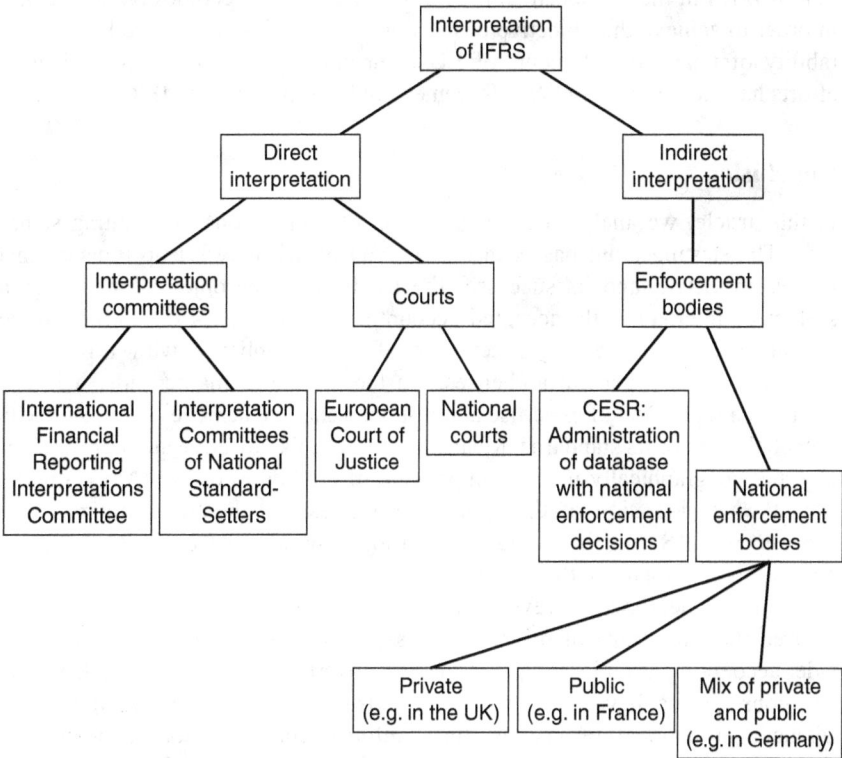

Figure 4 Interpretation of IFRS in the European Union.

having the purpose of providing information only. However, it has to be considered that previous rulings of the European Court of Justice referred to the interpretation of a directive, which principally becomes only effective with its transposition into national legislation. The fact that it can often not be unambiguously judged whether the case at question concerns a provision of national law or of Community Law may explain the reservation of national courts to call the European Court of Justice for interpretation. In contrast, the IFRS Regulation is directly effective European Law implying that national courts should appeal to the European Court of Justice in every case with a material impact.

Whereas the IFRIC bases the interpretation of the Standards on the concepts and general principles in the IASB Framework, the European Court of Justice is likely to base its interpretations of IFRS on the endorsement criteria, especially the 'true and fair view principle', since only IFRS that meet the endorsement criteria are applicable in the EU (Schön 2004a). That is one of the reasons why the European Court of Justice's interpretations of IFRS may not be compatible with future interpretations originated by the IFRIC. The 'competition' between interpretations of IFRS issued by the IFRIC, interpretations resulting from enforcement decisions of national supervisory bodies and judgements of the European Court of Justice is highly problematic, because it threatens the uniform application of IFRS in the European Union (Kirchner 2005). It becomes obvious that – in order to achieve the objective of the IFRS Regulation to increase the comparability of financial statements of EU companies – many more co-ordination efforts have to be made in the enforcement and interpretation of IFRS.

Conclusion

In this article, we analysed the legalization of transnational accounting standards. The starting point has been the creation of privately set up transnational bodies, the IASC and its successor the IASB, with the objective to design a system of internationally accepted accounting standards. As the IASB has no formal authority to require acceptance of and compliance with IFRS, it is dependent on two general audiences. On the private or market side, it has to establish a reputation of expertise and responsiveness to achieve acceptance with potential users of its standards. Means to achieve this objective are a professionally and geographically mixed composition of the bodies of the IASC Foundation, the consideration of the applicant's interests in the 'democratized' due process of IFRS and the granting of various implicit and explicit choices of accounting treatments in the Standards.

At the same time, however, we have seen that accounting has not only spurred the emergence of private norm systems. Most Western countries consider accounting as an important element to govern their respective markets and, as a consequence, have issued national provisions. Yet, there are significant differences in national provisions, their enforcement and, more generally, in national regulatory approaches. These differences have not only hampered the use of privately set accounting rules in the European context, where IFRS are endorsed and enforced in the complex multilevel setting. Private standards and accounting rules have also become subject to a regulatory competition between different systems, with the European Union and the SEC, respectively the FASB, being the most important actors.

In the process, two aspects are of particular interest. First, regulators on both sides have pressured the IASB to adapt its norms and rules to their peculiar needs. In this competition for influence, the SEC and the FASB retain a dominant influence on the IASB. Explanations for this observation are, on the one hand, internally conflicting interests in the European Union due to economic and cultural differences among the EU Member States. On the other hand, the attractiveness of US capital markets will prevail for the near future and will attract an increasing number of EU companies seeking to get listing.

Apart from the interesting finding of transnational legalization depending on political processes of co-ordination and competition both within the European Union and in the transatlantic relationship, the legal and technical implications of the endorsement and enforcement mechanism are worth further considerations. In particular, the compatibility of IFRS with the EU economic and legal environment as a precondition for the endorsement and application of IFRS in the EU has been of interest. A consequence of certain perceived incompatibilities is a legal uncertainty about the application of IFRS in the European Union. From the demonstration of the incompatibility of the accounting for financial instruments under IFRS and the specific circumstances of European banks as well as the differences in IFRS goodwill accounting and the EU Accounting Directives, we highlight the weaknesses of the endorsement mechanism and general difficulties in the field of legalization of transnational professional accounting standards.

Finally, we show that to ensure a uniform application of IFRS a harmonization of enforcement mechanisms such as enforcement actions of supervisory bodies is required. Drawn from past experiences with national court decisions, one may argue that the creation of specific national IFRS accounting practices should only rarely occur in the EU Member States. However, as the function of IFRS financial statements is likely to be extended from the sole purpose to provide information to the determination of distributable and taxable profits in the future, a transnational co-ordination of court rulings might become necessary. The role that the European Court of Justice will play with respect to the harmonization of enforcement of IFRS in the European Union is still an open question.

To conclude, we believe that despite a continuous convergence of national legal, financial and economic systems, remaining crucial differences still seem to impede a transnationally uniform application of one set of accounting standards. Although a worldwide increasing adoption of IFRS can be noticed, the institution of the endorsement mechanism in the European Union reveals that there is only a restricted readiness to delegate the power of rule-making in accounting to outsiders. The endorsement decisions that the European Commission has been taking so far make clear that the objectives to make applicable the entire set of IFRS in the European Union on the one hand and to regard the EU-specific circumstances and interests on the other hand are sometimes incompatible and therefore require the European Commission to make difficult trade-offs.

Notes

* The authors want to thank participants of the Zürich Center for Comparative and International Studies Workshop on 'Hard Law, Soft Law, and Private Legalities' and participants of the Accounting Workshop at the University of Mannheim (Area Accounting and Taxation) for their helpful comments. The authors are especially grateful to Dirk Lehmkuhl and Christian Brütsch for their intensive work on previous drafts of the paper.

1 It should be noted that there is also a case for a competition of accounting systems. Sunder (2002), for example, argues that a free choice between different sets of accounting standards would be more efficient than the mandatory use of a single set of globally applied accounting standards. See also Ballwieser (2001), Kirchner (2000) and Ordelheide (1998) for further discussion.

2 In April 2001, when the IASB took over the responsibility for the setting of IFRS, it approved a resolution to adopt International Accounting Standards (IAS) having been developed by its predecessor, the IASC, and Interpretations originating from the Standard Interpretations Committee (SIC), the predecessor of the International Financial Reporting Interpretations Committee (IFRIC).

3 According to the definition in IAS 1.11, IFRS comprise IFRS having been issued by the IASB since 2001, IAS having been developed by the IASC before 2001 and Interpretations originated by the IFRIC or the former Standing Interpretations Committee (SIC).

4 According to the IASB's aim to become a global standard-setter, the scope of users of IFRS is expanding constantly. Beside the mandatory use of IFRS for consolidated accounts of listed corporations in the EU since 2005 and the change-over to IFRS in Australia in 2005, there are numerous countries applying IFRS instead of developing their own national standards and certain stock markets that require the preparation of financial statements according to IFRS as a condition for listings. See for further details Wagenhofer (2005).

5 See for an overview over the structure of the IASC Foundation www.iasb.org/about/structure.asp (accessed 22 June 2006).

6 See for details IASC Foundation: Annual Report 2005. Available at: www.iasb.org/NR/rdonlyres/B95A11CA-A8E1-4B81-BF1C-CBF18C33F65F/0/10_845_1ASCFANNUALREPORTS.pdf (accessed 6 December 2006).

7 See www.sec./gov/news/speech/spch040605dtn.htm (accessed 2 March 2006).

8 See for the Norwalk Agreement www.fasb.org/news/memorandum.pdf (accessed 5 March 2006).

9 Member States may permit or require publicly traded EU companies to prepare their individual accounts according to IFRS (Art. 4a IFRS Regulation). Furthermore, they may permit or require non-listed EU companies to prepare their consolidated accounts and/or their individual accounts according to IFRS (Art. 4b IFRS Regulation).

10 The Lisbon European Council decided in 2000 that the International Market for Financial Services should be completed until 2005. See Presidency Conclusions from the Lisbon European Council, 23 and 24 March 2000.

11 Between 1998 and 2004 German listed parent companies have had the option to prepare their consolidated accounts according to IFRS or US GAAP instead of German GAAP (§ 292 a German Commercial Code). In this case of a 'dynamic reference' IFRS and US GAAP remained private norms that had become part of the national legal group accounting rules. The methodology of the dynamic reference in

Germany has been highly criticized as it refers to IFRS and US GAAP in their respective current form (Kirchhof 2000): if there are changes in IFRS or US GAAP, the new provisions are automatically integrated into national law. As a consequence, the mechanism of dynamic reference implies a de facto delegation of the authority to set legal norms to the non-legitimated IASB and FASB which may be disputable from a constitutionalistic perspective (Hommelhoff 1996).

12 Judgement of the European Court of Justice of 27 June 1996, Case C-234/94, European Court reports 1996, p. I-03133, here para. 18. See for a controversy on the role of the true and fair view principle in the endorsement of IFRS, Alexander (2006), Nobes (2006), and Wüstemann and Kierzek (2005 and 2006b).

13 See van Hulle (2004) for a detailed discussion of the endorsement criteria.

14 The Accounting Regulatory Committee was set up according to the EU-specific comitology rules that govern the delegation of implementing powers from the Council to the Commission. See Council Decision of 28 June 1999 laying down the procedures for the exercise of implementing powers conferred on the Commission (1999/468/EC), Official Journal, L 184, 17 July 1999, pp. 23–26.

15 If the Council affirms the Commission's proposal with a qualified majority or does not take a decision at all within three months, the Commission should take the required measures for the adoption of the respective IFRS. In case the Council rejects the proposal, the Commission is obliged to repeat the endorsement procedure and to bring a modified proposition before the Council. See for details Art. 5 of the Council Decision (1999/468/EC).

16 See for details as regards the endorsement of IAS 39 Whittington (2005).

17 See for details Wüstemann and Kierzek (2006b); Hennrichs (2005).

18 See Judgement of the European Court of Justice of 2 March 1999, Case C-179/97, European Court reports 1999, p. I-01251, here para. 9–11.

19 See Final Report of the Committee of Wise Men on the Regulation of European Securities Markets. Available at: ec.europa.eu/internal_market/securities/docs/lamfalussy/wisemen/final-report-wise-men_en.pdf (accessed 22 June 2006).

20 Until 2001, a market-based enforcement mechanism in the form of an institutional oversight of financial statements by a supervisory body has only existed in about half of the EU Member States (Fédération des Experts Comptables Européens 2001).

21 See for details relating to the FRRP Hines, McBride, Fearnley and Brandt (2001) and Cooke, Choudhury and Olusequn Wallace (2001).

22 See for details relating to the AMF, Dao (2005).

23 See also Wüstemann (2002).

24 See Wüstemann and Kierzek (2006a) for a detailed discussion of the EU's efforts to harmonize the enforcement of IFRS in the EU.

25 See SEC Press Release: Chairman Donaldson Meets with EU Internal Market Commissioner McCreevy. Available at: www.sec.gov/news/press/2005-62.htm (accessed 16 July 2005).

26 See for figures Kiefer (2003: 86).

27 See CESR Press Release: Meeting between CESR Chairman Arthur Docters van Leeuwen and US SEC Chairman Christopher Cox. Available at: www.cesr-eu.org (accessed 2 March 2006).

28 See Fédération des Experts Comptables Européens (2001) for the figures.

29 Some Member States already refer to IFRS for purposes of the determination of taxable profit. See Ernst & Young/Centre for European Economic Research (ZEW) (2004). See Schön (2004b) for an evaluation of the Commission's deliberations on the appropriateness of IFRS as a 'starting point' for purposes of the determination of taxable profits in the EU.

30 See for an overview over the status of the implementation of the IFRS Regulation in the Member States: europa.eu.int/comm/internal_market/accounting/ias_en.htm# options (accessed 25 February 2006).

31 See Judgement of the Court (Fifth Chamber) of 27 June 1996. Waltraud Tomberger v Gebrüder von der Wettern GmbH, Case C-234/94, European Court reports 1996, p. 3133; Judgement of the Court (Fifth Chamber) of 14 September 1999. DE+ES Bauunternehmung GmbH v Finanzamt Bergheim, Case C-275/97, European Court reports 1999, p. 5331; Judgement of the Court of 7 January 2003. Banque internationale pour l'Afrique occidentale SA (BIAO) v Finanzamt für Großunternehmen in Hamburg, Case C-306/99, European Court reports 2003, p. 1.

Bibliography

Abbott, K. W., Keohane, R. O., Moravcsik, A., Slaughter, A.-M. and Snidal, D. (2000) 'The Concept of Legalization', *International Organizations*, 54 (3): 401–419.

Accountancy Age (2003) 'Share options delay is a false dawn for opponents', 21 August 2003: 6.

Alexander, D. (2006) 'Legal Certainty, European-Ness and *Realpolitik*', *Accounting in Europe*, 3: 65–80.

Ballmann, A., Epstein, D. and O'Halloran, S. (2002) 'Delegation, Comitology, and the Separation of Powers in the European Union', *International Organizations*, 56 (3): 551–574.

Ballwieser, W. (2001) 'Konzernrechnungslegung und Wettbewerb', *Die Betriebswirtschaft*, 61 (6): 640–657.

Black, H. C. (1996) *Black's Law Dictionary*, 6th edn, Minnesota: West Publishing Co.

Brown, P. and Tarca, A. (2005) 'A Commentary on Issues Relating to the Enforcement of International Financial Reporting Standards in the EU', *European Accounting Review*, 14 (1): 181–212.

Canor, I. (1998) *The Limits of Judicial Discretion in the European Court of Justice: Security and Foreign Affairs Issues*, Baden-Baden: Nomos Verlagsgesellschaft.

Committee of European Securities Regulators (2002) *Charter of the Committee of European Securities Regulators*. Available at: www.cesr-eu.org/ (accessed 22 June 2006).

Committee of European Securities Regulators (2003) *Standard No. 1 on Financial Information – Enforcement of Standards on Financial Information in Europe*. Available at: www.cesr-eu.org/ (accessed 22 June 2006).

Committee of European Securities Regulators (2004) *Standard No. 2 on Financial Information – Coordination of Enforcement Activities*. Available at: www.cesr-eu.org/ (22 June 2006).

Committee of Wise Men on the Regulation of European Securities Markets (2000) *Initial Report of the Committee of Wise Men on the Regulation of European Securities Markets*. Available at: ec.europa.eu/internal_market/securities/docs/lamfalussy/wisemen/initial-report-wise-men_en.pdf (accessed 22 June 2006).

Cooke, T. E., Choudhury, M. and Olusequn Wallace, R. S. (2001) 'United Kingdom – Individual Accounts', in D. Ordelheide and KPMG (eds) *Transnational Accounting*, 2nd edn, New York: Palgrave, pp. 2571–2716.

Council of the EC (1978) Fourth Council Directive 78/660/EEC of 25 July 1978 based on Article 54 (3) (g) of the Treaty on the annual accounts of certain types of companies, *Official Journal L 222*, 14 August 1978, pp. 11–31 (quoted as *Fourth Company Law Directive*).

Council of the EC (1983) Seventh Council Directive 83/349/EEC of 13 June 1983 based on Article 54 (3) (g) of the Treaty on the annual accounts of certain types of companies, *Official Journal L 193*, 18 July 1983, pp. 1–17 (quoted as *Seventh Company Law Directive*).

Dao, T. H. P. (2005) 'Monitoring Compliance with IFRS: Some Insights from the French Regulatory System', *Accounting in Europe*, 2: 107–135.

Eriksen, E. D. and Fossum, J. E. (2002) 'Democracy through Strong Publics in the European Union?', *Journal of Common Market Studies*, 40 (3): 401–424.

Ernst & Young/Centre for European Economic Research (ZEW) (eds) (2004) *Company Taxation in the New EU Member States*, 2nd edn, Frankfurt am Main, Mannheim: Ernst & Young.

European Commission (1995) *Communication from the Commission: Accounting Harmonisation: A New Strategy Vis-à-Vis International Harmonisation*, COM (1995) 508.

European Commission (2000) *Communication from the Commission to the Council and the European Parliament: EU Financial Reporting Strategy: The Way Forward*, COM (2000) 359 final.

European Commission (2001) *Proposal for a Regulation of the European Parliament and of the Council on the Application of International Accounting Standards*, COM (2001) 80 final.

European Financial Reporting Advisory Group (2003) *ED 3 Business Combinations, Proposed Amendments to IAS 36 Impairment of Assets, and 38 Intangible Assets*. Available at: www.efrag.org/doc/1109_ED3Finalcommentletter.pdf (accessed 22 June 2006).

European Parliament and Council (2002) Regulation 1606/2002 of the European Parliament and of the Council of 19 July 2002 on the application of international accounting standards, *Official Journal L 243/1*, 11 September 2002, pp. 1–4 (quoted as *IFRS Regulation*).

European Parliament and Council (2003) Directive 2003/51/EC of the European Parliament and the Council of 18 June 2003 amending Directives 78/349/EEC, 86/635/EEC and 91/674/EEC on the annual and consolidated accounts of certain types of companies, banks and other financial institutions and insurance undertakings, *Official Journal L 178*, 17 July 2003, pp. 6–22 (quoted as *Modernization Directive*).

Evans, C. (2004) 'SEC warns EU on derivatives', *Accountancy*, 2 February 2004. Available at: www.accountancymagazine.com/main.asp?StoryID=6322 (accessed 29 June 2006).

Fédération des Experts Comptables Européens (2001) *Enforcement Mechanisms in Europe*. Available at: www.fee.be/publications/default.asp?library_ref=Y&content_ref=108 (accessed 6 December 2006).

Fédération des Experts Comptables Européens (2002) *Discussion Paper on Enforcement of IFRS within Europe*. Available at: www.fee.be/publications/default.asp?library_ref=Y&content_ref=273 (accessed 6 December 2006).

Financial Reporting Review Panel (2006) *Operating Procedures*. Available at: www.frc.org.uk/documents/pagemanager/frrp/Operating%20Procedures.pdf (accessed 9 March 2006).

Flower, J. and Ebbers, G. (2002) *Global Financial Reporting*, New York: Palgrave.

Gehring, A. (2001) *Abschlussprüfung, Gewissenhaftigkeit und Prüfungsstandards*, Baden-Baden: Nomos.

Hennrichs, J. (2005) 'Zur normativen Reichweite der IFRS – Zugleich Anmerkungen zu den Urteilen des EuGH und des FG Hamburg in der Rechtssache "BIAO"', *Neue Zeitschrift für Gesellschaftsrecht*, 8 (19): 783–797.

Hines, T., McBride, K., Fearnley, S. and Brandt, R. (2001) 'We're off to see the wizard', *Accounting, Auditing & Accountability Journal*, 14 (1): 53–84.

Hommelhoff, P. (1996) 'Deutscher Konzernabschluß: International Accounting

Standards und das Grundgesetz', in R. Böttcher (ed.) *Festschrift für Walter Odersky zum 70. Geburtstag am 17. Juli 1996*, Berlin: de Gruyter, pp. 779–797.

Hopwood, A. G. (1994) 'Some Reflections on the Harmonization of Accounting Within the EU', *European Accounting Review*, 3 (2): 241–253.

Investor Relations Business News (2002) 'FASB, IASB to Converge Standards', 7: 11.

Kiefer, M. (2003). *Kritische Analyse der Kapitalmarktregulierung der US Securities and Exchange Commission*, Wiesbaden: Gabler.

Kirchhof, P. (2000) 'Gesetzgebung und private Regelsetzung als Geltungsgrund für Rechnungslegungspflichten?', *Zeitschrift für Unternehmens- und Gesellschaftsrecht*, 29 (4–5): 681–692.

Kirchner, C. (2000) 'Der Wettbewerbsfaktor "Entscheidungsnützlichkeit von Rechnungslegungsinformationen": Eine Institutionenökonomische Analyse', in T. Schildbach and A. Wagenhofer (eds) *Wettbewerb und Unternehmensrechnung*, Sonderheft 45 der Zeitschrift für betriebswirtschaftliche Forschung, Düsseldorf, Frankfurt am Main: Verlagsgruppe Handelsblatt GmbH, pp. 41–68.

Kirchner, C. (2005) 'Zur Interpretation von internationalen Rechnungslegungsstandards: das Problem "hybrider Rechtsfortbildung"', in D. Schneider, D. Rückle, H.-V. Küpper and F. W. Wagner (eds) *Kritisches zu Rechnungslegung und Unternehmensbesteuerung, Festschrift zur Vollendung des 65. Lebensjahrs von Theodor Siegel*, Berlin: Duncker & Humblot, pp. 201–217.

Kostelitz, J. (2002) 'Tackling the Tower of Babel', *The Secured Lender*: 34–40.

Leuz, C. and Wüstemann, J. (2004) 'The Role of Accounting in the German Financial System', in J. P. Krahnen and R. H. Schmidt (eds) *The German Financial System*, Oxford: Oxford University Press, pp. 450–481.

Miller, P. B. W., Redding, R. J. and Bahnson, P. R. (1998) *The FASB: The People, the Process, and the Politics*, 4th edn, Boston et al.: Irwin/McGraw-Hill.

Nobes, C. W. (2006) 'Revenue Recognition and EU Endorsement of IFRS', *Accounting in Europe*, 3: 81–89.

Ordelheide, D. (1998) 'Wettbewerb der Rechnungslegungssysteme IAS, US-GAAP und HGB', in C. Börsig and A. Coenenberg (eds) *Controlling und Rechnungswesen im Internationalen Wettbewerb*, Stuttgart: Schäffer Poeschel, pp. 15–53.

Raffegeau, J., Dufils, P., Lopater, C. and Arfaoui, F. (2001) *Mémento Pratique Francis Lefebvre – Comptable 2001*, Levallois: Editions Francis Lefebvre.

Reynolds, B. (2003) 'Tweedie Warns on Derivatives', *Accountancy*, 17 December 2003. Available at: www.accountancymagazine.com/main.asp?StoryID=6203 (accessed 29 June 2006).

Richard, J. (2001) 'France – Group Accounts', in D. Ordelheide and KPMG (eds) *Transnational Accounting*, 2nd edn, New York: Palgrave, pp. 1129–1215.

Schipper, K. (2005) 'The Introduction of International Financial Reporting Standards in Europe: Implications for International Convergence', *European Accounting Review*, 14 (1): 101–126.

Schön, W. (2004a) 'Kompetenz der Gerichte zur Auslegung von IFRS', *Betriebs-Berater*, 59 (16): 763–768.

Schön, W. (2004b) 'International Accounting Standards – A "Starting Point" for a Common European Tax Base?', *European Taxation*, 40 (10): 426–440.

Schulze-Osterloh, J. (2004) 'Internationalisierung der Rechnungslegung und ihre Auswirkungen auf die Grundprinzipien des deutschen Rechts', *Der Konzern*, 2 (3): 173–177.

Sunder, S. (2002) 'Regulatory Competition Among Accounting Standards Within And

Across International Boundaries', *Journal of Accounting and Public Policy*, 21 (3): 219–234.

van Helleman, J. and Slomp, S. (2002) 'The Changeover to International Accounting Standards in Europe', *Betriebswirtschaftliche Forschung und Praxis*, 54 (3): 213–229.

van Hulle, K. (2004) 'From Accounting Directives to International Accounting Standards', in C. Leuz, D. Pfaff and A. Hopwood (eds) *The Economics and Politics of Accounting*, Oxford: Oxford University Press, pp. 349–375.

Wagenhofer, A. (2005) *Internationale Rechnungslegungsstandards – IAS/IFRS*, 5th edn, Frankfurt am Main: Überreuter.

Wessels, W. (1998) 'Comitology: Fusion in Action. Politico-Administrative Trends in the EU System', *Journal of European Public Policy*, 5 (2): 203–234.

Whittington, G. (2005) 'The Adoption of International Accounting Standards', *European Accounting Review*, 14 (1): 127–153.

Wüstemann, J. (2002) *Institutionenökonomik und internationale Rechnungslegungsordnungen*, Tübingen: Siebeck Mohr.

Wüstemann, J. (2003) 'Disclosure Regimes and Corporate Governance', *Journal of Institutional and Theoretical Economics*, 159 (4): 717–726.

Wüstemann, J. (2004) 'Evaluation and Response to Risk in International Accounting and Audit Systems: Framework and German Experiences', *The Journal of Corporation Law*, 29 (2): 449–466.

Wüstemann, J. and Kierzek, S. (2005) 'Revenue Recognition under IFRS Revisited: Conceptual Models, Current Proposals and Practical Consequences', *Accounting in Europe*, 2: 69–106.

Wüstemann, J. and Kierzek, S. (2006a) 'Das Europäische Harmonisierungsprogramm zur Rechnungslegung: Endorsement und Enforcement von IFRS', *Betriebs-Berater*, 61 (Supplement to Vol. 17): 14–22.

Wüstemann, J. and Kierzek, S. (2006b) 'True and Fair View Revisited – A Reply to Alexander and Nobes', *Accounting in Europe*, 3: 91–116.

Zeff, S. A. (2002) 'Political Lobbying on Proposed Standards: A Challenge to the IASB', *Accounting Horizons*, 16 (1): 43–54.

4 The harmonization of private commercial law

The case of secured finance

Edward S. Cohen

Contemporary capitalist economies are centred around the flow of finance in the form of credit. Creditor–debtor relationships are at the heart of the networks of contracts and organizations that link together the major sectors and actors in the economy. The emergence of transnational credit finance, however, has posed a variety of challenges for states and their legal systems. The forms that credit takes are the product and object of legal regulation, and the differences in the ways that legal orders conceptualize and govern credit finance are substantial and deeply rooted. In their attempts to promote and regulate transnational commerce, states, international institutions, financial institutions, and legal professionals are now engaged in multiple arenas to find strategies to overcome these differences through the harmonization of the legal regimes governing finance. These actors share a common project of achieving an international consensus on the principles of financial law, and to use this as a standard to guide the reform of national legal systems.

In this chapter, I focus on one area of financial law – the law of secured transactions – in order to explore the dynamics of the larger project of harmonizing private commercial law. The drive for legal harmonization, I suggest, is an important though neglected element of the contemporary phenomenon of legalization and the ultimate goal of this essay is to contribute to our understanding of the sources and impact of legalization itself. My analysis advances three claims concerning legalization, which move from the more general to the more focused. First, I challenge emerging rationalist and functionalist accounts of legalization in the global economy. The process of legalization, I argue, renders problematic existing boundaries between the national and the international, challenges our understanding of the public/private divide, and requires close examination of the activities of legal experts and their interaction with national and international institutions. Second, I emphasize the role and importance of private international commercial law and legal processes in the legalization of global governance. While often ignored in the treatment of legalization, private international law is central to the legal infrastructure of transnational commercial activity. Third, my account focuses on the constitution of the norms and principles that shape transnational legal frameworks, and on the movement of these norms and principles across and within national boundaries. In the process of legalization, power relationships and differentials are enacted through, and must be understood within, the contest over the norms and principles that inform institutions. In my discussion of this contest, I place special emphasis on the strategy of internationalizing national legal models, which is central to the current process of harmonizing commercial law.

Legalization and the transnational political economy

The study of international law has long been a neglected step-child in mainstream international relations and political economy. For the most part, scholars in these areas have dismissed legal phenomena as at best symbolic representations of more fundamental relationships of power and wealth, and at worst as simple distractions. But this situation is now changing. Developments in a variety of areas – increasing contestations over the nature of intellectual property, growing activism concerning the rights of consumers in an age of digital production and consumption, sustained movements for market-oriented legal reform throughout the globe, an explosion in transnational commercial law-making, etc. – make it clear that legal rules and institutions are now a central field on which contests are fought over the regulation of global capitalism. Instead of dismissing international legal processes and institutions as side-shows, we need to approach them as constitutive elements in the conflicts over power and wealth in contemporary capitalism.

What explains this growing relevance of law, usually referred to as 'legalization', in the global political economy? To this point, the most influential approach to legalization in the social sciences is the rationalist model centred around the analysis of international regimes (Goldstein *et al.*, 2000). This model conceptualizes emerging legal orders as more or less institutionalized arrangements through which states resolve collective action obstacles and thus secure mutual benefits. In this approach, the primary reason that states promote legalization is to find ways for the effective collective governance of transnational economic and political processes, and to provide the means to resolve disputes through legitimate common norms. As this model views legalized regimes as contributing to a distinctive form of global governance – one which relies on the resolution of conflict through collective norms rather than interest or power-based bargaining – much of the analytical focus is on the conditions under which such regimes are effective in shaping the behaviour of states. All instances of legalized relationships are measured against an ideal-type of a fully institutionalized regime, characterized by clear sources of authority in treaties and formal agreements, a dispute resolution system that uses the founding treaties to develop a coherent body of interpretation and precedent, and a reliable means for enforcing its rules.

Whatever its virtues, however, this model fails to capture the variety of ways in which law and legal processes shape the current political economy. (Finnemore and Toope, 2001) Instead of starting with regimes, my account emphasizes the construction of transnational spaces, and the flows of capital, goods, and persons through these spaces, as a central feature of the global political economy. Following Sassen (1996, 2000), I focus on the structural rearrangement in the nature and operation of political and economic power that is part of the emergence of transnational relationships since the 1970s. This rearrangement, which centres on the reconfiguration of states to facilitate the deeper integration of markets, has been driven by and been dependent upon the hegemonic position of the US state and financial markets. Two aspects of this project have been crucial for the analysis of legalization. First, it requires a substantial reform and reconfiguration of the legal structures and rules governing national and international markets. Second, to the degree that it has led to the emergence of networks of economic activity that escape traditional forms of control by the nation-state, it has generated a demand for new kinds of legal regimes to help shape and regulate transnational markets and activity.

In response, various actors – states, private business, professionals, etc. – have attempted to fashion new legal orders to stabilize and regulate these spaces and networks.[1] This move to law involves the emergence of legal rules and standards, and the construction or revitalization of institutions (or 'sites') for the articulation and enforcement of legal rules. But these efforts add a new twist to the transnational political economy. Emerging legal processes and institutions engage new and various actors and interests in the governance of the global economy, which may modify and/or challenge the goals of hegemonic power. They also complicate the process of governance itself, by multiplying the sites and agents over which power and authority must be exercised. The resulting ambiguity leads to a constant struggle over the shape and relationship of legal orders, a struggle based on ongoing transnational contests over principles, wealth and power.

From these foundations, I suggest a very different picture of the nature of legalization, one centred on the following three themes. First, the pluralism of legal institutions, norms, and orders is a defining feature of the governance of transnational economic relationships. In addition to the state-based regimes, we can observe a variety of legal orders – public and private, national, international, and transnational – of varying shape and dynamics, including the highly institutionalized WTO dispute resolution system, the very informal world of commercial arbitration, and civil society compacts such as the forest certification system. Nor is there any necessary common trajectory in the development of these different kinds of legal systems; indeed, there are good reasons to believe that legal pluralism is a defining feature of legalization today. Moreover, these different orders (and the actors and institutions that constitute them) do not exist in isolation, but are in constant interaction with each other. There is not, nor will there likely be, any fixed allocation of issues or problems to specific autonomous orders.

Second, it is a mistake to assume that states are always the dominant actors in shaping legalization. While they remain central actors, states and their representatives are joined in the construction and enforcement of legal orders by a variety of other public and private agents. These include multilateral institutions and banks, private corporations and business associations, non-governmental organizations, and professional experts (especially, but not exclusively, lawyers) and their associations. In this chapter, I place special emphasis on the role of professional experts – particularly legal reformers – in articulating and circulating norms and principles for the legal governance of commercial relationships. But the larger point is that any one of these kinds of actors, or various coalitions between them, can be the driver of the legalization process, and that relationships between these actors are often in flux. In addition, as Slaughter (2004) has emphasized, we ought not to assume that policy-makers in any state are a unified group. Rather, the various sub-groups of regulators are often linked in dense cross-national networks which often include these other kinds of actors as well.

Third, the heavy functionalist influence on the dominant model obscures the ways in which relationships of, and contests over, power are implicated in legalization. As in any legal order, the construction of transnational legal frameworks is played out through legal discourses in which principles, norms, and rules play a central part. Following Braithwaite and Drahos (2000), I emphasize the role of these discourses in creating and diffusing the shared understandings on which the governance of economic relationships is built. Legal expertise and the particular concerns of legal specialists, in turn, are often at the forefront of debates over the shape of legal orders. But the work of these discourses and specialists is informed and constrained by power relationships, while they also shape the way power and interests are understood. Legalization projects almost always combine considerations of power, interests, and normative vision; states and private interests must articulate their goals in terms of legal–normative projects, and legal norm entrepreneurs and advocacy networks must link their goals to the power and/or interest agendas of other actors. My account places special emphasis on the role of epistemic communities of legal experts as key players in the shaping of legal regimes though the articulation of normative legal-agendas. The key questions, as Sell and Prakash (2004) demonstrate, concern the ways these specialists are attached to projects of power and influence, projects which can involve professional interests, state agendas, the aims of private actors, or any combination of these factors. An adequate understanding of particular legal orders and the relationships between them, I suggest, requires careful investigation of the ways in which legal conceptions are articulated to and against specific agendas of power.[2]

The political economy of private international commercial law

Private international commercial law is constituted by rules that directly shape the activity of businesses (and other actors) – rules regarding contract practices, the definition of property rights, dispute settlement, the management of insolvent firms, corporate governance, corporate finance, etc.[3] They create the essential legal framework through which markets and corporations are constructed and within (and around) which they operate.[4] For the most part, these rules emerge from national legal systems. As a result, any international commercial actor and/or transaction is likely to be subject to multiple, and often conflicting, national rules. Since the mid-nineteenth century, Western legal systems have responded to this problem with the development of rules of 'conflicts of law', which aim to determine which national rule(s) applies to any specific international commercial activity. This sub-discipline of conflicts of law has long been understood as the essential core of private commercial international law. The basic principle that shapes practice in this area of law, then, has been that international commercial actors and transactions are best governed by being 'nationalized', subjected to the most appropriate national legal order.

Over the past three decades, however, many state officials, business representatives, practising lawyers, and legal scholars have concluded that the strategy of nationalization through conflicts of law rules can no longer provide adequate legal regulation for transnational commerce. In this view, the reality that commercial transactions are increasingly transnational in character means that the attempt to find the appropriate national locus of for their regulation is increasingly futile, while the persistence of significant national legal diversity becomes in itself a further obstacle to deeper economic integration itself. On the basis of these concerns, a project for the reform and modernization – or the 'harmonization' – of private commercial international law has taken root since the 1970s. At the heart of this project is the development of common principles of private commercial law, and the diffusion of these principles throughout the various sites and institutions in which commercial law is articulated and enforced, and international commerce is regulated by law.[5]

While the idea of legal harmonization has existed for a century or more, the contemporary project is closely linked to the restructuring of the global political economy initiated by US policy-makers and business in the 1970s (Cutler, 2003; Wiener, 1999). The connection is not simply chronological. The private law strategy of nationalizing commercial disputes was well adapted to the conditions of the system of 'embedded liberalism' described by Ruggie (1982). In order for the project of deepening economic integration to succeed, many of the basic substantive and procedural foundations of private commercial law within and between states needed to be reformed. The harmonization project took off because many of its long-standing advocates found new support among policy-makers, business representatives, and legal professionals, support generated by a recognition of the new structural conditions in the global economy. In the area of private commercial law, though, it is important to emphasize that the focus is less on the 'legalization' of new areas of activity than on changing the content of bodies of existing law and the orientation of existing legal institutions. Harmonization aims at creating a legal framework that facilitates (while regulating) the integration of markets and the movement of capital and investment across national borders.[6]

At the centre of the harmonization project are three (often intertwined) networks of actors, which together form a 'transnational policy coalition'. I draw this concept from two sources. In her analysis of policy diffusion and change,

Stone identifies 'transnational policy communities' as '... experts and professionals [who] share their expertise and information and form common patterns of understanding regarding policy through regular interaction (international conferences, government delegations and sustained communication)' (2004: 559). In order to grasp the active role of these networks in advancing policy or legal change, though, I combine Stone's approach with that of Khagram *et al.*, who identify a 'transnational coalition' as '... sets of actors linked across country boundaries who coordinate shared strategies or sets of tactics to publicly influence social change' (2002: 7). A transnational policy coalition, I suggest, is a coalition of networks which share a commitment to promote policy change at various sites in the transnational system. It pulls together networks and actors motivated by different concerns – normative advocacy, political power, and economic interests – but share a common policy agenda. In the emerging transnational system, I contend, transnational policy coalitions are crucial drivers of policy development and change, in all areas of law and regulation involving the global economy. They pursue various projects, such as harmonization, in order to advance a common agenda for the governance of specific parts of the global system.

In the area of legal harmonization, transnational policy coalitions usually include three types of networks. First, there is a transnational network of legal experts – academics and practitioners – who advance harmonization goals on the basis of claims of professional expertise and shared normative goals. A crucial aim of these experts is to mobilize emerging networks of private law policy makers and bureaucrats from key states and international institutions, the second type of network, which have the authority necessary to reform national and international commercial law. The third network is made up of business interests, represented by national and international business organizations, with specific interests in the development of key areas of commercial law. These networks and their members work together in a variety of fora – national legal reform efforts; the development of model laws; the negotiation of international agreements; the shaping of judicial interpretation – to advance a common set of principles for commercial law. As such, the project of legal harmonization illustrates many of the players identified in the social science literature on the role of networks in transnational policy-making – epistemic communities (legal experts), intergovernmental networks (private law policy-makers), advocacy coalitions, and non-state actors and interests (business). However, as I will emphasize below, it is inadequate to characterize any one of these networks as one 'type'. In practice, each network can exhibit the characteristics of different types of network, often at the same time, a dimension facilitated by the regular movement of individuals between these networks.[7]

While this transnational policy coalition works to advance the harmonization project, though, this project faces significant opposition from counter-networks of experts, officials, and interests. At present, the key conflicts are generated by the perception that the harmonization agenda privileges principles of commercial law and practice derived from Anglo-American models of capitalism. In many cases, this has generated resistance from those who defend alternative models of capitalism, a resistance which sometimes turns into an alternative harmonization project. As a result, the field of commercial law-making has become the scene of a continuing struggle over which principles, norms, and rules should constitute the standard for a regime of commercial law capable of promoting and regulating a transnational economy. By examining this ongoing political process, we can gain insight into some of the key sources and dynamics of the legalization of the global political economy.

In order to advance this goal, the analysis in the rest of this chapter centers on one ongoing area of reform in private international commercial law – the law concerning secured transactions. The efforts to reform this particular area of commercial law, an important part of the modern law of credit finance, illustrate the complexity and fluidity that is characteristic of the processes of legalization in the contemporary world. My analysis identifies a key dynamic in the politics of legalization – the attempts of the harmonizing coalitions to 'internationalize' one national legal regime as the foundation of a global standard of secured transactions law, to use this standard to guide legal change in specific fora (private and public, national and international) and the resistance faced by this project. The push for secured transactions law reform, I suggest, provides a good case for furthering our understanding of how legal norms and principles cross key national and sectoral boundaries, a process which is central to the ways in which legalization is manifested in the contemporary political economy.

Credit finance and the law of secured transactions.

In this section, I provide an introduction to the nature and role of secured finance and review the basics of secured transactions law, which governs secured financial relationships. I then explain the basics of the contemporary US law of secured transactions, known as the 'Article 9' approach, on the basis of which the harmonization coalitions are attempting to build a new global standard for secured finance law.

Secured finance and modern capitalism.

In contemporary capitalist economies, credit finance is provided to businesses by a variety of actors, particularly banks, commercial finance companies, and suppliers. It comes in two general forms, 'unsecured' and 'secured'. Unsecured credit is provided by a lender on the basis of a close analysis of the creditworthiness of the borrower; the interest rate at which such credit is offered will vary with the lender's assessment of the riskiness of the borrower. Secured credit is provided in exchange for some form of collateral; unsecured credit is advanced without any exchange of collateral. When a secured credit agreement is arranged, the borrower agrees to offer some part or aspect of its property as collateral to secure the repayment of the loan; the lender, then, attains what is termed a 'security interest' in that property.

Secured financing has great advantages for creditors, which are important in understanding its role in business finance (McCormack, 2004: Chapter 1). First, the taking of a security interest in an asset gives the lender some control over its use, and thus some increased oversight of the borrower's activities. (This is an advantage only in some situations; in other contexts, lenders prefer to avoid the costs of such oversight with unsecured loans.) Second, most modern legal systems allow secured creditors to take possession of the asset in which collateral is given upon default of the debtor. In regular commercial relationships, it is a relatively simple matter for creditors – upon demonstration of default – to attain a court order allowing them to take possession of the asset in question. Third, most modern bankruptcy/insolvency systems grant some 'priority' to secured creditors; '... the taking of security maximizes the creditor's prospects of recovery in the event of the debtor's insolvency' (McCormack, 2004: 5). In the case of unsecured loans, creditors have to take their chances with what is usually regarded as the cumbersome and unpredictable process of insolvency law. The fewer obstacles a legal system puts in the way of secured finance, the more secured lenders – especially commercial banks and commercial finance companies – benefit.

For many legal and economic analysts, these specific benefits translate into general advantages for society as a whole. Put simply, the more security for creditors, the more credit is provided to the economy; the result is greater efficiency and economic growth (Fleisig, 1998). In this view, banks and other creditors are reluctant to lend without security to all but the largest and most established businesses. Without the possibility of secured financing, small and medium-sized businesses, and newly established firms more generally, are likely to be either frozen out of credit markets or charged much higher interests rates for loan capital. By bringing more business into the credit markets and expanding the supply of credit, then, the existence of secured financing leads to higher rates of economic activity, benefiting borrowers specifically and the public more generally. There remains much debate among specialists concerning this argument, but it is widely accepted in recent movements to harmonize secured transactions law.

The law of secured transactions

As modern commercial law developed along with capitalism, it was faced with the questions of what sorts of assets could be used as collateral for loans and the closely related issue of ownership of that collateral. 'Traditionally, security interests were often limited to the following two types: non-possessory security interests over immovables and possessory security interests over movables' (IMF, 2002: 4). Simply put, if a borrower wanted to offer as collateral for a loan a form of movable property (essentially, not land or fixed buildings), the lender would have to acquire possession of that property until the loan was paid. By the late nineteenth century, the increasing importance of mobile forms of wealth led creditors to push for a new legal regime. In different ways, the legal systems of the major capitalist economies developed legal forms to accommodate financial transactions based on 'non-possessory security interests over movables', such as inventories, goods, and accounts receivable. The result was a proliferation of different types of legal devices to govern different forms of secured transactions, each with its own slightly different implications for how credit was arranged and how the security interests created would be handled in bankruptcy, closely tied to different approaches to the law of property (Tajti, 2002a).

By the mid-twentieth century, national systems of secured credit law displayed great variation in the ways in which security interests could be created and enforced. There remained wide differences in the kinds of assets – especially moveable assets – that could be used to secure a loan, and the circumstances in which this could be done. The level of formality necessary when arranging secured financing, and thus necessary to prove the existence of a security interest, varied widely. In some states, a wide range of secured loans required public registration (often with different registration systems for different devices), while in others no such registration was necessary. The ability of creditors to seize the assets of a debtor in default differed widely. In some jurisdictions, this could be done without any formal legal process in some situations, while in other jurisdictions (especially civil law systems) such forms of 'self-help' were usually prohibited. Insolvency law treated secured creditors very differently; while some gave them absolute priority, others tried to balance their claims more evenly with those of unsecured creditors. At the heart of these differences lay contrasting judgments concerning the role and nature of credit, the rights of different kids of creditors, and the ways to protect debtors from predatory creditors (Wood, 1998). Legal regimes that leaned towards the interests of creditors allowed market actors substantial leeway in creating new security devices and granted creditors substantial freedom to enforce their claims as they saw fit. At the other end were legal regimes that were suspicious of non-traditional forms of credit and concerned about the ability of creditors to manipulate debtors into vulnerable situations. These systems embodied more precise limitations on the forms of secured credit agreements and required lengthy formal procedures before secured creditors could seize the assets of defaulting debtors. In addition to protecting some forms of debtors, these legal regimes were common in bank-dominated forms of capitalism, and protected the dominance of large banks in the provision of commercial finance.

Article 9 and secured transactions law

The policy coalition behind the current project for harmonizing secured transactions law is united behind a set of principles, a model of an appropriate legal framework, derived from the Uniform Commercial Code (UCC), itself the product of an attempt to 'modernize' and 'systematize' commercial law in the United States (Rubin, 1997). Article 9 of the UCC amounted to a fundamental reorganization and redefinition of secured transactions law across the US, one which fundamentally distinguishes US law from both its common law cousins and from the civil law tradition. (Bridge *et al.*, 1999, Scott, 1994). What is the significance of this approach for the way property rights and power are distributed in secured transactions? Article 9's adoption marked the acceptance of a wide range of assets as the basis for security interests, deference to the choices of market agents in setting the terms of secured credit, and simplification of the legal formalities of secured finance arrangements. It provided a legal framework that better fit the emerging dynamics of the post-Second World War financial system in the US. Although there is much debate surrounding the exact relationship, it has also coincided with a major expansion in the market for secured credit in the US. There is less controversy regarding the benefits of Article 9 for the financial institutions that provide such credit, in relationship to borrowers and especially unsecured creditors. The growth of the market provides more business for these institutions which, in combination with their expertise in writing financing contracts, leads to more power for secured creditors over the assets and decisions of borrowers. Combined with the strengthening of the role of private enforcement and the priority rules, Article 9 establishes a clearly creditor-friendly legal framework for commercial finance. Whatever their views on the efficiency impact of secured credit, almost all the commentators agree that this is a legal regime from which secured creditors have gained significantly (Scott, 1997).

The success of Article 9 in the US, and the UCC more generally, had the unanticipated effect of transforming the world of international private commercial law-making. The Article 9 approach to the law of secured finance provided a model around which a community of experts and advocates developed. As a set of principles that moved beyond both traditional common and civil law approaches, it presented an opportunity to build a new international basis for private financial law. By the 1970s, a transnational network of experts on secured transactions law had developed, dominated by legal scholars and practitioners whose authority derived from their understanding of the Article 9 model, which they offered as the most 'efficient' and 'modern' approach in the field. These epistemic claims, however, were coupled with a commitment to advocacy of legal reform, a project to reconstruct and harmonize secured finance law around the world. In the view of these experts, reforming legal systems around the principles of Article 9 would be a key step in opening up new sources of credit finance around the world, which in turn would deepen economic integration, stimulate investment and growth, and help alleviate poverty (Fleisig, 1996, 1998; Goode, 1998).

Reconstructing the law of secured transactions: internationalizing Article 9

The emergence of an effective harmonization project, however, required the mobilization of policy-makers and private interests into a broader transnational policy coalition. It was the transformations of the global political economy in the 1980s and especially the 1990s that created the conditions in which this coalition could emerge. The neo-liberal project put the issue of legal harmonization on the agenda of major states (especially the US) and international institutions, in areas ranging from trade policy to services, intellectual property, and financial regulation. Market liberalization in developing economies, and the subsequent opening of East European and Central Asian economies to the global market place, created new contexts in which to pursue the neo-liberal governance agenda. At the same time, these market openings led commercial finance institutions to take seriously the idea of expanding their lending activity into contexts where the existing legal and policy environment had prevented their activity. In this context, an expert community was able to attach itself to coalitions of policy makers and private interests to create a transnational policy coalition to advance the reform of secured transactions law.

The resulting attempts at legal change, while still very much in progress, illustrate some of the key dynamics of contemporary legalization. The harmonization project is led by a transnational policy community, and aims to internationalize the principles of the Article 9 approach, establishing this model as the global standard for secured transactions law. The key features of this model – ease of creation and enforcement of security agreements, the variety of assets that can be treated as security, the priority it gives to secured creditors – are seen as uniquely able to facilitate private credit creation across national boundaries. Legal reform efforts proceed in a number of fora simultaneously – national, regional, and international, private and public, involve a variety of strategies, and engage a diverse set of actors and institutions. In the process, reform efforts are faced with resistance and generate new patterns of conflict, through which differentials of *power* and authority are engaged in, and shape, the substance of legal change itself. In the following account, I begin with an overview of the development of the harmonization project, then look more closely at the policy coalition driving it, and then consider the nature and impact of a counter-reform coalition.

Fora

The harmonization project for secured transactions law began in the 1980s, with domestically initiated reform efforts in key common law states.[8] Legal reform commissions and initiatives appeared in the United Kingdom, Canada, Australia, and New Zealand, which had the mission of reviewing existing laws on security interests in light of the perceived success of law reform in the US and of ongoing attempts to reconsider insolvency law (Ziegel, 1997). While strong forces have prevented much change in English and Australian law, in the 1990s most Canadian provinces adopted new Personal Property Security Acts (PPSA) based closely on Article 9 of the UCC, and New Zealand adopted a similar approach at the national level.[9] In these cases, the basic principles of the Article 9 approach were successfully adapted to legal systems more deeply shaped by English law than was the case with pre-UCC commercial law in the US, but the 'success' of this strategy turned out to have an unexpected impact. The

Canadian PPSA's, though based on similar principles, provide models of a 'modern' secured transactions law less directly tied to US law. As a result, the Canadian approach has earned a degree of authority and respect that makes it especially useful for reformers working in developing states with common law systems, which are usually still much closer in structure to English law, and in states where there is resistance to the influence of US law.[10] Here, the adaptation of a national legal model to another national context contributed to emergence of a more 'international' legal standard.

In the early 1990s, in response to the sudden emergence of a number of East European and Central Asian countries attempting to make the transition to market economies, states, regional organizations, and multilateral institutions developed active legal reform programmes and institutions. The most important product of these efforts was the Model Law on Secured Transactions prepared in 1994 by the European Bank for Reconstruction and Development (EBRD). Developed with the involvement of major Anglo-American and Continental experts and practitioners, this model law attempted to provide a guide to law reformers that relied heavily on the Article 9 and PPSA standards, incorporating them into a format suitable to the civil law traditions of the emerging market economies. This law, and the more general 'Core Principles' distilled from it, remains the basis of an active effort by the EBRD to oversee the creation of 'modern' credit finance laws and institutions in the states of the former Soviet sphere.[11] By the late 1990s, similar efforts to integrate secured finance law reform with larger legal and political reform projects had begun under the authority of the Asian Development Bank (ADB) and the Organization of American States (OAS).[12]

The issue of secured credit law has increasingly drawn the attention of multilateral institutions. As the World Bank and IMF give more attention to issues of legal reform and institution-building, corporate governance, and the 'financial architecture', the issue of secured finance has been the focus of more study and policy-making. For these institutions, secured credit law is (along with other key financial market issues) at the intersection of the concerns for facilitating access to capital and thus ultimately development in emerging economies. In the wake of the financial market crises of 1997–1998, moreover, secured credit reform came to be seen as a piece of any approach to stabilize global and developing country financial markets. In practice, both institutions have responded by – in some situations – including standards for secured transaction law reform as part of the package of legal and institutional reform required of states receiving financial assistance. While it does not always become part of the conditions required for loans, the reform of secured transaction law is now part of the agenda for all multilateral development institutions.

The success of these national and multilateral efforts, in turn, brought renewed energy to the idea of developing a more formal, international approach to legal harmonization. Over the course of the twentieth century, states had created three international institutions or organizations to address the role of private international law in shaping global commerce – the Hague Conference for Private International Law ('Hague Conference'), the International Institute for the Unification of Private Law (UNIDROIT), and the United Nations Commission on International Trade Law (UNCITRAL)[13] Although these institutions claimed broad mandates to harmonize parts of private international law, for most of their existence their work had been limited to addressing relatively narrow points in the conflicts of law. The emergence of the issue of legal harmonization on the broader agenda of neo-liberal political economy, however, has reinvigorated the work of these institutions. Over the past two decades, significant agreements on the harmonization of substantive areas of law – particularly in the areas of contracts and insolvency/bankruptcy – have been produced by all three of these institutions. By the mid-1990s, both UNIDROIT and UNCITRAL were working on agreements concerning key areas of credit financing, and began to turn their attention to secured finance, an area previously considered too difficult for any real progress on harmonization (Burman, 2003). Most importantly, in 2001 UNCITRAL began work on the development of a Legislative Guide on Secured Transactions, which is meant to provide general legal models as guidance to states interested in modernizing their secured finance regimes. This process has become an important focal point for the harmonization project on secured transactions, and a context for the emergence of a counter-harmonization coalition.[14]

This brief overview of one harmonization project illustrates the plural contexts and dimensions of the process of contemporary legalization. National and regional legislatures, court systems, development banks, and international institutions all play important rules in shaping the development of legal rules for global commerce. In each case, and in the relationships between these sites, we can observe a variety of different kinds of activities, from the articulation of principles and standards through the legislative adoption of specific legal rules. At the same time, there is no clear hierarchy in the allocation of functions, problems, or authority in the legal reform process. What we see is a fluid process in which different aspects of a common reform agenda are addressed in different parts simultaneously at various sites. In the current context, legalization involves the generation and modification of multiple legalities, and the constant but unpredictable effects of the interaction of these legalities furthers the indeterminacy of the overall process of legalization. So, for instance, the original Article 9 reform model has been reworked into a set of alternative approaches – especially the Canadian PPSA's and the EBRD model law – which often compete with one another for adherents. The situation is clearly much more complex and layered than the rationalist model of legalization would have us expect. But the picture remains incomplete, and we need to look more closely at the actors involved in this sector of legalization to get a fuller sense of how the process works.

Actors

The project to reform and harmonize secured transactions law is driven by a transnational policy coalition which draws together networks of legal experts, policy-makers, and private interests. The members of this coalition work in the variety of institutional contexts discussed above to advance their shared agenda for harmonization of laws along the lines of Article 9 principles. Indeed, it is the activity and agendas of this coalition that animates the work of all significant aspects of the harmonization movement – legal scholarship and advocacy, policy reform, and policy implementation. The members of this policy coalition share membership in overlapping networks which bring together those active in the legal, political, and economic worlds of credit finance, and provides crucial linkages between the various fora in which legal harmonization is pursued. Regular work on reform projects, constant informal interaction, and significant movement of actors between different institutional sites provide the glue that holds the coalition together and empowers it to act to advance a common agenda.[15]

The first pillar of this coalition is a group of lawyers, legal academics, and legal officials who are part of a transnational network of experts in credit and bankruptcy law. This network first took shape in the 1970s, as common law states began to show more interest in the innovations of the UCC. Two decades later, key participants took advantage of the changed circumstances of the 1990s to articulate and sell a project of law reform as a necessary response to some of the new challenges of financial regulation and economic development. The membership is primarily of North American and European background, but experts from developing nations – with substantial legal training and in some cases employment in developed states – play an increasing role in the law reform movement. These experts share significant prestige within national and international legal circles, and have a history of varied experience in commercial law harmonization projects, including membership on advisory boards to multilateral institutions, designing legal reform projects as consultants for specific states, and representing industry and bar associations in the development of harmonization projects.[16] They use their epistemic prestige and position to attempt to engage these institutions in the law reform project, while providing the legal conceptualization and expertise necessary for such institutions to participate effectively in the processes of legal change.

The second pillar is formed by a network of public officials at national states and international institutions, who share and advance the goal of the harmonization of secured transactions law. Key officials at the major regional and multilateral development and financial institutions have played central roles in advancing – but also modifying – the secured transactions law reform agenda. The work of UNCITRAL provides another example. In the 1970s, the Secretariat developed an interest in this area, and commissioned a comparative study of legal regimes, which was to form the basis of a model law development project. In 1980, however, the Assembly – made up of representatives of states – decided that the time was not ripe for such a project, and it was not until the mid-1990s that UNCITRAL returned to work on the issue (Tajti, 2002a: 323–324). In another case, the EBRD project and the World Bank's work on secured transactions reform in Eastern Europe can be traced to the initiative of some United States Agency for International Development (USAID) officials working in the region in the early 1990s. Officials from key states have played a similar role. National policy officials have also, at times, played a decisive role in the harmonization project. In the US case, for example, key officials of the Private International Law division of the State Department's Legal Advisor's Office played a leading role during the 1990s in inserting secured transactions law onto the agenda of various domestic and international bodies.

The third pillar of this policy coalition is a made up of representatives of the industry and business organizations most directly affected by secured transactions law. Their involvement is often difficult to trace, as such groups lack official representation at most of the organizations that actually put together agreements, but we do have some direct evidence of this involvement, from the UNCITRAL process. Unlike most other international law-making bodies, interested non-governmental organizations are permitted to participate in these deliberations, though they do not have voting rights. At the working group on security interests, groups such as the International Chamber of Commerce (ICC), the Union of Industrial and Employers Confederations of Europe (UNICE), and the International Association of Restructuring, Insolvency and Bankruptcy Professionals (INSOL) are all active participants in the deliberations, and are often asked to assess which of a set of alternative proposals would be most likely to garner the acceptance of the business community. In this case, the most prominent private sector agent is the Commercial Finance Association (CFA), an association of banks and financial institutions specializing in providing finance to business.[17] The CFA's role in the development of a secured transactions legislative guide includes but extends well beyond the activities described above. From the beginning of the working group's activities, CFA representatives have been in close contact with the UNCITRAL secretariat and the state delegations.

The project of harmonizing secured transactions law, then, is driven by a policy coalition which includes actors and networks drawn from various institutions and sites – national, regional, and international; private and public – in the global political economy. States and public international institutions play an important part in this aspect of legalization, as the rationalist model suggests, but only to the extent that they are implicated in, and are animated by, one or more transnational networks. This coalition works to enroll the major sites of power and authority in private commercial law in the harmonization project, operating simultaneously at different sites and on different aspects of legal reform. Legalization in this context emerges as a process in which the locus of policy initiative shifts between different institutions and actors, depending on the dynamics of each institution, the changing contexts they face, and the shifting priorities of the larger political economic context. Neither an emphasis on the interest calculations of states, nor a functionalist account of inherent system needs, is enough to make sense of the process of this dimension of legalization.

Resistance to reform: contests of principle, interest, and power

The fluidity of the legalization process, however, does not mean that power differentials and conflicts of interest are not central to the shape of emerging transnational legal regimes. Rather, relationships and conflicts of power and interest are best understood as implicated in the substance of the legal regimes promoted by different actors and institutions. Legal principles and norms do not float freely across national and structural boundaries; they are shaped and constrained by professional, political, and economic interests. This dynamic relationship is well demonstrated in the emergence of counter-harmonization networks and the nature of the resulting contest over the future of international commercial law. As efforts to harmonize secured transaction law have gained more traction over the past decade, they have led to more explicit resistance at the national, regional, and international levels. The counter-harmonization forces are not as clearly defined or focused as their opponents, and present a variety of (sometimes contradictory) alternatives. But the general outlines of the conflict are clear. The most active opponents of the harmonization agenda attempt to protect the vitality of forms of capitalism in which the relationship of banks, financial markets, and credit are incompatible with the system on which the Article 9 model is based. And, like their opponents, these counter-harmonization networks link normative ideals, professional networks, and political and economic interests in intricate combinations.

One major source of opposition to Article 9 harmonization derives from advanced industrial nations, in particular Great Britain and Germany. While the US and UK systems are often lumped together in discussion of varieties of capitalism, the English legal and financial system has its own, deeply rooted approach to dealing with credit finance. To this point, the legal and financial establishment in London has successfully resisted pressures to adopt Article 9 style reforms, maintaining that English law and practice are fully adequate to the needs of contemporary commercial and financial activity. The impact of English law in shaping key areas of global finance provides an important material interest to support this opposition; indeed, it is common for English (and other) experts to suggest that the export of the UCC system is driven by the interests of US and US-trained lawyers and legal academics. Here, the ongoing competition between London and New York law and lawyers to shape the rules of global commerce finds another important outlet (Beaverstock *et al.*, 2002). While resisting domestic reform, moreover, English practitioners have played little role in regional or international contexts where secured transactions law is engaged. To this point, the continued power and attraction of London as a financial center seems to have protected the English legal order from the pressure of the harmonization project.[18]

The case of Germany is somewhat different. The well known bank-centered system of commercial finance is not easily compatible with Article 9-style secured finance, and attempts to follow the harmonization model would require significant changes throughout the German system of commercial law. And, as in the English case, the German system provides alternative ways of dealing with commercial finance that seem successful on their own terms. But German experts and officials have been much more active at the regional and international level in trying to limit the harmonization project. In contrast to the English case, the German system of bank-dominated financial capitalism has been much more influential abroad, especially in Central and Eastern Europe (Tajti, 2002b). As a result, German representatives (and some representatives of similarly structured economies) have worked in a number of regional and international venues to preserve room for competition between models of commercial finance. Their opposition takes two major forms – active promotion of German-style legal arrangements in emerging market economies, and attempts to deflect attempts to establish the Article 9 model as the international norm for secured credit law. The latter initiative has been especially prominent in the ongoing UNCITRAL efforts to develop a legislative guide to secured transactions.

Opposition to Article 9 harmonization also comes from many developing states and emerging market economies, where legal norms regarding secured lending, often deeply tied to a whole set of practices – involving financial institutions, the role of notaries, insolvency regimes, registration systems for securities, etc. – are incompatible with an Article 9 regime. In addition, many of these states have inherited forms of civil law tradition that remain hostile to much secured lending in its modern forms. Here, again, principles and interests are linked, as the positions of key legal and political actors are closely tied to these practices. Resistance to legal change is often bolstered as well by a suspicion and fear of the opening to foreign actors that reform could generate (Moglia Claps and McDonnell, 2002). In many cases, established legal agents and institutions have employed substantial political influence to frustrate proposed reforms. It is important to note, however, that over the past two decades many lawyers from these states have received advanced training in the US and have returned as advocates of legal reform and modernization along the lines of US law. Indeed, developing states are sometimes represented by such actors at regional and international sites, where they can often be voices for the harmonization project. In most cases, however, this has yet to translate into substantial domestic change.[19]

These conflicts of interest and power, in turn, have generated an ongoing conflict of principles in this (and other) areas of private law harmonization. To this point, attempts to establish the Article 9 principles as the global standard of secured credit law have met with only limited success. The principles themselves have been reworked into competing models, and critics have been able successfully to mobilize the claim of respect for legal diversity to prevent the consolidation of support around a clear, hegemonic statement of the legitimacy of the Article 9 approach. In addition to successful resistance in specific national contexts, the limits of the reform movement can be seen in two multilateral fora in which attempts have been made to develop model secured transactions laws. The first concerns the efforts of multilateral banks to develop guidelines on legal reform for aid recipients. To this point, these banks have concluded that there is too much resistance to the full-scale adoption of the Article 9 model around the world. In response, their model laws and legislative guides attempt to incorporate Article 9 principles as much as possible while adapting them to the structure and needs of competing legal orders. This is precisely the approach of the EBRD, ADB, and (to a lesser extent) the OAS model laws. It is reflected in the stated understandings by the IMF, World Bank, and ADB that, while modernization of security interest law is necessary, it need not follow one common path, and needs to be adapted to specific local traditions and situations. The second example is the ongoing efforts of UNCITRAL to develop a legislative guide on secured transactions law to guide national reform efforts. This effort has been dominated by members of the harmonization network and was first undertaken with a clear commitment to establishing a consensus in support of the Article 9 principles. Despite their efforts, however, it seems that the desire to present a 'unitary' legislative guide has yielded to the pressure of opponents, and the current draft documents now accept a dual track approach similar to that of the development banks.

It is necessary, finally, to point out who is not involved in the process of transnational commercial law reform. With rare and only sporadic exceptions, there is no effective presence of consumers, unions, or any other 'social' interests in the private law dimensions of the regulation of the global economy. This is true not only at the drafting stage, but includes the internal processes in which such agreements are ratified by states. There is no doubt that regimes of secured credit law can have a major impact on the distribution of property rights in commercial life, especially between creditors and debtors. While conflicts between creditors and debtors often play an important role in national political conflict, representatives of debtors (and consumers generally) are not participating in the shaping of secured finance law at the transnational level. These and other interests have become an important force in public international economic law-making, but they have made little impact in the world of private international commercial law.

Commercial law harmonization and the global political economy

In the end, the picture of legalization that emerges from this case is much more complex and messy than we would expect from the rational–institutionalist model. It is clear that the recent movement for harmonization of international commercial law gains its impetus from the dominant position of the US political economy in the transformation of the transnational system. This structural position created a context in which a variety of actors could undertake the reorganization of commercial law through the internationalization of key principles and models derived from US law. In the process, these agents and the networks in which they are placed could mobilize and indeed empower a variety of institutions in this project. It is here, however, that the story becomes more complicated. The transnational system that is emerging is fundamentally multi-layered and diverse, and is not often amenable to the easy translation of national models into international standards. The multiplication of fora – each with its own particular dynamics of power and purpose – and actors – with a variety of interests and motivations – means that attempts to create and/or reform the legal regulation of global commerce will end up with much more varied and uncertain results than agents of change often intend.

This brings the discussion back to where it began, but analysis of the secured transactions harmonization project allows us to emphasize two central implications for the broader study of legalization. First, it seems clear that legalization is a process that is producing multiple legalities rather than one stable legal framework for the global political economy. Projects for legalization focus on specific problem or issue areas, but must contend with the variety of interests and institutions that have (or claim) some degree of jurisdiction over that problem. As projects take on momentum, more actors are likely to get involved, sometimes of their own initiative and sometimes because they are mobilized by supporters of the legalization project itself. In the process, each project is likely to meet some degree of opposition, which can vary from resistance to legalization to the development of an alternative approach to dealing with the problem at hand. In such situations, which are more and more common, it is likely that we will see multiple legal regimes or frameworks developed at different sites in the global system. Rather than progressing towards a uniform resolution, though, the competition and conflict of interests and ideas is likely to continue and turn into a conflict of legalities. While this may pose a problem for some actors, it can also allow others strategically to manipulate the diversity of legal regimes for their own goals. The multi-layered structure of the transnational political economy, then, will tend towards the multiplication of legal regimes, not their consolidation. This is a phenomenon that the rationalist model of legalization does not, and probably cannot, explain effectively.

Second, the secured transactions harmonization project illustrates the central role of networks of actors – public and private, national and international – in shaping the turn to law. While states and public officials play an important part in these networks, they are by no means the only or most important sources of legalization, nor do they necessarily determine the substantive content of legal harmonization. Indeed, my research suggests that transnational policy coalitions are essential to the building, reforming, and enforcement of legal regimes in the global political economy. Because of the complex multiplicity of the institutional environment, actors with only one primary institutional location can rarely carry out a legalization project on their own. The strategies through which actors pull together transnational policy coalitions, then, are a central dynamic in understanding legalization.[20] I have placed particular importance on the role of epistemic communities of legal experts in the emergence and activity of these networks. The main significance of these experts is their ability to formulate and clarify the substantive principles and rules upon which any particular aspect of legalization is based. Policy coalitions need a substantive vision around which to animate their activities, and expert networks can exert substantial influence through their ability to articulate and manipulate the legal norms over which policy networks struggle (Sell and Prakash, 2004). Expert networks, of course, are not free to lead other actors in any direction they desire; I hope my account has made that clear. But the importance of these networks, and the larger transnational policy coalitions of which they are a part, suggests that the study of legalization must move beyond the parameters of the rationalist–institutionalist project in order to fully grapple with the changing role of law in the global political economy.

Notes

1 The construction of legal orders is one way of attempting to establish effective regulation and governance over transnational economic activity. It often coexists with other approaches, such as regulatory co-operation, the development of private standards, control over market access, etc. My emphasis in this essay, on the distinctive elements of legalization, is not meant to discount the importance of these other elements of regulatory governance. For a thoughtful discussion of the distinctive role of legal orders, see Finnemore (2000).

2 These themes are explored in much more depth in the Introduction.

3 In the legal literature, this is contrasted with public international law, which is concerned with the behaviour of states. Thus, most issues of international trade or environmental policy are classified as public law as they primarily address the choices of states, not private actors directly. Many of the rules of private law, of course, are generated by states through legislation and judicial interpretation, but the 'public'/'private' distinction is based on the objects of the rules, the actors whose behavior the rules constrain (or empower). As in other areas, though, there is growing evidence that the utility of this distinction is quickly eroding.

4 Nonetheless, the study of private international law has been neglected by social scientists, and is widely considered a purely technical discipline even amongst legal experts (Ramsay, 2001). A growing number of social scientists and legal scholars are challenging this view, however, and exploring more critically the role of private commercial law in the constitution of regulatory capitalism (Appelbaum *et al.*, 2001; Braithwaite and Drahos, 2000; Cutler, 2003; Muir Watt, 2003; Wai, 2002; Weiner, 1999).

5 For an insightful analysis of the idea and project of legal harmonization, see Leebron (1996).

6 Importantly, the US became an active player in international private law harmonization only in the mid-1960s, and this involvement expanded significantly in the 1970s. Prior to this, the movement was primarily an affair of continental European states. See Cutler (2003) for an overview of the history of the harmonization movement.

7 See the classic works of Haas (1992) on epistemic communities, Slaughter (2004) on intergovernmental networks, and Keck and Sikkink (1998) on advocacy networks. My approach to understanding the role of transnational policy coalitions, though, is indebted to Sell and Prakash's (2004) argument that there are no sharp divides between the strategies of different sorts of coalitions (business, NGOs, etc.) in the transnational context. The mobilization of epistemic authority, normative advocacy, and power are part of all attempts at policy change, though different networks often have to rely on (or specialize in) one kind of strategy.

8 Buxbaum (2003) provides the best single overview and assessment of these developments from the perspective of a specialist.

9 The Canadian reform project actually dates back to the late 1960s, with Ontario adopting the first provincial 'Personal Property Security Act' (PPSA) in 1967. Beginning in the late 1980s, the pace of the adoption of similar legislation by the other provinces picked up, and Quebec reformed its civil law in a similar direction as well.
10 Interview with expert active in legal reform efforts in the developing world.
11 The EBRD Model Law is available at: www.ebrd.com/country/sector/law/st/core/modellaw/modellaw.pdf. The Core Principles for a Secured Transactions Law is available at: www.ebrd.com/country/sector/law/st/about/prin/index.htm (both accessed 7 July 2006).
12 For the ADB project, see ADB (2000). A presentation and overview of the OAS Model Law by two of its key developers can be found in Kozolchyk and Wilson (2002).
13 The Hague Conference dates back to the late nineteenth century, and was established to resolve conflicts of law issues among the civil law systems of continental European states. UNIDROIT was created in 1926 to promote more substantive harmonization of laws among the same legal systems. UNCITRAL was formed in 1966 to provide a forum to address issues of private law harmonization outside the highly polarized venue of the United Nations Conference on Trade and Development (UNCTAD). It was only with the formation of UNCITRAL that non-European civil law states, especially the US, began to play an active role in international private law projects.
14 My discussion of the work of UNCITRAL is based on interviews with participants and observers involved in this project, and on my own observation of the ongoing negotiations.
15 For a study that emphasizes the importance of a similar kind of policy coalition in another area of legalization, anti-trust and competition law and policy, see Portnoy (2000).
16 The American Bar Association (ABA) and International Bar Association (IBA) are especially active in legal reform and harmonization efforts.
17 For the membership and activities of the CFA, see its website at http://www.cfa.com (accessed 6 June 2006).
18 To be sure, some English experts (especially Roy Goode) have been key players in making the case for the harmonization of secured credit law. But their influence in this area has been much greater abroad than at home. The same qualification applies to the German case discussed below.
19 For an excellent analysis of this kind of dynamic, see Dezalay and Garth (2002).
20 The analysis of these strategies and their outcomes is a central emphasis of Braithwaite and Drahos (2000).

Bibliography

Appelbaum, R., Felstiner, W. and Gessner, V. (eds) (2001) *Rules and Networks: The Legal Culture of Global Business Transactions*, Oxford: Hart Publishing.
Asian Development Bank (ADB) (2000) *Law and Policy Reform at the ADB Vol. II, 2000 Edition*, (December). Online, available at: www.adb.org/Documents/Others/Law_ADB/lpr_2000_2.asp?p=lawdevt (accessed 6 July 2006).
Beaverstock, J. V., Doel, M. A., Hubbard, P. J. and Taylor, P. J. (2002) 'Attending to the World: Competition, Cooperation and Connectivity in the World City Network', *Global Networks*, 2 (2): 111–132.
Braithwaite, J. and Drahos, P. (2000) *Global Business Regulation*, Cambridge: Cambridge University Press.
Bridge, M., Macdonald, R., Simmonds, R. and Walsh, C. (1999) 'Formalism, Functionalism, and Understanding the Law of Secured Transactions', *McGill Law Journal*, 44 (November): 567–664.

Burman, H. (2003) 'The Commercial Challenge in Modernizing Secured Transactions Law', *Uniform Law Review*, 8 (1/2): 347–352.

Buxbaum, H. (2003) 'Unification of the Law Governing Secured Transactions: Progress and Prospects for Reform', *Uniform Law Review*, 8 (1/2): 321–339.

Cuming, R. C. C. (1997) 'The Internationalization of Secured Financing Law: The Spreading Influence of the Concepts UCC, Article 9 and its Progeny', in R. Cranston (ed.) *Making Commercial Law: Essays in Honour of Roy Goode*, Oxford: Clarendon Press.

Cutler, A. C. (2003) *Private Power and Global Authority*, Cambridge: Cambridge University Press.

Dezalay, Y. and Garth, B. (2002) *The Internationalization of Palace Wars*, Chicago: University of Chicago Press.

Finnemore, M. (2000) 'Are Legal Norms Distinctive?', *New York University Journal of International Law and Politics*, 32: 699–705.

Finnemore, M. and Toope, S. (2001) 'Alternatives to "Legalization": Richer Views of Law and Politics', *International Organization*, 55 (3): 743–758.

Fleisig, H. W. (1996) 'Secured Transactions: The Power of Collateral', *Finance and Development*, (June): 44–46.

Fleisig, H. W. (1998) 'Economic Functions of Security in a Market Economy', in J. Norton and M. Andenas (eds) *Emerging Financial Markets and Secured Transactions*, London: Kluwer Law International.

Goldstein, J., Kahler, M., Keohane, R. and Slaughter, A. (eds) (2000) 'Special Issue: Legalization and World Politics', *International Organization*, 54 (3).

Goode, R. (1998) 'Security in Cross-Border Transactions', *Texas International Law Journal*, 33 (Winter): 47–52.

Haas, P. M. (1992) 'Introduction: Epistemic Communities and International Policy Coordination', *International Organization*, 46 (1): 1–35.

International Monetary Fund (IMF) (2002) 'Development of Standards for Security Interests', Paper Presented at IMF Seminar on Current Developments in Monetary and Financial Law, Washington, DC, May 7–17. Online, available at: www.imf.org/external/np/leg/sem/2002/cdmfl/eng/pdb.pdf (accessed 9 July 2006).

Keck, M. and Sikkink, K. (1998) *Activists Beyond Borders*, Ithaca, NY: Cornell University Press.

Khagram, S., Riker, J. V. and Sikkink, K. (2002) 'From Santiago to Seattle: Transnational Advocacy Groups Restructuring World Politics', in S. Khagram, J. V. Riker and K. Sikkink (eds) *Restructuring World Politics: Transnational Social Movements, Networks, and Norms*, Minneapolis, MN: University of Minnesota Press, pp. 3–23.

Kozolchyk, B. and Wilson, J. (2002) 'The Organization of American States' Model Inter-American Law on Secured Transactions', *Uniform Law Review*, 7: 1–64.

Leebron, D. W. (1996) 'Lying Down with Procrustes: An Analysis of Harmonization Claims', in J. Bhagwati and R. E. Hudec (eds) *Fair Trade and Harmonization: Prerequisites for Free Trade? Volume 1*, Cambridge, MA: The MIT Press, pp. 41–117.

McCormack, G. (2004) *Secured Credit under English and American Law*, Cambridge: Cambridge University Press.

Moglia Claps, G. and McDonnell, J. (2002) 'Secured Credit and Insolvency Law in Argentina and the U.S.: Gaining Insight From a Comparative Perspective', *Georgia Journal of International and Comparative Law*, 30: 393–442.

Muir Watt, H. (2003) 'Choice of Law in Integrated and Interconnected Markets: A Matter of Political Economy', *Electronic Journal of Comparative Law*, 7 (3). Online, available at: www.ejcl.org/73/art73-4.html (accessed 6 July 2006).

Portnoy, B. (2000) *Constructing Competition: Antitrust and the Political Foundations of Global Capitalism*. Unpublished Doctoral Dissertation, Department of Political Science, The University of Chicago.

Ramsay, I. (2001) 'The Politics of Commercial Law', *Wisconsin Law Review*, 565–575.

Rubin, E. (1997) 'The Code, The Consumer, and the Institutional Structure of the Common Law', *Washington University Law Quarterly*, 75 (Spring): 11–68.

Ruggie, J. G. (1982) 'International Regimes, Transactions, and Change: Embedded Liberalism in the Post-War Order', *International Organization*, 36 (4): 379–415.

Sassen, S. (1996) *Losing Control?* New York: Columbia University Press.

Sassen, S. (2000) The State and Economic Globalization: Any Implications for International Law? *Chicago Journal of International Law*, 1: 109–116.

Scott, R. (1994) 'The Politics of Article 9', *Virginia Law Review*, 80 (November): 1783–1851.

Scott, R. (1997) 'The Truth About Secured Financing', *Cornell Law Review*, 82 (September): 1436–1465.

Sell, S. and Prakash, A. (2004) 'Using Ideas Strategically: The Contest Between Business and NGO Networks in Intellectual Property Rights', *International Studies Quarterly* 48: 143–175.

Slaughter, A. M. (2004) *A New World Order*, Princeton, NJ: Princeton University Press.

Stone, D. (2004) 'Transfer Agents and Global Networks in the "Transnationalization" of Policy', *Journal of European Public Policy*, 11 (3): 545–566.

Tajti, T. (2002a) *Comparative Secured Transactions Law*, Budapest: Akademiai Kiado.

Tajti, T. (2002b) 'Viehwig's *Topics*, Article 9 UCC, the "Kautelanische Sicherheiten" and the Hungarian Secured Transactions Law Reform', *The Vindobona Journal of International Commercial Law and Arbitration*, 6 (1): 93–131.

United Nations Commission on International Trade Law (2001) 'Possible Future Work in Security Interests: Note by the Secretariat', A/CN.9/496.

Wai, R. (2002) 'Transnational Liftoff and Juridical Touchdown: The Regulatory Function of Private International Law in an Era of Globalization', *Columbia Journal of Transnational Law*, 40: 212–274.

Wiener, J. (1999) *Globalization and the Harmonization of Law*, London: Pinter.

Wood, P. (1998) 'World-Wide Security – Classification of Legal Jurisdictions', in J. Norton and M. Andenas (eds) *Emerging Financial Markets and Secured Transactions*, London: Kluwer Law International.

World Bank Working Group on Debtor–Creditor Regimes (1999) 'Building Effective Insolvency Systems: Debtor–Creditor Regimes', Paper Presented at World Bank Conference on Building Effective Insolvency Systems, Washington, DC, September 14–15. Online, available at: www4.worldbank.org/legal/insolvency_ini/WG10-paper.htm (accessed 9 July 2006).

Ziegel, J. (1997) 'Harmonization of Private Laws in Federal Systems of Government: Canada, the USA, and Australia', in R. Cranston (ed.) *Making Commercial Law: Essays in Honour of Roy Goode*, Oxford: Clarendon Press.

5   Multi-stakeholder initiatives to combat money laundering and bribery

Mark Pieth

Introduction

Intensified economic globalisation has had positive and negative effects. It has left nation states struggling to deal with the negative fall-out (Haufler 2001: 11; Jenkins 2001: 2ff.). National regulation against abuses has, however, proven increasingly ineffective, especially since companies have the freedom to move their hazardous activities to under-regulated areas (Haufler 2001: 1, 7). States have stepped up cooperation and coordination on a bilateral as well as a multilateral basis: international organisations and treaties are becoming more and more relevant to the regulation of international trade relations (Brütsch and Lehmkuhl in Chapter 2 of this volume). However, the traditional instruments of international law are frequently considered too cumbersome and slow. Increasingly, international law is created by unconventional means: 'task forces'[1] prove to be far more expedient, since they prefer 'soft law' to treaty law (Black 2001: 11; Brütsch and Lehmkuhl in Chapter 2 of this volume). Political enforcement by peer-pressure is becoming more relevant than juridical instruments (courts and tribunals) (Brütsch and Lehmkuhl in the Introduction to this volume). Furthermore, regulation goes well beyond lawmaking by legislators and government bodies; non-state actors are contributing extensively, especially in the area of regulating international trade relations.

However, after a phase of enthusiasm for self-regulation (Haufler 2001: 7ff.), some of the drawbacks have now become apparent. Effectiveness depends largely on independent monitoring and complaint procedures, transparency is not always guaranteed. Furthermore, doubts remain about whether self-regulatory instruments are able to go beyond the narrowly defined self-interest of those in control.

In more recent times, therefore, short of reverting fully to state regulation, self-regulatory instruments are conceptualised as multi-stakeholder initiatives (see below) or as instruments of co-regulation, co-opting the different interest groups into the mechanisms themselves or linking self-regulation to state regulation.

This paper will follow up on two recent examples of so-called 'multi-stakeholder initiatives' and discuss their creation, the respective political and legal context, and give some details on their operation, in order to analyse them as current examples of the role of non-state actors in regulation. Finally, the paper will address some of the critique levelled against these initiatives and discuss the challenges.

The examples

On the one hand the so-called 'Wolfsberg Principles', a multi-stakeholder initiative in the financial services industry aimed at standardising customer-due-diligence procedures, is presented. On the other hand the 'Partnering Against Corruption Initiative (PACI)' is put into its wider context.

Wolfsberg

In 1999, after a series of reputational disasters for the banking industry (in the US especially, the 'Salinas' and the 'Bank of New York scandals'; in Europe, the fallout of the various 'Abacha' cases), two leading banks could be convinced by civil society representatives, interested in combating corruption (the NGO Transparency International and the research unit Basel Institute on Governance), to form the nucleus of a group whose aim it was to develop customer-due-diligence standards in private banking. With the help of these protagonists, the group rapidly grew to the now 11 key industry players, controlling roughly 60–70 per cent of the world market in private banking. The Wolfsberg Anti-Money Laundering Principles on Private Banking – the Group is named after the UBS conference centre 'Wolfsberg' where these first standards were written in autumn 2000 (Pieth and Aiolfi 2003: 259ff.),[2] were rapidly followed by further standards on preventing the financing of terrorism, on correspondent banking, on anti-money laundering issues in the context of investment and commercial banking and texts relating to the risk-based approach. In 2002, the AML Principles on Private Banking were updated in the light of recent developments.[3] After initial hesitation, the relevant national financial regulators and their international organisations (especially the 'Basel Committee on Banking Supervision' as well as the 'Financial Action Task Force on Money Laundering') met annually at the 'Wolfsberg Forum'.[4] The Wolfsberg initiative has managed to establish itself as a key policy interlocutor with the regulators and international bodies; the standards are increasingly referenced and quoted even by non-members as 'best practices' of the industry.[5] However, the group has not grown since 2000 and it has not established monitoring mechanisms of its own (obviously the area is highly supervised by regulators, who sometimes refer to the Wolfsberg standards in their decisions).[6] Furthermore, the annual 'Wolfsberg Forum' serves as a sounding board and as a means to include some of the next largest 50 banks worldwide into the discourse on standards.

Partnering Against Corruption Initiative (PACI)

On 28 February 2005 (at the Annual Meeting of the World Economic Forum in Davos, the representatives of three sectorial groups of companies participating in the World Economic Forum went on stage and published an industry code against corruption (the so-called 'Partnering Against Corruption Principles for Countering Bribery'[7]): the presidents and CEOs of now about 100 companies in the construction and engineering industry, in the mining business as well as some oil and gas corporations signed a compact, which had been proposed by a working group made up of industry representatives and facilitators of the World Economic Forum, the NGO Transparency International and the Basel Institute on Governance (including the Chairman of the OECD Working Group on Bribery). Whereas the Wolfsberg Principles focus on customer-due-diligence and the prevention of money laundering in the financial services industry, the PACI Principles establish the foundations for corporate compliance codes to prevent bribery. They deal in particular with definitional aspects (gifts as well as political and charitable contributions and so-called facilitation payments) and with the treatment of third parties, both 'upstream' and 'downstream' (in order to prevent indirect bribery, the code gives an answer to the question of how far the responsibility for due-diligence in the selection and instruction of suppliers, agents, subsidiaries, joint-venture partners and other contractual partners should reach from an industry standpoint).

The code is open to further participants and all protagonists are currently lobbying for the inclusion of additional signatories, especially as some big players in the oil and gas industries have so far been reticent to sign up.[8] The three sectorial group leaders within the Davos framework which presented the initiative to the media[9] promised publicly to help introduce a monitoring mechanism for the initiative, thereby deliberately putting their reputation at risk.

The context

From the 1970s onwards, the pace of economic globalisation intensified and increasingly transnational corporations were criticised for their tendency towards the exploitation of under-regulated and economically or politically dependent areas. At first, states in the South attempted to counteract uncontrolled self-interest by public regulation in a nation state context. Soon they had to realise, however, that this approach was economically no longer sustainable and a general move towards de-regulation, motivated in the South by the need to attract investors set in (Jenkins 2001: 1ff.). International organisations like the World Bank, the IMF and the OECD supported this drive towards de-regulation in the 1980s, even if there were some attempts to prevent some of the worst excesses of globalisation, e.g. by the OECD with its Guidelines on Multinationals of 1977, revised on 27 June 2000.[10]

In 1990, after the East–West détente, a new phase in the history of globalisation commenced: its positive and negative impacts became more and more visible and states as well as international organisations were forced to take counter-measures, especially against ecological damage and exploitation of the labour force (Haufler 2001: 14, 17; Jenkins 2001: 19ff.; Utting 2002: 75ff.).

An intensive discourse set in, as to what extent these tasks could be managed by self-regulation and, in several instances, companies and groups of companies started experimenting with social accountability initiatives, together with NGOs.[11] The acceleration of globalisation made society more vulnerable to organised crime, terrorism and new dimensions of transnational economic crime, since the liberalisation of goods and services, the new means of data transmission and travel simplified cross-border transactions (Passas 1998, 1999: 399ff.). An era of re-regulation set in. This time, however, the driving forces were not so much nation states, but international organisations and members of the civil society. Whereas NGOs proved forceful in pushing even the largest TNCs to re-consider their environmental and labour policies,[12] the fight against economic and organised crime remained primarily a state function. In particular, since 1990 a regulatory boost in the area of prevention of money laundering and corruption set in. The following chapter gives a quick overview over the development and addresses specifically the issue of the main actors in regulating.

Combating money laundering

Public sector initiatives

Originally a limited concept, introduced in the core area of fighting organised crime by the UN Convention against illegal drugs,[13] money laundering was rapidly extended to other predicate crimes. Initial attempts to harmonise criminal law (especially by defining the offence, introducing forfeiture rules and a minimum standard with respect to mutual legal assistance),[14] were soon supplemented by regulatory and preventative rules, in particular on 'know your customer'-policy (Pieth 2004: 23ff.; Pini 2004: 227ff.). The political change was brought about not so much by conventions[15] but by 'soft law', especially the 'Forty Recommendations' of an informal group created by G7 and later extended to the OECD scope and beyond, the 'Financial Action Task Force on Money Laundering' (FATF).[16] The rules on customer identification pre-dated action against money laundering and were originally developed within a self-regulatory context.[17] In Switzerland, in 1977 after the so-called 'Chiasso scandal' (Capus 2004: 123), the primary role of such an instrument was to prevent state regulation. In 1988 the standards had just been elevated from a national to an international model text,[18] when the FATF picked them up and integrated their approach into its work to develop a series of Anti-Money Laundering Recommendations that were to be adopted in their first version in 1990. AML legislation is, therefore, from the outset a mixture of 'hard law' and 'soft law', of traditional government-led 'hierarchical' regulation and self-regulation as well as mixed, negotiated, solutions. Clearly, the emergence of the FATF was an effort within the wider agenda of countries in the North to control financial flows worldwide. To some extent, it could be explained to the countries of the South as serving their interests in tracing stolen assets.

Since then, the standards against money laundering have been broadened in every sense, and the scope of predicate offences has been extended in the Recommendations of the FATF to all (serious) offences. The professions addressed in the preventative concepts have been drastically extended to include all kinds of 'gate-keepers' (a category reaching far beyond fiduciaries and tradi- tional financial intermediaries to include lawyers and precious metal dealers etc.). The geographic scope of the AML-initiatives now spans the world, well beyond the FATF and its satellite organisations.[19] Those jurisdictions which were perceived as un-cooperative were put on a black list and coerced into coop- eration.[20] International recommendations have continuously and studiously been implemented in national law, especially since the FATF has engaged its con- stituency in a rigorous peer-evaluation process. The ratings may have dramatic economic effects, as they decide on the position of companies domiciled in a specific country. They may also influence the cost of transactions with certain financial institutions. Countries and institutions blacklisted may find it difficult to do business with the rest of the (more) regulated world.

Why would, under these circumstances, a group of key competitors in private banking, one of the areas most at risk, get together and draft a private business standard on customer-due-diligence?

Private sector initiatives

REASONS

In order to situate the Wolfsberg initiative of private banks correctly in the mul- titude of self-regulation instruments, it needs to be stressed that the domain the principles deal with was already heavily regulated and more regulation was just about to come (the 'Basel Committee on Banking Supervision' was at the time preparing its new customer-due-diligence paper),[21] a set of politically, if not legally, binding 'recommendations' to member states). Bankers perceived these moves as yet another threat of over-regulation by less-than-sensitive regulators. Instead, the Wolfsberg process was to prepare the ground for a change of para- digm towards a 'risk-based approach', engaging the responsibility of the profes- sion in a far more in-depth way than the 'rule-based approach' traditionally adopted by regulators. A risk-based approach allows financial institutions to find solutions more closely attuned to their needs (Pieth 2004: 23ff.).[22] Therefore, the Wolfsberg papers must primarily be seen as offers to regulators to enter into collective negotiations on standards and standard-setting procedures.

The main advantage to be drawn from the process, both by legislators and banks, was to be that they could achieve harmonisation of standards amongst key competitors, especially the US, European and Japanese companies, whose activities were based on rather diverging regulatory environments, far more expediently than through inter-governmental negotiations. Additionally, the

Principles had a direct impact, even on under-regulated off-shore centres, as they apply also to all subsidiaries of the participants, wherever they do business. One of the major tasks of Wolfsberg is, therefore, to reduce the risk of regulatory arbitrage amongst the big players in private banking, later on extended to other forms of banking.

Of course, a standard of this type improves the public perception of a company, the primary goals of the Wolfsberg standards are, however, of an even more directly pecuniary nature: agreeing amongst competitors and above all with key regulators on 'best practices' allows the reduction of risk and costs: if the standards on customer identification seem high in comparison with everyday practice in the industry today, they also put a limit on what needs to be done and help manage legal risks (by defining adequate compliance with the new standards). They are, above all, an instrument for expectation management.

The Wolfsberg banks would, however, have been unable to come together without the help of facilitators from civil society and former representatives of the FATF. What was in the deal for them? Going back to the original motivation for the initiative, their goal was the reduction of the availability of services to corrupt officials. Making it more difficult to launder corruption funds was considered an essential condition to effectively combat bribery. It is following this logic that makes the Wolfsberg Group currently consider a further statement to address the specific risk of becoming a conduit for corrupt transactions.

HOW DOES THE WOLFSBERG GROUP OPERATE?

The Wolfsberg Group meets up to four times a year under a rotating dual chairmanship (traditionally one European and one US banker). The structure of the meetings is very informal, decisions are prepared in working groups and intensively discussed also in the plenary. Decisions are taken by unanimity, after consultations of the responsible bodies in every member institution (typically the board).

CRITIQUE

Not astonishingly for a private initiative with such public impact, critique has been voiced: Wolfsberg has in particular been criticised for its 'elitist' approach and for not monitoring the compliance with its standards. On monitoring – to address this issue first – it must, however, be pointed out that all banks are under the tight supervision of regulators and that offering detailed language on customer-due-diligence issues to regulators may backfire easily if something 'goes wrong': Wolfsberg banks could find themselves sanctioned by regulators on the basis of their own private standards.

Furthermore, The Group has deliberately decided to remain small, in order to maintain its discussion culture and to be able to take decisions by unanimity. However, the Wolfsberg Forum, especially in its most recent form, has opened up substantially: the papers, produced by the Wolfsberg Group during the last years, were subjected to the scrutiny of the next 50 largest banks and key regulators. The comments are being integrated into the final version of these texts.[23]

RECENT DEVELOPMENTS

In the original phase leading up to the first standards, Wolfsberg was very much a multi-stakeholder group, initiated by civil society members, advised by former officials and by farsighted members of the private sector.[24] Since Wolfsberg has managed to establish itself as accepted interlocutor with regulators, there is a tendency to move towards a pure private sector group. A shift in topics, but also in the participants delegated by banking institutions, indicates a move from policy-orientated activities to a technical emphasis. Not all participants are equally aware that losing the multi-stakeholder element would transform the Group into a mere lobbying institution for multinational banking interests. Using the power triangle with government/intergovernmental input, private sector efforts and civil society engagement as the three corners, the influence of the

Figure 5 Original actor constellation of the Wolfsberg Principles.

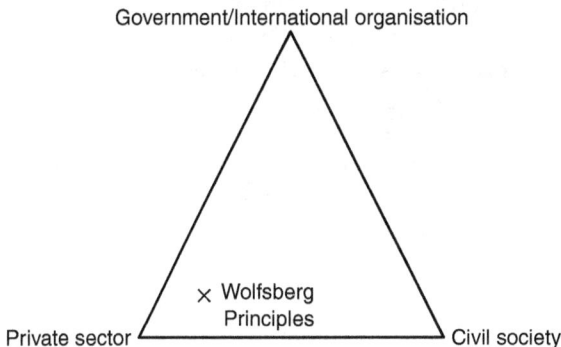

Figure 6 Contemporary actor constellation of the Wolfsberg Principles.

various actors can be visualised. The original Wolfsberg Group was already based very strongly on private sector and civil society contributions, the public interest manifested itself indirectly through the regulatory environment and former members of the FATF and national FIUs as 'translators' and 'motivators'.

As a pure private sector group, Wolfsberg would lose a lot of its appeal: it would become vulnerable to all the criticism directed at traditional instruments of self-regulation, such as that they are self-serving, undemocratic, intransparent and ineffective since they lack the control by non-involved observers or by the representatives of public interest.

SUMMARY

Wolfsberg is more than a pure private sector representation. As a multi-stakeholder group it gained credibility, both because the key institutions in private banking were ready to sign up and to submit to an intensive group process (four meetings a year and one open forum), but also because representatives of NGOs and academia have been participating. The motivation of the private sector to participate, however, has always hinged on more direct economic interests: to prevent a next regulatory push or at least influence its direction to establish a level playing field amongst key competitors, in order to marginalise those who fall below the bench mark and to ameliorate the reputation of the sector altogether. In summary, they have become a standard setting power, despite the fact that they are purely private and not necessarily representative for the industry as a whole.

Combating corruption

Public sector initiatives

Although the negative consequences of corruption, especially transnational bribery in Third World countries, were obvious long before the 1990s (Eigen and Pieth 1999: 1ff.), earlier efforts to draft international treaties failed[25] due to North–South and East–West differences. The East–West détente around 1990 changed the landscape dramatically. As formerly 'controlled' territories opened up to international commerce, the need to reduce the risk of unfair competition amongst exporters became paramount. At the same time, it was more obvious that endemic corruption in the local justice systems and administrations in the East and the South made investors vulnerable. It was, therefore, ultimately the concurrent effect of first world interests with NGO pressure that allowed corruption to move up the political agenda, in the 1990s (Aiolfi and Pieth in Fijnaut and Huberts 2002: 350f.; Sacerdoti 2000: 29ff.; Eigen 1999 in Eigen and Pieth 1999: 293ff.). The OECD started its work on transnational commercial corruption in 1989 and adopted a first Recommendation in 1994,[26] it revised the Recommendation in 1997[27] and shortly afterwards adopted a Convention[28] focusing on the criminal law aspects to transnational bribery. Much of this work has been accomplished in a sparring relationship between the NGO Transparency International, founded in 1993, and the OECD Working Group on Bribery.

Especially in the 1990s several regional organisations (OAS,[29] Council of Europe,[30] the EU etc.) developed their own anti-corruption conventions, some of which cover a vast area of topics. The most recent brick in the anti-corruption building is the comprehensive UN Convention Against Corruption, which entered into force in December 2005. Concurrently, Multilateral Development Banks (MDBs)[31] as well as, bi- and multilateral development agencies stepped up the efforts to prevent bribery dramatically.

The various instruments create a complex web of anti-corruption rules, sometimes causing difficulties for national legislators attempting to implement them all at once. They follow very different rationales: whereas the OECD initiative is primarily directed at fostering a level playing field for exporters, the regional texts seek to harmonise law, in order to enable mutual legal assistance amongst neighbours. In the context of the Council of Europe, an additional aim was to upgrade Eastern European legal standards to help enable the enlargement of the European Union. The EU started off by following a very narrow remit of protecting its own financial interests and gradually broadened the approach to corruption within the Community's Member States in general (Salazar 2003: 137ff.).

Only at first sight has the evolution on anti-corruption followed the traditional ways of international law more closely than those on money laundering: the OECD standards on corruption evolved primarily with the help of Recommendations, merely in the last minute were criminal law rules translated (from the so-called Agreed Common Elements) into a legally binding instrument. The key instrument used to make soft law tough, the peer review process,[32] was combined here with treaty law. The OECD Convention has another common denominator with the AML instruments: it does not request unification of criminal law. Rather, it adopts the principle of 'functional equivalence', which allows Member States a substantial margin of appreciation (Aiolfi and Pieth 2002: 351ff.).

OECD-ICC-industry standards

Already in 1977, when the UN was involved in a first attempt to draft an anti-corruption treaty, the International Chamber of Commerce (ICC) developed a code of conduct[33] meant to supplement the UN Treaty. Since this Treaty was not finalised in its time, the ICC text remained dead letter. Together with the OECD Convention of 1997 the code obtained a new 'raison d'être'. Correspondingly it was revised in 1996 and again in 1999.[34] The rules are currently again under review for a 2005 amendment. Their main focus is prevention of corruption and they address some delicate issues, like the relations to third parties. They remain, however, rather generic and do not focus on any sector in particular. They do not require signing up by companies. Equally generic are the business principles developed by Transparency International[35] together with a core group of businesses. In many points, this text goes beyond the current ICC standard.

The language, however, does not always apply the same precision in definition as a purely legal text would.[36] Furthermore, both the ICC and the Transparency International Business Principles (TI/BP) do not require actual declarations of commitment by companies. A further 'industry standard' on corruption emerged when the UN decided, after adoption of its Anti-Corruption Convention in 2003, to add a 'tenth principle' to the 'Global Compact'.[37] This text is, on the face of it, merely a Statement of Principle without any detail; it does, however, require an annual self-declaration on implementation.

Following the Wolfsberg example, after 2000 a series of sectorial industry groups were created to define specific anti-corruption standards. They were all initiated by civil society and co-chaired by industry and NGO members. It was believed that corruption prevention raised different problems in each sector (the construction, the defence, the extractive industries, the power systems manufacturers, the pharmaceutical industry, the insurance sector, etc.). While this may be true for some particular issues (like the treatment of so-called 'signature bonuses' in the oil industry) overall, the issues dealt with in the industry standards tended to gravitate towards a common denominator of topics: issues relating to the definition of corruption, especially distinctions within the 'grey area' of donations, hospitality and facilitations payments on the one hand, and the treatment of third parties and intermediaries (suppliers, agents, joint venture partner, foreign subsidiaries) on the other hand.[38] Since most of these standards are still in the making, no specific reference will be made here before their actual publication.

The benefit of sectorial groups was rather seen in the confidence building and disciplining effect of face-to-face groups of big companies. Such compacts are useful in oligopolistic markets (turbines, fast trains, oil and gas, mining, aircraft manufacture, pharmaceuticals, etc.). Even where a formalised monitoring/complaints/arbitration procedure is not foreseen, such groups can allow companies who compete for huge contracts, sometimes deciding over the success or failure of entire corporations, to meet in a secure environment, facilitated by disinterested parties to agree on a no-corruption policy. Many such groups are currently working on texts, often the companies are however shy to carry through the actual process to the signature stage. Apparently, the issue of corruption is – in many sectors and many areas of the world – still too hot a topic.[39]

Overall, the main consequence of public sector activities has been to raise the risk for the private sector and for managers. Especially companies and managers in the North are now facing criminal, civil, administrative and fiscal sanctions for bribery, also of foreign officials. They are motivated to make sure that their key competitors implement similarly expensive compliance concepts. Industry standards with the necessary detail and monitoring mechanisms are considered useful. They allow the members of the group to present themselves as cooperative and sound business partners.[40] Foremost, industry standards are, however, an instrument of expectation management.

Partnering Against Corruption Initiative (PACI)

DAVOS

A group of three facilitating bodies, the World Economic Forum (WEF), Transparency International (TI), and the Basel Institute on Governance, was asked by key players in the construction sector to create a multi-stakeholder group on corruption. The idea was launched by Alan Boeckmann, President of Fluor, at the WEF Annual Meeting in 2003.[41] A working group made up of 15 Engineering and Construction company representatives and the facilitators adapted the TI Business Principles to the needs of the sector. The text was then adopted for signature by member companies of the WEF's 'E&C Governor's Group' at the Davos meeting in 2004.[42] Concurrently, other company groups were showing an interest in making similar efforts, especially the Metals and Mining and the Oil and Gas groups. For the Davos 2005 meeting, intensive lobbying by all parties made it possible to substantially enlarge the scope of participants. The E&C text was now used for all three sectors and so far a total of over 100 companies have signed.[43]

The next immediate challenge for the companies in question is the development of a follow-up mechanism as announced by the chairmen of the three Governors' Groups participating at the press conference in January 2005.[44]

SITUATING PACI

Situating PACI on our 'power diagram' makes a slightly different picture than with respect to Wolfsberg. Public influence is stronger, not only through the strict regulatory environment (Convention texts as opposed to Recommendations) but also the direct participation of officials in the international forums during the actual process. Furthermore, the civil society element is stronger than in Wolfsberg, the WEF is acting as a neutral convenor, TI as a pressure group on the topic and the Basel Institute on Governance as the technician of the multi-stakeholder concept.

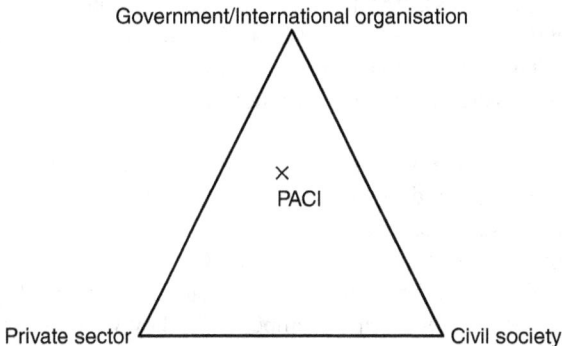

Government/International organisation

×
PACI

Private sector   Civil society

Figure 7 Actor constellation PACI.

MONITORING

There is widespread agreement that the follow-up issue is decisive for the credibility of any attempt at self-regulation (Australian Task Force 2000: 51ff.; Haufler 2001: 8; Jenkins 2001: 27; Utting 2002: 82). A broad variety of options is available.

Monitoring can be informal. This will be the case where companies do not actually sign but merely publicly (unilaterally) declare, that they are following a specific standard. But even where an actual Group has been constituted (for example, the Wolfsberg model), monitoring can remain informal. Formalised monitoring mechanisms can either be based on self- or mutual evaluation by group members or on independent third party monitoring. According to the construction, a softer form can be selected or, in the extreme case, certification by a professional certifier (e.g. ISO) could be applied and certification could even be made a condition for participation. Which model the group chooses – group or third party monitoring – depends on the make up of the group: a small group of market leaders in an oligopolistic market will most likely rely on the group process, a large group consisting of SMEs or a mixture of larger and smaller companies will more likely opt for third party monitoring.

Monitoring focuses on abstract compliance with standards. Another approach would be to base the evaluation of compliance on complaints heard by a tribunal. Some tribunals even have the authority to impose private monetary sanctions. An example on a national basis is the Swiss bankers' agreement on customer-due-diligence.[45] The choice of an adequate monitoring mechanism for PACI is currently under way and will be decided by the members of the three Industry Groups in Davos in January 2006.

THE FUTURE OF PACI

Situating PACI. It is planned to expand PACI yet further and to invite the participation of other sectors. Already now, a serious difficulty is arising from the many competing anti-corruption instruments in the private sector (including the ICC, TI Business Principles (BPs), PACI, Global Compact and the various sectorial groups' compacts). In many respects, ICC, TI BPs and PACI ought to be treated as equivalents. They are no longer specific to a certain sector, they are generic as they cover the issue of bribery prevention on a mid-level of abstraction.

The Global Compact should not be seen as a competing instrument at all: with its one-sentence statement and its broad constituency, its role is rather that of an umbrella text. The Global Compact should consider ICC, TI BPs, PACI, International Federation of Consulting Engineers (FIDIC) and the like as translations of its basic principles and efforts into more concrete language. Ideally, the semi-abstract standards would merge. In December 2005 they went as far as to reach a consensus to mutually accept each other as equivalents.

Apart from these instruments, there will probably remain some more focused

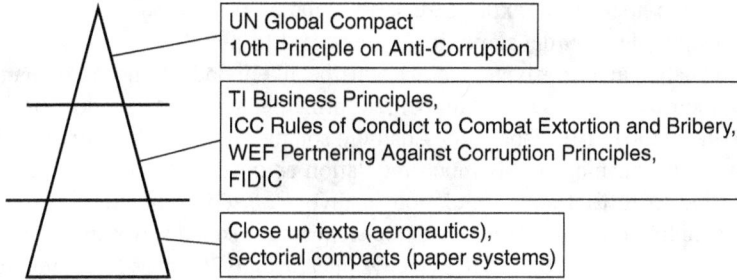

Figure 8 Global compact: norms, principles, text.

compacts, like the Aeronautic Industry's text on the selection, employment and remuneration of agents ('Clovis Principles'). Furthermore, industry-specific groups of the Wolfsberg type (small groups of strong oligopolistic competitors) will be necessary in certain sectors to make a real difference (e.g. Power Systems).

RELEVANT CONSTITUENCY

Another problem that PACI is currently facing is how to make the group grow. Even though the text was very successful in securing signatures, some major competitors in the engineering and construction industry as well as, especially, the oil and gas sector have still not signed. In fact, in the oil and gas industry some of the largest TNCs are still refraining from joining the group for a variety of reasons: some companies are maintaining that their standards are going way beyond the PACI standards, some are unconvinced that signing will be good for their reputation and finally, several others are holding back for as long as their main competitors have not joined (the fear of 'free riders'). Facilitators are currently facing the arduous task of trying to convince the timid.[46]

Analysis

The advent and the demise of self-regulation

The history of self-regulation has been told many times over as the issue became prominent over the last two decades (Black 2001: 4ff.; Haufler 2001: 7f., esp. 10; Jenkins 2001; Knill and Lehmkuhl 2002; Utting 2002; Brütsch and Lehmkuhl in Chapter 2 of this volume). Most authors mention the deregulation and privatisation processes of the 1980s as a crucial starting point (Haufler 2001: 7ff.; Jenkins 2001: 4; Utting 2002: 61ff.). In search of concepts to contain the negative impact of uncontrolled economic globalisation, the Nation State was out of its depth and intergovernmental regulation frequently turned out to be a very cumbersome process.

Not only the private sector itself, but also public entities encouraged self-regulation. High hopes were expressed: self-regulation was supposed to be cheaper, more flexible, less burdensome, it was expected to mobilise expertise (particularly available in the private sector) and the likelihood of the participants to follow their own rules seemed higher, as 'principle and agent are collapsed into one' (Black 2001: 16). Especially Australia sought to reduce the cost of (public) regulation by farming out as much regulation as possible to the private sector. Laws tried to restrict state regulation in favour of self-regulation;[47] the public sector supplied minimal standards and checklists for sound self-regulation (Australian Task Force 2000: 59ff.). NGOs increasingly favoured self-regulatory instruments over complex and non-transparent international treaty negotiations. While this approach opens the door to NGOs to influence the rules, it raises issues of legitimacy within civil society. In lieu of the elected parliament (or parties, trade unions etc.), private companies and self-appointed single-issue-representatives dominate this type of regulation.

No wonder that self-regulation very rapidly lost its appeal and critical opinions of the concept gained in prominence: self-regulation came to be considered ineffective (Black 2001: 10; Jenkins 2001: 26; Klauser 1994: 53; Ruch 2004: 449), non-transparent (Marti 2000: 582; Minogue 2001: 14; Ruch 2004: 409; Tsingou 2001 (VII. 1.)), self-serving (Minogue 2001: 9f.; Pitofsky 1998: 1; Ruch 2004: 449) and undemocratic (Delmas-Marty 2004: 260; Klauser 1994: 52; Marti 2000: 580; Tsingou 2001 (VII. 1.)).

Co-regulation

Instead of fully reverting to 'Command and Control' (CAC)-type regulation (Black 2002: 2ff.), a new paradigm emerged: non-state-regulators have definitely pushed their way into regulation, even in traditional CAC areas like criminal law. They were integrated into decision making bodies (cf. e.g. in financial services supervision).[48] We are currently witnessing the emergence of 'hybrid regulatory networks' and new forms of mixed regulation or 'co-regulation' (Black 2001: 6ff.; Brütsch and Lehmkuhl in Chapter 2; Haufler 2001: 12). There is clearly a link between the less hierarchical forms of regulation applied by the international task forces referenced above, the soft-law and peer-review arrangements, and the entry of non-state actors into international regulation. The civil society and the private sector play a decisive role not only in rule-making but also in the application of rules: monitoring mechanisms controlling implementation of the AML and anti-corruption rules of international bodies frequently rely on the cooperation of non-state actors.[49]

Multi-stakeholder initiatives

Multi-stakeholder initiatives were first developed in the area of labour practices and the protection of the environment (cf. for details Utting 2001: 75ff.; also Haufler 2001: 14, 17; Jenkins 2001: 19ff.). Frequently, they are partnerships between the private sector and NGOs or joint public–private initiatives (Utting 2001: 61f.). They were considered a viable 'third way' between government regulation and corporate self-regulation (ibid.: 66). In many cases, the impetus to form such an initiative came from civil society, but this is not a fundamental element of their definition. The aim of this approach is to overcome some of the merited criticism of traditional self-regulation: if the non-industry members of the group do their job well, they will assume a control-function from within and will see to it that the agenda of the group is not dominated entirely by business interests. They will also have to insist on the establishment of a credible monitoring or complaints procedure to enforce the standards. It is their task to see that the group respects general interests and to seek ways of convincing the participating companies that commercial interests run in parallel to public interests, at least with a view to a long term perspective. This is obviously a tall order for groups and individuals who typically have little economic power to back them. Their power basis is either public opinion, potential consumer reaction (Haufler 2001: 9, 11, 23) or simply the force of the argument. In this respect it has helped both in the Wolfsberg and the PACI experience, to establish a link to the public sector, in order to allow influencing the agendas of international organisations, as the strongest motivator for the private sector to embark on a self-regulatory experiment has traditionally been the anticipation of public regulation (Australian Task Force 2000: 7; Black 2001: 9f.; Haufler 2001: 3, 22f.).

Conclusion

Wolfsberg and PACI are representatives of a new era of regulation. They are not entirely driven by a private agenda: on the contrary, AML and anti-corruption are key issues in the fight against transnational corporate crime. Heavy public regulation attempts to control these activities and the private sector is recruited into the fight on a preventative level. It is, however, in the interest of the business world to contain efforts and manage risk (including legal and reputational risk). Their own efforts in translating the standards onto an operational level serve the purpose of levelling the playing field vis-à-vis competitors and of controlling the cost of risk management. On the other hand, these standards are not simply part of a hierarchical regulatory structure: with a 'risk-based approach' to money laundering and with the rules on employing intermediaries to prevent corruption, the private sector is genuinely contributing to the fight against transnational economic crime with its own means, reaching beyond public rules. Overall, Wolfsberg and PACI are elements of a system of co-regulation in emerging international law against commercial crime.

Civil society is probably in the most difficult situation since its representatives are often the main initiators and motivators of the initiative, at least in its early stages. If the initiative does take off, they rapidly become superfluous, even though the initiative changes its character without them. On the other hand, their means to set the process in motion are frequently weak, sometimes crude and the prospects are usually uncertain.

Notes

1 Originally a US concept: introducing an ad hoc multi-agency structure to deal with a specific problem in the international area, cf. especially the Financial Action Task Force on Money Laundering and the Chemical Action Task Force on Precursor Chemicals for Illicit Drug Production.
2 www.wolfsberg-principles.com.
3 Wolfsberg Anti-Money Laundering Principles on Private Banking, revised version 2002.
4 The most recent Wolfsberg Forum took place in May 2006. It has been frequented by roughly 100 bankers, regulators, and representatives of international organisations (BCBS, FATF, Worldbank, IMF, OECD).
5 For example by the Association of Banks in Singapore (ABS), cf. Lee in Pieth and Aiolfi 2004: 96.
6 For example, recently the Federal Reserve Bank, when sanctioning ABN AMRO in 2004.
7 Partnering against Corruption Principles for Countering Bribery, an initiative of the World Economic Forum in partnership with Transparency International and the Basel Institute on Governance, Davos January 2005.
8 Cf. Wall Street Journal Europe, 27 January 2005, A1, A6: 'Big firms take stand on bribes'.
9 Alan L. Boeckmann, Chairman and CEO of Fluor Corporation, USA; Wayne W. Murdy, Chairman and CEO of Newmont Mining Corporation, USA; and Tan Sri Hassan Marican, President and CEO of Petronas, Malaysia.
10 The OECD Guidelines for Multinational Enterprises, revised version 2000.
11 Cf. especially the example of Shell in Nigeria.
12 Take the consequences of the Brent Spar debacle for Shell. A consumer boycott effectively prevented the company from simply submerging a disused oil platform and taught the TNC a lesson it will not easily forget.
13 United Nations Convention against Illicit Traffic in Narcotic Drugs and Psychotropic Substances, December 19, 1998.
14 Art. 3, 5 and 7 UN Convention (fn. 22).
15 The Council of Europe Convention 141 and the EU-Regulation of 1991 are mere reflections of the standards agreed on by the FATF in 1989.
16 The 40 Recommendations of the Financial Action Task Force on Money Laundering (FATF), Paris 1990, revised 1996 and 2003.
17 For Switzerland, for example the first Due Diligence Agreement (DDA) was crafted by the Swiss Bankers Association in 1977, and has since then been updated every five years. The most recent version (Version 06, DDA 03) was adopted on 1 July 2003.
18 Basel Statement of Principles of 12 December 1989, written by the Cooke Committee of the Bank of International Settlements (BIS).
19 Cf. the Caribean Financial Action Task Force (CFATF), the South American Financial Action Task Force (GAFI SUD), the Middle East and Northern African Financial Action Task Force (MENA FATF), the Asia/Pacific Group on Money Laundering (APG), and the Eastern and Southern African Anti-Money Laundering Group (ESAAMLG).
20 The so-called 'NCCT' Process (for Non-cooperative Countries and Territories). Online, available at: www.1.OECD.org/FATF/NCCT_EN.HTM.
21 'Basel Committee on Banking Supervision' (BCBS), Customer-due-diligence for Banks, Basel October 2001.
22 Cf. the new Wolfsberg paper relating to 'A risk-based approach for managing money laundering risks', 2005.
23 Cf. fn. 9.
24 Especially Hans-Peter Bauer of UBS and Shaukat Aziz of City Group.

25 Cf. the work of the Economic and Social Council (ECOSOC) and its Commission on Transnational Cooperation, later the Committee on an International Agreement on Illicit Payments from the mid-1970s until the project was abandoned in 1979.

26 Recommendation of the Council on Bribery in International Business Transactions, 27 May 1994, C (94) 75 final.

27 Revised Recommendation of the Council on Combating Bribery in International Business Transaction, adopted by the Council on 23 May 1997.

28 Convention on Combating Bribery of Foreign Public Officials in International Business Transactions, adopted on 21 November 1997.

29 Inter-American Convention against Corruption of 29 March 1996.

30 Criminal Law Convention of 27 January 1999, Civil Law Convention of 4 November 1999, European Union Protocol to the Convention on the Protection of European Communities' Financial Interests of 27 September 1996 and the Convention on the Fight against Corruption of 26 May 1997.

31 Cf. Worldbank 2000.

32 Peer review, An OECD tool for cooperation and change, OECD 2003.

33 On the ICC Rules of Conduct and their history, cf. Heimann 2004.

34 Cf. ICC Rules of Conduct: Extortion and Bribery in International Business Transactions, revised version October 2005.

35 Business Principles for Countering Bribery, an initiative of Transparency International and Social Accountability International, December 2002 and the following revisions.

36 Cf. especially Art. 5.1 Bribes and 5.4 Facilitation Payments with fn. 3.

37 www.unglobalcompact.org; cf. Kell and Ruggie 1999.

38 Since most of these standards are still in the making no specific references will be made here before their actual publication.

39 *The Economist*, 2 March 2002, 11, 67ff.

40 The PACI Initiative has held talks both with the World Bank and the EBRD, suggesting that these institutions request sound anti-corruption compliance systems for the contractors they deal with. It is believed that PACI is a crucial contribution to such a system.

41 Boeckmann, World Energy, 6 April 2003, 2ff.

42 Business Principles for Countering Bribery in the Engineering and Construction Industry, an Initiative of the World Economic Forum, Transparency International and the Basel Institute on Governance, January 2004.

43 www.weforum.org/paci.

44 The Wall Street Journal Europe, 27 January 2005: 'Big firms take stand on bribes', A1 and A6; Basler Zeitung 29. Januar 2005: '23 Unternehmen gegen Korruption', 21.

45 Cf. fn. 27, Agreement on the Swiss Banks' code of conduct with regard to the exercise of due diligence (CDB 03): Article 11 foresees a fine of up to CHF10 million for non-compliance decided on by an independent supervisory board.

46 Cf. the Wall Street Journal Europe (fn. 49).

47 Productivity Commission, Office of Regulation Review (1998), A Guide to Regulation (second edition).

48 In the UK, cf. the AML guidelines adopted by the joint Money Laundering Steering Group (news version 14 March 2005; for Switzerland the AML regulation of the Swiss Federal Banking Commission of 18 December 2002 referring in its Art. 14 explicitly to the self-regulation instrument of the Swiss Banker's Association on KYC (cf. fn 47).

49 For example on the role of civil society and the private sector in the OECD monitoring: Private sector and civil society are systematically interviewed and make oral as well as written submissions within the framework of so-called Phase 2 evaluations. Online, available at: www.oecd.>orgcorruption>anti-bribery convention>country reports on the implementation of the convention>procedure of self- and mutual evaluation phase 2.

References

Aiolfi, G. and Pieth, M. (2002) 'How to Make a Convention Work: The Organisation for Economic Co-operation and Development Recommendation and Convention on Bribery as an Example of a New Horizon in International Law', in: C. Fijnaut and L. Huberts (eds) *Corruption, Integrity and Law Enforcement*, The Hague: Springer, pp. 350ff.

Australian Task Force (2000) *Industry Self-Regulation in Consumer Markets*, Report prepared by the Taskforce on Industry Self-regulation, Canberra.

Black, J. (2001) 'Decentring Regulation: Understanding the Role of Regulation and Self Regulation in a "Post-Regulatory" World', in: M. Freeman (ed.) *Current Legal Problems* vol. 54. Oxford: Oxford University Press, pp. 103–146.

Black, J. (2002) 'Regulatory Conversations', *Journal of Law and Society* 29 (1), in: D. Campbell and S. Picciotto (eds) 'New Directions in Regulatory Theory', *Special Issue of the Journal of Law and Society*, 29 (1): 163–196.

Boeckmann, A.L. (2003) 'Taking a Corporate Stand Against Corruption', *World Energy Magazine*, 6 (4): 2–5.

Capus, N. (2004) 'Country Report: Combating Money Laundering in Switzerland', in: M. Pieth and G. Aiolfi (eds) (2004) *A Comparative Guide to Anti-Money Laundering, A Critical Analysis of Systems in Singapore, Switzerland, the UK and the USA*, Cheltenham UK/Northampton USA: Edwar Elgar Publishing, pp. 114–226.

Delmas-Marty, M. (2004) *Le relativ et l'universel, les forces imaginantes du droit*, Paris: Éd. du Seuil.

Eigen, P. (1999) 'Internationale Zivilgesellschaft – Einleitung', in: M. Pieth and P. Eigen (eds) *Korruption im internationalen Geschäftsverkehr: Bestandesaufnahme, Bekämpfung, Prävention*, Basel: Luchterhand, pp. 293–296.

Eigen, P. and Pieth, M. (1999) 'Einführung: Altes Thema – neue Strategie', in: M. Pieth and P. Eigen (eds) *Korruption im internationalen Geschäftsverkehr: Bestandesaufnahme, Bekämpfung, Prävention*, Basel: Luchterhand, pp. 1–8.

Fijnaut, C. and Huberts, L. (2002) *Corruption, Integrity and Law Enforcement*, The Hague: Verlag.

Haufler, V. (2001) *A Public Role for the Private Sector: Industry Self-Regulation in a Global Economy*, Washington: Carnegie Endowment for International Peace.

Heimann, F. (2004) 'The ICC Rules of Conduct and the OECD Convention', in: F. Vincke and F. Heimann (eds) *Fighting Corruption; A Corporate Practices Manual*, Paris: ICC Publishing, pp. 13ff.

Jenkins, R. (2001) *'Corporate Codes of Conduct, Self-Regulation in a Global Economy'*, in: UN Research Institute for Social Development, pp. 1–44.

Kell, G. and Ruggie, J. (1999) *Global Markets and Social Legitimacy: The Case of the 'Global Impact'*, United Nations. (Online, available at: www.unglobalcompact. org.)

Klauser, P. (1994) 'Selbstregulierung versus staatliche Regulierung I', in: Europainstitut an der Universität Basel (ed.) *Ein schweizerisches Börsengesetz im europäischen Kontext: Tagungsband* Basel: Europainstitut der Universität Basel, pp. 51–64.

Knill, Ch. and Lehmkuhl, D. (2002) 'Private Actors and the State: Internationalization and Changing Patterns of Governance', *Governance: An International Journal of Policy, Administration, and Institutions*, 15 (1): 41–67.

Lee, M. (2004) 'Country Report: Anti-Money Laundering Laws and Regulations in Singapore', in: M. Pieth and G. Aiolfi (eds) *A Comparative Guide to Anti-Money Laundering, A Critical Analysis of Systems in Singapore, Switzerland, the UK and the USA*, Cheltenham UK/Northampton USA: Edwar Elgar Publishing, pp. 64–99.

Marti, A. (2000) 'Selbstregulierung anstelle staatlicher Gesetzgebung?', in: *Zentralblatt für Staats- und Verwaltungsrecht*, 11/2000: 561–586.

Minogue, M. (2001) *Governance-Based Analysis of Regulation, Centre on Regulation and Competition Working Paper Series*, Paper No. 3, Manchester: Centre on Regulation and Competition, Institute for Development Policy Management, University of Manchester.

OECD (2000) *OECD Guidelines for Multinational Enterprises*, Meeting of the OECD Council at Ministerial Level, Revision 2000. Paris: OECD.

OECD (2003) *Peer Review, An OECD Tool for Cooperation and Change*, Paris: OECD.

Passas, N. (1998/1999) 'Globalization, Criminogenic Asymmetries and Economic Crime', in: *European Journal of Law Reform*, 1 (4): 399–424.

Pieth, M. (2002) 'Staatliche Intervention und Selbstregulierung der Wirtschaft', in: C. Prittwitz, M. Baumann K. and Günther (HrSg.) (eds) *Festschrift für Klaus Lüderssen*, Baden-Baden: Nomos, pp. 317–325.

Pieth, M. (2004) 'International standards against money laundering', in: M. Pieth and G. Aiolfi (eds) *A Comparative Guide to Anti-Money Laundering, A Critical Analysis of Systems in Singapore, Switzerland, the UK and the USA*, Cheltenham UK/Northampton USA: Edwar Elgar Publishing, pp. 3–61.

Pieth, M. and Aiolfi, G. (2004) 'The Private Sector Becomes Active: The Wolfsberg Process', *Journal of Financial Crime*, 10 (4): 359–365.

Pini, M. (2004) 'Country Report: Costumer Due Diligence in Switzerland', in: M. Pieth and G. Aiolfi (eds) *A Comparative Guide to Anti-Money Laundering, A Critical Analysis of Systems in Singapore, Switzerland, the UK and the USA*, Cheltenham UK/Northampton USA: Edwar Elgar Publishing, pp. 227–258.

Pitofsky, R. (1998) *Self Regulation and Antitrust*, Remarks prepared for the D.C. Bar Association Symposium (18 February 1998, Washington, D.C.). Online, available at: www.ftc.gov.

Productivity Commission, Office of Regulation Review (1998) *A Guide to Regulation*, second edition. Canberra: Office of Regulation Review.

Ruch, A. (2004) '*Regulierungsfragen der Gentechnologie und des Internet*', Referat für den Schweizerischen Juristentag 2004, in: *Zeitschrift für Schweizerisches Recht* 4/2004°II, Halbband: p. 373.

Sacerdoti, G. (2000) 'To Bribe or not to Bribe?', in: OECD (ed.) *No Longer Business as Usual, Fighting Bribery and Corruption*, Paris: OECD, pp. 29–49.

Salazar, L. (2003) 'Profili penalistici dell'attuazione in Italia delle convenzioni anticorruzione dell'OCSE e dell'Unione Europea', in: G. Sacerdoti (ed.) *Responsabilità d'impresa e strumenti internazionali anticorruzione: Dalla Convenzione OCSE 1997 al Decreto no. 231/2001*, Milano: Egea, pp. 137–163.

Schweizerische Bankiervereinigung (2003) *Agreement on the Swiss banks' code of conduct with regard to the exercise of due diligence (CDB 03)*, Basel: Swiss Bankers Association. Online, available at: www.swissbanking.ch.

Tsingou, E. (2001) Governance in the Financial Markets: Understanding Self-Regulation, Paper presented to the ISA International Convention, Panel S 1-4 'The Politics of Banking', Hong Kong: University of Amsterdam.

United Nations Convention Against Illicit Traffic in Narcotic Drugs and Psychotropic Substances, adopted on 19 December 1988. Online, available at: www.unodc.org/pdf/convention_1988_en.pdf.

Utting, P. (2001) 'UN–Business Partnership: Whose Agenda Counts?' *Transnational Associations: The Review of the Union of International Associations*, 3: 118–128.

Utting, P. (2002) 'Regulating Business Via Multistakeholder Initiatives: A Preliminary Assessment', in: R. Jenkins, P. Utting and R. Alva Pino (eds) *Voluntary Approaches to Corporate Responsibility: Readings and a Resource Guide*, UN Research Institute for Social Development, part 2, pp. 61–130.

Wolfsberg (2000) *Wolfsberg Anti-Money Laundering Principles on Private Banking*, adopted 30 October 2000, revised in May 2002. Online, available at: www.wolfsberg-principles.com.

World Bank (2000) *Helping Countries Combat Corruption: Progress at the World Bank Since 1997*, Washington: The World Bank. Online, available at: www.worldbank.org.

World Economic Forum (2004) *Business Principles for Countering Bribery in the Engineering and Construction Industry*. Online, available at: www.weforum.org/paci.

World Economic Forum (2005) *Partnering Against Corruption Principles for Countering Bribery*. Online, available at: www.weforum.org/paci.

6 Legalization, transnationalism and organic agriculture

William D. Coleman and Austina J. Reed

The complex interdependence and ever more dense networks of interconnections that characterize social living under globalization are transforming local places. As Tomlinson (1999: 9) writes, 'Putting it simply, connectivity means changing the nature of localities and not just occasionally lifting some people out of them.... The paradigmatic experience of global modernity for most people ... is that of staying in one place but experiencing the "displacement" that global modernity *brings to them*'. The consequence of this kind of development, Tomlinson (1999: 12) adds, is that local practices and lifestyles need to be examined and evaluated in terms of their global consequences. These insights provide the initial motivation for a study of growing legalization in one of the most determinedly local sectors of economic activity: organic farming. Organic farmers and the local places in which they work and live have become spliced into a complex system of local, national and global legalities, a system in turn that is changing how they work.

The organic agricultural movement began as a local response by a small number of farmers primarily in wealthier countries to the 'modernization' and 'chemicalization' of mainstream agriculture. In challenging these tendencies toward monocropping, growing farm extensity, and expanded use of pesticides, herbicides and chemical fertilizers, organic farmers favoured polycultural practices, chemical-free farming, and less industrial farming practices. They believed that farming had to function in harmony with its environment and in ways that kept soils rich and animals free of chemicals. The values, norms and, ultimately, the rules for proceeding in this way were formulated locally, often informally. As social movements, organic producers and their supporters in many countries became strong political critics of dominant approaches in farming.

As environmentalists, consumer advocates for safe and healthy foods, and smaller farmers raised awareness about the effects of monocultural, industrial agriculture, a growing awareness of the organic movement developed. In response to this higher visibility, demand for organic food has risen swiftly over the past 15 years. This enhanced awareness of organic approaches to farming and increased demand for organic products have begun to change the local practices and commercial networks of organic producers. Some producers have increased the size of their farms and moved to more monocultural growing. The buyers of their products have changed from consumers in local farmers' markets and health food stores to large retail chains, which often distribute their products regionally, if not nationally. Some of the large businesses purchasing organic products now come from other countries as rising consumer demand makes international trade in organic foods more profitable.

These changes in the political economy of organic production have raised the horizon of local organic farmers to national and global levels. They have also created pressures for a rationalization and legalization of organic farming. Initial efforts at norm production and definition of rules came from private co-operative producers' organizations. These private organizations, in turn, entered into national networks, and eventually international ones. All the while, organic producers have guarded jealously the power to define standards and to certify whether farm products meet these standards. As distribution networks became nation-wide and international trade increased, farmers' own private sites of authority were joined by those of states increasingly interested in the legal realms of standard-setting and certification. These changes have sparked divisions within the organic movement over what their core principles should be.

As a consequence, we argue in this chapter that a highly pluralistic, some-times contradictory, and often chaotic legalization has occurred when it comes to organic production. Legal pluralism and hybrid arrangements involving private and public actors characterize the system. Private regulation has remained an important part of these legal arrangements, but it has expanded from the local level to encompass the national and global levels as well. This pluralization of centres of norm production has fostered an increasing differenti-ation between the social system of organic farming and its regulation.

We develop our argument in this chapter in the following way. First, we present an overview of the changing political economy of organic production. We then turn to identify the key legal points of reference in organic farming: standard-setting, accreditation and certification. In moving next to trace the growing transnational legalization in the organic sector, we begin with a case study of nation-state activity in North America, comparing developments in the United States of America and Canada. All the while stressing the parallelism in national and global legalization processes, we then examine the growth of legal practices at the global level. In this discussion, we divide the analysis into two periods, legalization before and after 1995, with the creation of the World Trade Organization and the revision of the rules of the international trade regime being the key turning point.

The political economy of the global organic movement

Organic farming is not new. Some would say that it refers to the approach to farming followed for millennia. At its most basic level, it refers to commodities that are produced without artificial fertilizers or pesticides, relying instead on organic-based fertilizers like manure and vegetable-based compost, and natural pesticides like predator animal species (Jones 2003: 18). In addition, organic agriculture does not permit use of artificially compounded growth regulators, livestock feed and additives or genetically modified organisms. Behind this basic definition, however, lies a social philosophy for many practitioners and consumers. As the International Federation of Organic Agriculture Movements (IFOAM) reports (2004), 'Utilizing both traditional and scientific knowledge, organic agricultural systems rely on practices that promote and enhance biodiversity, biological cycles and soil biological activity. It is based on minimal use of off-farm inputs and on management practices that restore, maintain or enhance ecological harmony'. The scientist and organic farmer Bill Liebhardt (2003: 33–34) expands further on these ideas:

> Organic agriculture, I believe, is a holistic way of looking at the world and the role of human activities in it. It is the integration of our responsibilities to others – present and future generations – in the way we produce the food and fibre we all require and our duties to enhance and maintain the natural environment which is both our resource base and our own personal setting. It extends beyond the farm gate to the community, both local and global. As a movement it is a goal not fully realised and still evolving as the criteria continue to change along with our understanding of human and ecological needs.

Although organic agricultural practices thus defined are by no means new, the founding and growth of social movements promoting these practices are relatively recent events. Many trace the scientific and advocacy roots of the contemporary movement to the work of several pioneers such as Rudolf Steiner, Robert Rodale, Albert Howard and Eve Balfour who published their work in the 1920s, 1930s and 1940s. For example, Howard, a British scientist, made the argument for organic methods based on his analysis of experiments in farming practices in India and other parts of Asia. In the introduction to his book, *The Agricultural Testament*, published in 1940, he wrote: 'The maintenance of the fertility of the soil is the first condition of any permanent system of agriculture. In the ordinary processes of crop production fertility is steadily lost: its continuous restoration by means of manuring and soil management is therefore imperative' (Howard 1940).

The first label for organically produced goods came from a movement in Germany that grew up around the ideas of Rudolf Steiner in the 1920s. The Demeter movement issued its first label in 1928. The second such label came probably from the Soil Association in the UK in 1967. In both cases, these labels tended to be based on a set of guiding principles rather than on detailed production rules. Such local standards and labels are not surprising. Differences in soil type, climate, topography, resources, and culture all warrant rules that relate to very specific local conditions.

As the implications of these basic ideas were elaborated, they increasingly contradicted the 'modern', productivity and efficiency-focused practices of agriculture that had evolved in Europe, North America, Australia, New Zealand, parts of Central and South America and elsewhere. These practices had moved away from polycultural planting which tended to weaken soil fertility less and towards the use of chemical fertilizers to replenish soils ravaged by monocultural planting. In addition, in efforts to improve yields, these modern practices made increasingly extensive use of synthetically compounded herbicides to control weed growth and pesticides to keep insect populations down. The organic movement gradually became more politically active as it sought alternatives to these perceived destructive practices.

This rapid growth in the use of chemical fertilizers, herbicides and pesticides became a crucial concern for the ecological social movements that gathered strength in the 1960s and early 1970s. Many farmers in these movements embraced organic agriculture as part of their alternative vision for an ecologically oriented world. Consistent with this holistic focus, organic farming tended initially to be very local. Organic growers set up relatively small operations that were designed to provide alternative foods for the farm owners and their families and for nearby communities. This pattern of development continued through the 1970s and 1980s into the early 1990s.

For reasons that are not completely clear, the very small size of organic farming and the existing pattern of incremental, slow growth changed in the early 1990s. Several events brought more attention to organically grown foods: breakdowns in the systems for food safety in Europe and in North America illustrated best by the repeated crises from mad cow disease; a growing concern about the impact of additives in foods on human and animal health; increasing public debate about patterns of food consumption and health; and worries about genetically modified organisms. Demand for organic products began to expand rapidly in OECD countries in the 1990s, particularly in the European Union countries and in North America. An estimated 97 per cent of revenues in organic product sales come from these two areas (Sahota 2004: 25). In the US, total certified organic acreage grew by 150 per cent between 1992 and 2001 (Dimitri and Greene 2002: 1). In the EU, organic hectares grew by 67 per cent in the three year period 1998–2000 alone (Duchateau 2003: 2). The total land area under organic management as a percentage of total agricultural area reached 11.60 in Austria, 10 per cent in Switzerland, 8 per cent in Italy, 4.2 per cent in the UK and 4 per cent in Germany by 2004 (Yussefi 2004: 16). In the US, the figure was about 2 per cent. Worldwide markets for organic foods are thus expanding rapidly, with annual growth rates of 15 to 30 per cent in Europe, the US and Japan, the largest markets, in the period 1997 to 2002. By 2002, the total global market for organic food and drink was estimated at US$23 billion (Sahota 2004: 21). The size of the market is expected to continue to grow to about 102 billion by 2010 (Lohr 2001: 68).

This rise in demand, coupled with expectations that growth levels will continue to be high in OECD countries, has led to increasing levels of international trade in organic products. For example, imports have a 30 per cent market share of consumption in Austria, 25 per cent in Denmark, 40 per cent in Germany, 60 per cent in The Netherlands, 70 per cent in the UK and 80 per cent in Canada

(Lohr 2001: 70). In response to these opportunities, developing countries have taken an increasing interest in organic production. Commercial production has begun in 27 African countries, 25 in the Caribbean and Latin America, and 15 in Asia (ibid.: 77). Corresponding changes have come to the International Federation of Organic Agricultural Movements (IFOAM). In 1990, it had 93 members, with 80 per cent of these based in the OECD countries. This number increased to 243 by 1995, 462 by 2000, and 724 by 2003. Over the same period, the percentage from non-OECD countries rose to 41.[1]

The rapid growth in organic production and consumer demand in the OECD countries has brought with it changes to the political economy of the sector. In the US, there has been movement away from the small farm model; for example, in California, five giant farms control one-half of the USD 400 million organic market (Pollan 2001). These farms are working more frequently with conventional agribusiness firms. Pollan (2001) reports that Gerber's, Heinz, Dole, ConAgra and A.D.M have all created or acquired organic brands. And some of the original small organic food processors have themselves grown quickly.

Companion changes have taken place on the distribution side. For example, in 1991 in the US, conventional retailers had about 5 per cent of organic sales, compared to 30 per cent for direct farm and local market sales, and 65 per cent for natural foods and organic specific retailers. A decade later, conventional retailers had 45 per cent of the market, natural foods and organic specific retailers 45 per cent, and direct farm and local market sales accounted for only 5 per cent of sales (Dimitri and Greene 2002: 3). By this time as well, organic products were being sold in 73 per cent of mainstream supermarkets in the US (Robinson 2004). Similar developments are found in European countries. Conventional supermarkets have 77 per cent of organic sales in Austria, 70 per cent in Denmark, 45 per cent in France, 90 per cent in Sweden, 60 per cent in Switzerland, and 65 per cent in the UK (Lohr 2001: 74).

These changes in the political economy and structure of the organic sector have two important consequences. First, they are tending to pull apart organic foods as a consumer product from the members of the holistic social movements that gave life to organic production in the first place. These movements debate, for example, whether an 'organic Twinkie' is a contradiction in terms (Pollan 2001). When they view the 2000 acre industrial organic farms in California, they wonder about the future for the small farmers present at the creation of organic agriculture. Second, proponents of the organic movement query whether international trade in organic foods is consistent with their emphasis on local communities and sustainable environments.

Legalization and the organic movement

The numerous changes in the political economy of organic production are accompanied by ever-increasing legalization on a global scale. Once organic products enter mainstream production and distribution channels, fundamental questions arise: What does the term 'organic' mean? What farming practices are implied? What additives are permitted when it comes to something like an organic TV dinner? Is an organic TV dinner even consistent with the idea of organic production? How do I know whether a product labelled 'organic' is actually so? Within countries, is it acceptable that organic products are governed by private and local systems of self-regulation? Is national regulation necessary? And when markets grow to the point that international trade in organic commodities becomes attractive and important, further questions arise. Does the legal meaning of 'organic' vary from one country to the next? Are there any global norms guiding the understanding of organic production? Is it possible to agree on global norms and rules to facilitate international trade in organic products? Are emerging country-wide and public regulatory systems acting as barriers to trade?

In order to investigate these kinds of questions, we need to begin with a review of how legalization comes to order organic production. Four interlinked legal processes are involved: standards, certification, accreditation, and enforcement (ITC 1999: 9–11; Meidinger 2006: 60). These processes are becoming common in many fields as international legalization increases. When consumers purchase organically grown coffee, for example, they are normally informed of the quality of the coffee through a label. Of course, there is little to stop a coffee seller from labelling a given stock of beans as 'organic'. Accordingly, organic producers developed ways to certify that their products are actually produced according to organic farming principles. Certification, then, is a procedure for verifying that a product conforms to certain standards. The standards involved may be established by private or by state organizations. Once a given stock of coffee beans has been certified as conforming to a set of standards in this way, they may obtain a certain certification mark (label or seal) to this effect. If the beans are to be certified in this way, it also means that all operators in the production chain – growers, roasters, exporters, importers, wholesalers, retailers – are themselves certified as operating in ways consistent with the standards involved.

Of course, consumers might very well ask how they can be certain that this certification process itself has been followed. To be assured, they would like the procedures of any body involved in certification to be transparent and independent of the producers and other businesses involved. If the certification organization was owned by some of these businesses, then they might have less confidence in the label on their bag of coffee beans. For these reasons, certification bodies themselves can be evaluated according to how well their procedures fit with these ideas of transparency and independence. If a given coffee certifying authority is evaluated well, it may be awarded accreditation status. Consumers thus know that the certified label comes from an accredited certifying body.

Enforcement in such systems comes in various forms (Meidinger 2006: 75). Certification can be revoked by an accrediting body. As large retailing firms become more involved in the business and committed to given labels, market pressures make the costs of cheating more significant and activists become highly attentive to the quality of the foods on the shelves as well. In addition, as we see below, the state can step in to provide legal back-up to each of the processes of standards-setting, accreditation and certification.

Behind these certifying and accrediting aspects of legalization lie a set of standards outlining the norms by which organic production, processing, and distribution must be carried out. These standards take both general and more specific forms. For example, at the core of virtually all organic standards is the norm that the fertility and biological activity of the soil must be maintained and increased. Such a general norm would be accompanied by more specific ones addressing how the soil might be fertilized; how pests might be controlled; and how the given commodity is harvested. These standards become the norms which certifying authorities will use in inspecting a coffee farm and upon which they will give the owner of the farm the right to certify the coffee beans grown as organic or not.

The complexity of the legalization process – certification, accreditation, standards – grows once increased amounts of organic commodities are traded. For example, suppose our consumers of organically grown coffee live in Canada, where coffee beans are not produced. Who certifies the beans? Are they certified in the originating country or in the receiving country? If they are certified in the exporting country, will Canada agree that the standards upon which the certification is based are valid ones? Suppose that the certifying authority in the exporting country is itself accredited. Will Canada recognize that accreditation? Or perhaps we should put ourselves in the position of coffee growers in Kenya. Suppose that they want to sell their beans into both EU and US markets. What happens when the standards favoured by these two major economic powers differ or when the processes for accrediting certifying authority are not the same. In the following two sections, we demonstrate that legalization in the organic field has become a complex mixture of public and private systems of certification, accreditation, and standards-making involving multiple, overlapping sites of authority from the most local to the global levels.

National regulation and organic production: the examples of the USA and Canada

In North America, similar to other developed countries, the organic production chain has grown more complex, involving not only more people in the actual processes of producing and selling organic products but also more people who are willing to buy organic products on a regular basis as part of their daily or weekly shopping routines. In these respects, it has evolved from a small fruit and vegetable co-op run by local farmers and their families, to large supermarket chains with entire aisles dedicated solely to organic foods. The web of relationships that tie organic producers, sellers, and buyers together has increasingly become more complicated and dense. The organic production chain that has emerged in recent years can be characterized as being both multi-national and global, with fewer and fewer personal or direct contacts established and sustained between organic growers and their buyers. Today, we find Canadian shoppers buying organic carrots from California, and US shoppers buying organic spaghetti from Italy – with both products carrying a different organic seal, but an organic label nonetheless. As the organic movement moves away from its local roots, and becomes something that creates transnational ties between producers, sellers, and buyers from different countries, pressures have increased for nation-states to take a greater role.

In Canada and the United States, similar to most OECD countries, national regulation in the form of a national standards system for organic products is a fairly recent development. The US has taken an earlier lead than Canada, but both countries had made visible legal attempts to regulate the organic production chain by the 1990s. The US Organic Foods Production Act (OFPA) came into effect in 1990, and the Standards Council of Canada ratified the first version of the National Standard for Organic Agriculture in 1999. These national organic standards systems put into place a set of requirements which all operators in the organic production chain are expected to follow if they wish to grow, buy, or sell organic products in these countries. Both the US and Canadian national organic standards systems are comprised of three interlinking legal processes: certification, accreditation, and standards. There are differences between the two countries in the actual content of the requirements, but overall the foundations of the system itself are remarkably similar. Governments set national standards for organic production and provide accreditation to organizations that, in turn, certify products as organic. Governments do not, however, actually certify these products. Instead, certification is the domain of private organizations. Thus, the state relies on self-regulation through private bodies for determining whether or not a certain product meets the necessary standards to be labelled organic.

What follows is a general description of the key characteristics of the two national standards systems, which allows us to examine these three interlinking legal processes in closer detail. We see from this analysis that national organic standard-setting in both countries has been driven and sustained in large part by the involvement of private actors whose interests in developing a flexible regulatory framework prompted discussions about national regulation in the first place. In turn, the involvement of these private actors in both the drafting and implementing stages of decision-making has fostered the emergence of a public–private partnership in national organic regulation. This partnership also has parallels with the transnational legalization processes that we discuss below.

Comparing national organic standards systems: the United States and Canada

The development of a national standards system in the United States demonstrates the extent to which public and private institutions are involved in the processes of regulating the organic production chain.[2] When the Organic Foods Production Act was passed as part of the 1990 Farm Bill, a regulatory framework was established, which placed the design and implementation of national organic standards firmly in the control of the US Department of Agriculture (USDA). Specifically, the OFPA delegated official responsibility to the Secretary of Agriculture to develop national standards regulating the procedures and methods involved in organic production and the handling of organic products, including, for example, types of approved substances as well as substances that are prohibited in crop and livestock production. The OFPA also recognized the establishment of a National Standards Organic Board (NSOB) whose mandate is to assist and advise the Secretary of Agriculture in implementing a national organic programme. The NSOB is made up of 15 members representing farmers and growers, handlers and processors, retailers, environmentalists, consumer and public interest groups, certifying agents, and scientists.

Over the course of ten years, from 1990 to 2000, the USDA organic regulations underwent two sets of revisions, one in 1997 and the other in March of 2000, before the final version was accepted and published in December of 2000 (Robinson 2004). In effect, national standards are defined so as to ensure that those operators who produce and handle organic products have complied with the provisions outlined in the OFPA. The standards cover three major agricultural operations: crop production, livestock production, and the handling of organic products. Organic crop production standards specify that no prohibited substances are applied to the soil in the three years leading up to the harvest of organic crops and only crop and animal waste materials may be used, soil fertility is maintained and soil erosion minimized, and crop rotation and cover crops are practiced. Organic livestock production standards stipulate that no synthetic (or growth) hormones or antibiotics are given to the animals and that these animals eat only 100 per cent organic feed. The origin of the livestock is to be carefully monitored and documented, and the health and safety of the animals are maintained at all times. Organic handling standards require that under no circumstance should organic products come into contact with non-organic products or any prohibited substances. One of the key roles of the USDA, then, is to ensure compliance with and enforcement of these national standards.

When it comes to enforcement, it is only through the certification process that the USDA can be confident that an operator's compliance with the national organic standards has been achieved and will be maintained over the duration of time that the operator expects to produce or handle organic products. Products may be identified as belonging to one of three groups: '100 percent organic', 'organic', or 'made with organic ingredients' (AMS 2000). In order to become a certified organic producer or handler, so that their products may eventually carry the organic label, these operators must provide detailed information demonstrating what efforts they have taken to meet national organic standards. The applicants are subjected to careful scrutiny of their methods and practices in the form of an organic systems plan describing the type of production or handling of products they intend to run as well as a monitoring plan which demonstrates how they intend to implement their organic plan. The USDA, however, does not actually certify the products and is not really involved in the certification process. Rather, it provides the standards upon which certification is based and the organic labels which are attached to the products. By early 2002, certifications had begun, and from this point on then, products would be expected to carry the USDA organic label, thereby verifying to customers buying organic products that these products had met all national organic standards to the USDA's satisfaction (Kortbech-Olesen 2003; Robinson 2004).

The actual responsibility for verification and certification rests with independent organizations that have committed themselves to ensuring any application of the organic plan submitted by an organic operator is absolutely consistent with national organic standards. This independent organization is referred to as an 'accredited certifying agent', and only a certifying agent that is recognized by the USDA as an independent and transparent organization can grant certification (AMS 2000). These accredited certifying agents are specifically responsible for reviewing applications and their organic systems plans, conducting on-site inspections annually of farms and handling operations, and when the applicant is found to have satisfied all regulations pertaining to organic production or handling, issuing a certificate to the operator so that the product can be marketed and sold as organic. The accredited certifying agent is also responsible for responding to any complaints filed against a certified operation. The National Organic Program maintains a close working relationship with the Agricultural Marketing Service (AMS) Compliance Staff, which is part of a larger federal agency that is the arm of the USDA charged with monitoring compliance with national standards throughout the organic production chain. The USDA does not directly deal, however, with complaints that are brought against certifying operators (Robinson 2004).

Since the full implementation of the National Organic Program in late 2002, there have been nearly 100 accredited certifying agents listed with the USDA. Of these independent organizations, more than half are considered 'domestic accredited certifying agents', and a great majority of these are private organizations (AMS 2004). Public organizations, namely individual state departments of agriculture, make up approximately 25 per cent of the domestic certifying agents. The other group listed by the USDA are 'foreign accredited certifying agents', which operate in countries other than the US and are involved in the certification of organic products that are later imported into the US.

The USDA alone is directly responsible for accrediting organizations as certifying agents. Organizations that seek accreditation with the National Organic Program have to demonstrate to the USDA their expertise, impartiality, and consistency in applying the national standards of certification to farmers and handlers involved in the organic production chain. Like the application process for certification that organic operators are expected to do, applying for accreditation status is a rigorous and time-consuming process for organizations that want to be recognized by the USDA as an accredited certifying agent of the National Organic Program. Applications are processed first through the Administrator's office of the AMS and provide detailed information about the personnel employed in the organization as well as their ability to adequately monitor and enforce the certification process (Robinson 2004). The USDA is also responsible for conducting on-site inspection of the organization's place of business. Once the USDA has found the organization to be in compliance with all national regulations, then the organization receives accreditation status for a five-year period and therein agrees to submit annually to USDA evaluations of their certification activities. This process also applies to foreign organizations seeking accreditation with the USDA and its National Organic Program. In the event that complaints are brought up against an accredited certifying agent, the USDA is solely responsible for responding to these charges.

Public legalization has proceeded less quickly in Canada where a national organic standards system is more privately based than the USDA's National Organic Program. Canada's National Standard for Organic Agriculture is best characterized as a private industry standard rather than a government standard. It is voluntary in character, providing guiding principles for organic production and sustainable organic farming systems.[3] Similar to the US national organic standards, then, the Canadian National Standard for Organic Agriculture specifies criteria pertaining to crop and livestock production, handling and transportation, and labelling. In order to issue a national voluntary standard, consensus first has to be reached between members of the Canadian General Standards Board (CGSB), a private sector body, and its Standards Committee on Organic Agriculture.

The Standards Committee on Organic Agriculture is made up of 115 members representing producers, users, regulatory, and general interest groups (CGSB 2004). Of these, only 41 actually hold voting privileges on the committee. The federal government is represented on the committee, but its representation is much smaller in relationship to all of the other groups present on the committee. As such, the federal government does not dominate the course of the standards development process as it has in the US. It has, however, consulted with the International Organic Accreditation Service about the conformity of its standards with international private standards, but thus far has not defined its own.

Accordingly, developing and maintaining Canada's national organic standards remain responsibilities of the CSGB. The CSGB must, in turn, follow the criteria for developing national standards which have been set by the Standards Council of Canada (SCC), a federal Crown corporation responsible for coordinating the private standard-setting bodies at the centre of Canada's National Standards System. Because Canada has adopted the general guidelines of the International Standards Organization (ISO) for accreditation and certification, as specified in the ISO-61 and ISO-65 requirements, the SCC is recognized internationally as an accreditation body. As such, it has the capacity to award accreditation status to organizations that demonstrate their compliance with these general principles (Agri-Food Trade Service 2004).

The second key difference, and one that is closely related to the first point, is that the accreditation of certifying bodies in Canada is strictly voluntary at the national level. Only the province of Québec has implemented a mandatory certification and accreditation system whereby the Conseil d'accréditation du Québec has authority to verify an independent certifying agent's compliance with its provincial organic standards. In the provinces outside of Québec, certification and the accreditation of certification bodies remain in the hands of private sector organizations. In fact, according to Agriculture and Agri-food Canada (Agri-Food Trade Service 2003, 2004), there are currently 46 certifying bodies in Canada, but only two of them have obtained accreditation status from the SCC. As well, the certification of organic products is voluntary under this system because, in effect, Canada does not differentiate between organic and non-organic products. The production and distribution of organic products need only to comply with Canada's specific regulations for food safety, packaging and labelling, health, and phytosanitary requirements for conventional agricultural food products (Storz *et al.* 2004).

Like many OECD countries, Canada has experienced a rapidly expanding market for organic products, both as an importer and an exporter of these goods. Canada is recognized as the sixth largest market for organic foods and beverages and is ranked as one of the five largest producers of organic grains and oilseeds in the world. The Canadian Organic Growers estimates that 'imports of organic products represent approximately 70 to 80 per cent of Canada's consumption' of organic products (Agri-Food Trade Service 2003). Moreover, recent figures show that anywhere from 80 to 90 per cent of organic imports come from the United States (Kortbech-Olsen 2003; Storz *et al.* 2004).

This point about international trade in organic products demonstrates the third key difference between national standards systems in Canada and the US. Unlike in the US where national regulation requires that foreign certifying bodies seek accreditation status through the USDA and that all organic imports carry the NOP certification label, in Canada foreign certifying bodies need not apply for accreditation with the SCC, nor comply with the Canadian organic standards for certification.[4] When it comes to exporting organic products and thereby gaining additional access to foreign markets, Canada has taken a particular position that demonstrates its continued support for the concept 'equivalence recognition', based on its compliance with ISO guidelines for accreditation and certification. We return to this notion of equivalence in the following section of the chapter on global legalization. In this approach, Canada differs from other governments like the US, the EU and Japan where certification of imported products is publicly regulated (Agri-Food Trade Service 2004).

Most recently, however, a number of private organic organizations – but acting in conjunction with the Organic Sector Development Program of the AAFC as part of a larger pan-Canadian project that has given rise to the Organic Regulatory Committee – launched an attack on this position (see, for example, Doherty 2004). They cite the rising costs that individual operators carry because they each must seek separate agreements if they wish to gain access to these foreign markets. In the interests of Canadian consumers of organic imports, these organizations raise the thorny issue of compliance with Canadian national standards, suggesting a general lack of enforcement mechanisms at the national level that would provide the necessary scrutiny and oversight to guarantee an organic product's authenticity, regardless of its place of origin.

Legalization on a global scale

By global legalization, we refer to the development of norms and legal rules by private or public bodies, whose domain of activity is broader than the limits of a territorial nation state and includes more than one major world region. Global legalization in organic production and trade is particularly evident when it comes to the development of standards and the norms and rules for accreditation of certifying organizations. Certifying organizations, themselves, tend to operate within nation states, as we have illustrated in our case studies of the US and Canada. Over the past decade, however, the larger of these have taken on a multinational form, that is, they have developed the capacity to certify production as organic in a number of nation states. Such a capacity, of course, is made possible, in part, by the global legalization in the standards and accreditation areas.

In the areas of standards definition and accreditation, private global organizations tended to be active before nation states in many parts of the world. With the growth of markets and the more concerted entry of nation-states into the field, parallel public and private systems of rules came to exist. The linkages between these parallel systems became a matter of greater concern as international trade increased. Pressures for coordination intensified following the World Trade Association Agreement in 1994, due to increased importance being given to public standards setting organizations in the new Agreement on Sanitary and Phytosanitary Measures and the existing Agreement on Technical Barriers to Trade. To see the importance of the changes that have resulted from the revised trade regime, we begin with a discussion of the situation before 1995.

Global legalization prior to 1995

As the organic movement continued to grow in Europe and in North America, the interest in sharing information and experiences across national lines increased. In response to this interest, a number of organizations took the initiative to create the International Federation of Organic Agriculture Movements (IFOAM) in 1972. As part of its mandate, IFOAM began to explore whether there would be any value in co-ordinating better the increasing number of certifying organizations. In particular, its members asked whether there would be some basic standards common to all organic production that might guide certifying organizations world-wide. This task was given over to IFOAM's Technical Committee and in 1980, it published the first set of basic standards as global guidelines for local and national certifying organizations across the world (Herrmann 2003: 71). IFOAM has continued to nurture and develop these standards to the present day. They are the first comprehensive statement of basic standards and have been influential in all further standards development, whether private or public. The Demeter movement began to publish its own set of global standards beginning in 1992 (Demeter 2004). Its influence is restricted to those growers and certifiers following the biodynamic ideas of Rudolf Steiner and his associates.

Public rule-making at the global level began to occur in 1992 through the Codex Alimentarius Commission.[5] Since 1963, the CAC has led efforts to protect the health of consumers and to work towards fair trade in foods by developing international food standards that could then be approved by nation state governments. In 1991, the European Union approved a comprehensive regulation (2092/91) setting out organic standards, certification processes, and other rules to govern the sector. With the US and Japan also interested in developing public national regulatory systems, a number of states raised the issue with the Food Labelling Committee of Codex whether a set of public international standards could be defined. The challenge was novel for the Commission because defining standards on the basis of a 'production system' was a relatively new area for international standardization (Doyran 2003: 30). The Committee began its deliberations in 1993, finalised them in 1998, and they were adopted formally by the Commission as a whole in 1999 at its 23rd Session (ibid.: 31).

Although the European Union had taken some inspiration from the IFOAM Basic Standards, it also departed from these standards in some ways. Similarly, the Food Labelling Committee drew to a significant extent on the IFOAM standards, but also on the EU and other standards, in devising its own. As a consequence, by 1999, two sets of complementary, but also competing global standards were in play, one private from IFOAM and one public from Codex.[6] Both sets of standards function as guidance documents for the development of national and local public and private standards. For example, India based its technical organic regulations on IFOAM standards and Japan referenced Codex in its regulatory law (Bowen 2004: 14). The IFOAM standards have an additional function related to accreditation and enforcement not found in the Codex ones.

To the extent that it took place in a formal way, accreditation of certifying organizations occurred at the local levels primarily and to a limited extent nationally. In response to some members, IFOAM's Standards Committee began evaluating certification bodies in 1987 (Herrmann 2003: 71). Evaluation consisted of visiting certification organizations, writing reports and then sharing them with other certifiers participating in the IFOAM system. With the growth in the sector developing rapidly at this time and with increasing interest in regulation being expressed by governments, IFOAM feared that responsibility for the integrity of the organic system might migrate from the private sector, organic growers and their organizations, to the public sector (Commins 2002). Such migration might lead to the involvement of other interests, particularly agribusiness, less concerned with organic principles.

Accordingly, in 1990, IFOAM reorganized itself by creating a Standards Committee to take over the development of basic standards, a Programme Evaluation Committee to conduct evaluations, and an Accreditation Committee to prepare an Accreditation Programme. At its General Assembly in 1992, IFOAM launched an Accreditation Programme to be implemented by a new IFOAM Programme Board. The International Standards Organization (ISO) raised concerns with reference to its standard for accreditation bodies (ISO 65).

It argued that standard setting and accreditation responsibilities should lie with separate organizations (Mallett 2003:89). In response, IFOAM set up a new company, International Organic Accreditation Services Ltd (IOAS) in 1997. IOAS is incorporated and located in the US.

Global legalization after 1995

After 1995, the context for legalization changed in two ways. First, developing countries became increasingly interested in gaining access to the growing developed country organic markets. As we saw in our discussion of the NOP in the US, access to these markets requires that any products exported by developing countries be certified as organic before they can be sold as such in the major importing jurisdictions (USA, EU, Japan). The governmental regulatory systems in these major jurisdictions differ when it comes to certification requirements. The situation is complicated further by large retailers in the OECD countries also requiring certification to a host of private standards. This legal diversity creates problems for trade even among OECD countries. For example, if organic Swiss chocolate manufacturers want to export their product to the UK, they need to use UK milk powder. The UK certification standards for organic milk production differ from those in Switzerland and imports must meet the UK standard (Aebi 2003:204). For developing countries, where certification and accreditation are at more rudimentary levels of development, such barriers are even more difficult to surmount.

As will also be evident from our discussion thus far, most certification procedures have been defined with reference to standards consistent with climatic conditions and soil properties in the OECD countries. With significantly different climatic and soil conditions, however, organic standards are bound to differ in developing countries (Twarog and Vassenaar 2003: 125). To date, developing countries have had rather little input in defining either basic standards or certification procedures. Developing countries have had fewer resources to participate fully at Codex meetings than do OECD countries and historically they were poorly represented in IFOAM. Admittedly, this latter situation is changing as we noted above.

The second change in the overall context for organic legalization relates to the multilateral trade regime. The WTO agreements gave the Codex Alimentarius Commission a new status in the governance of the trading system. Participants in this round of negotiations recognized that measures ostensibly adopted by national governments to protect the health of their consumers, animals and plants could become disguised barriers to trade as well as being discriminatory. Consequently, they concluded the Sanitary and Phytosanitary (SPS) and the Technical Barriers to Trade (TBT) agreements in the negotiations which established the World Trade Organization (WTO) in 1995.

The SPS Agreement acknowledges that governments have the right to take sanitary and phytosanitary measures necessary for the protection of human health. The SPS Agreement requires them, however, to apply those measures only to the extent required to protect human health. In its preamble, the Agreement suggests that agreement on harmonized international standards will facilitate these objectives and, in Article 3, enjoins member states to participate fully in the CAC in pursuit of these ends.

The TBT Agreement seeks to ensure that technical regulations and standards, including packaging, marking and labelling requirements, and analytical procedures for assessing conformity with technical regulations and standards do not create unnecessary obstacles to trade. Article 2.6 makes a similar statement to that found in Article 3 of the SPS Agreement on the importance of member-state involvement in international standard setting bodies like CAC. In addition, Article 2.7 asks states to accept 'equivalent technical regulations' of other states, even if these differ from their own, provided that they are satisfied that these regulations 'adequately fulfil the objectives of their own regulations'.

From the perspective of the organic sector, these changes gave added legitimacy to the public standards developed by Codex. They also added to the importance of both the IFOAM and Codex standards. Their legitimacy derives from the fact that states or private organizations could argue that their national or local standards could be seen to be 'equivalent' to one another because they meet accepted international standards. Establishing 'equivalence' was an important mechanism in the TBT Agreement for overcoming trade barriers. Not surprisingly, then, the number of organizations with IOAS certification grew from 13 in 1998 to 26 by 2003 (Willer and Yussefi 2004: 48).

For developing countries interested in gaining access to OECD countries' organic products markets, this notion of 'equivalence' was a crucial one. IFOAM then took the initiative to convene a conference on 'International Harmonisation and Equivalence in Agriculture' working in co-operation with the FAO and the United Nations Commission on Trade and Development (UNCTAD). This conference outlined the problem and recommended that further efforts be made to improve the access of developing countries to OECD markets. After the conference, IFOAM, FAO and UNCTAD created an International Task Force on Harmonisation and Equivalence in Organic Agriculture. The task force was asked to review existing organic agriculture standards, regulations and conformity systems in order to assess their impact on international trade and the degree of harmonization that was present. In addition, it was asked to identify opportunities for harmonization and for assessing equivalence of standards. Proposals for changes were to be submitted to governments, Codex, IFOAM and other appropriate organizations.

As in other aspects of legalization in this section, private sector accreditation and certification bodies have taken some initiative in seeking to facilitate equivalence assessment.

Several of the IFOAM Accredited Certification Bodies (ACB) recognized that all their standards were at least equivalent to the IFOAM Basic Standards and that each of their competence as a certification body was ensured by meeting IFOAM accreditation criteria. Beginning in 1997, the idea of a Multilateral Agreement on Equivalence and Mutual Recognition in Certification began to be developed by several of these ACBs taking into account an ISO 9000 report on mutual recognition agreements and model MLAs in other ISO settings. The agreement was finalized in 1999, with nine initial signatories (Simmons 2003: 100). By 2003, 22 of the 26 IFOAM ACBs had signed and these tended to be the larger ones involved in the international trade of organic products (Bowen 2004: 6). Even with the MLA in place, however, reaching agreement among these certification bodies is still a protracted and complex process.

Conclusion

In their introduction to this volume, Brütsch and Lehmkuhl argue that international legalization does not necessarily emerge through states acting rationally according to pre-determined sets of preferences. They also note that legalization is a profoundly social process emerging from practices and beliefs in society and through the interaction among these societies. Accordingly, they add, we must allow for the possibility that the activities of private actors will contribute to the norms and rules that come to influence what states do.

In this chapter, we have described a process of increasing global legalization in organic production and trade that supports these arguments. Organic growing of fruits and vegetables and raising of animals began locally and beyond the gaze of states, if not ignored by them. Firmly committed to supporting a productivist, and increasingly industrial agriculture model and politically beholden to the farmers involved, ministries of agriculture in the developed world were happy to let organic agriculture develop its own norms and rules. Reinforced by strong moral beliefs in nurturing soils and respecting the environment, the small numbers of growers and supporters in the organic movement came to separate understandings about what 'growing organic' meant in their respective localities. Gradually, they came together across state boundaries, formed their own international organization and eventually agreed upon a set of basic norms and rules that could be common to all growers in the organic world. In short, private actors in the organic movement were the catalysts for global legalization. States were largely on the sidelines.

Market forces were important in catalysing global legalization, particularly as international trade in organic products rose in response to consumer demand. Trade also triggered more interest in legal forms by states. They began to pay more attention to enforcement and thus to the processes of accreditation and certification. As states became more interested in what kinds of basic norms distinguished organic from conventional farming and in how organic products might be certified as such, a plurality of legal orders came into place. Private legal arrangements at the local, national and supranational level were not subsumed by state actions. Private actors were fearful of states watering down their standards in response to other corporate interests and persisted in asserting their autonomy from state regulation. In each legal domain of the sector – standards, accreditation, certification – private and state/intergovernmental actors coexist. In many areas, they co-operate with one another as developments at Codex and the writing of public international standards illustrate. Over the past 20 years, a series of transnational policy networks involving state and private actors have helped facilitate more complex and globally extensive legalization. None the less, this co-operation should not occlude the fact that these varying sets of standards and approaches to certification are also often in competition with one another.

In the organic sector at least, it is also evident that increasing global legalization is not accompanied by higher levels of rationalization. To the contrary, from the perspective of organic farmers in the less developed countries in the world, the resulting legal arrangements are a financial and political obstacle course. As Bowen (2004: 17) concludes: 'the current system is inefficient and some producers undoubtedly face insurmountable obstacles to some international markets because of the high cost of compliance with organic regulations. The long-term stability of the current system is also questionable in the face of rapid growth of organic markets and opportunities worldwide'. Nor does legalization necessarily bring harmonization. In fact, the entrenchment of different views of organic standards into hard law by states makes it that much more difficult to reach a common understanding among private and public actors at all levels of the system on such key issues as organic equivalence and basic standards. The 'move to law' has changed the relationships between public and private actors in ways that may frustrate reaching the kind of intersubjective understanding that is necessary for the global organic movement to respond adequately to the consumers who wish to buy their foods. In such circumstances, consumer confidence in enforcement and compliance with organic standards may be fragile.

Notes

1 Calculated based on information supplied to the authors by IFOAM.
2 Much of the following discussion on standards, certification and accreditation is drawn from the actual US regulation. See Agricultural Marketing Service (2000). Program Standards. Accessed on line on 3 March 2004 at: www.ams.usda.gov/nop/ NOP/standards.html; and National Organic Standards Board. Accessed online on 3 March 2004 at: www.ams.usda.gov/ nosb/index/html.
3 The following discussion draws on material provided in Canadian General Standards Board (2004). CSGB Info: Standard for Organic Agriculture. Frequently Asked Questions. Accessed online on 8 November 2004 at: www.pwgsc.gc.ca/cgsb/ 032_310/faq-e.html.
4 Analysis based on Canadian General Standards Board (2004). CGSB Info: Standard for Organic Agriculture. Frequently Asked Questions. Accessed online on 8 November 2004 at: www.pwgsc.gc.ca/cgsb/032_310/faq-e.html.
5 For information on the origins and development of the Commission, see Coleman (2006).
6 For a systematic comparison of the EU, Codex and IFOAM standards, see Schmid (2003).

References

Aebi, Patrick (2003) 'International and National Standards and Their Impact on Trade: the Swiss Perspective', in OECD (ed.) *Organic Agriculture: Sustainability, Markets, and Policies*, Paris: OECD/CABI Publishing, pp. 203–206.

Agricultural Marketing Service (2004) *USDA Accredited Certifying Agents*. Accessed on line on 8 November 2004 at: www.ams.usda.gov/nop?CertifyingAgents/Accredited.html.

Agricultural Marketing Service (AMS) (2000) *Program Standards. [Regulations]*. Accessed online 3 March 2004 at: www.ams.usda.gov/nop/NOP/ standards.html.

Agri-Food Trade Service (2003) *Canada's Agriculture, Food and Beverage Industry: Canada's Organic Industry*. Accessed online on 12 November 2004 at atn-riae.agr.ca/supply/3313_e.htm.

Agri-Food Trade Service (2004) *Organic Agriculture Market Access Issues*. Accessed online on 15 November 2004 at atn-riae.agr.ca/can/e3469.htm.

Bowen, Diane (2004) 'Current Mechanisms that Enable International Trade in Organic Products', Discussion Paper. International Task Force on Harmonization and Equivalence in Organic Agriculture, Tholey-Theley, Germany: IFOAM.

Canadian General Standards Board (2004) *CGSB Info: Standard for Organic Agriculture*. Accessed online 8 November 2004 at: www.pwgsc.gc.ca/cgsb/032_310/faq-e.html.

Coleman, W.D. (2006) 'Codex Alimentarius Commission', in W.D. Coleman and Nancy Johnson (eds) *Globalization and Autonomy Online Compendium*. Online. Available at: www.globalautonomy.ca/global1/glossary_entry.jsp?id=OR.0010 (accessed 17 July 2006).

Commins, Ken (2002) *The First Ten Years of the IFOAM Accreditation Programme*. Online. Available at: www.ioas.org/WEBSITE/0410%20History.htm.

Demeter (2004) 'History of the Biodynamic® Movement'. Online. Available at: www.demeter.net/ (accessed 12 November 2004).

Dimitri, Carolyn and Catherine Greene (2002) *Recent Growth Patterns in the US Organic Foods Market*, AIB 777, Washington, DC: USDA, ERS.

Doherty, Paddy (2004) *Organic Regulatory Committee [Letter]*. Accessed 15 November 2004 at lincensees.certifiedorganic.bc/ca/COI/ORCProvince.pdf.

Doyran, Selma H. (2003) 'Codex Guidelines on the Production, Processing, Labelling and Marketing of Organically Produced Foods', in Christina Westermayer and Berward Geier (eds) *The Organic Guarantee System: The Need and Strategy for Harmonisation and Equivalence*, Tholey-Theley: IFOAM/FAO/UNCTAD, pp. 30–36.

Duchateau, Koen (2003) 'Organic Farming in Europe: A Sustained Growth 1998–2000', *Statistics in Focus, Environment and Energy, Theme 8-2/2003*, Brussels: Eurostat.

Herrmann, Gerald A. (2003) 'A Short Overview on IFOAM's Organic Guarantee System', in Christina Westermayer and Berward Geier (eds) *The Organic Guarantee System: The Need and Strategy for Harmonisation and Equivalence*, Tholey-Theley: IFOAM/FAO/UNCTAD, pp. 71–73.

Howard, Sir Albert (1940) *An Agricultural Testament*, Oxford: Oxford University Press. Accessed online on 29 October 2004 at: journeytoforever.org/farm_library/ howardAT/AT1.html.

International Federation of Organic Agricultural Movements (2004) Online. Available at: www.ifoam.org/whoisifoam/index.html (accessed 29 October 2004).

International Trade Centre (ITC) (1999) *Organic Food and Beverages: World Supply and Major European Markets*, Geneva: ITC.

Jones, Darryl (2003) 'Organic agriculture, sustainability and policy' in OECD (ed.) *Organic Agriculture: Sustainability, Markets, and Policies*, Paris: OECD/CABI Publishing, pp. 17–31.

Kortbech-Olsen, Rudy (2003) *The US and Canadian Markets*. [Conference presentation]. FAO Seminar on the Production and Exports of Organic Fruit and Vegetables in Asia,

Bangkok, Thailand, 3–5 November 2003. Online. Accessed on 8 November 2004 at: www.intracen.org/mds/sectors/organic/faobkk.htm.

Liebhardt, Bill (2003) 'What is organic agriculture? What I learned from my transition', in OECD, *Organic Agriculture: Sustainability, Markets, and Policies*, Paris: OECD/CABI Publishing, pp. 31–50.

Lohr, Luanne (2001) 'Factors Affecting International Demand and Trade in Organic Food Products' in Anita Regmi (ed.) *Changing Structure of Global Food Consumption and Trade*, Washington, DC: USDA, ERS.

Mallett, Patrick (2003) 'Options for Accreditation: National and International Accreditation Systems', in Christina Westermayer and Berward Geier (eds) *The Organic Guarantee System: The Need and Strategy for Harmonisation and Equivalence*, Tholey-Theley: IFOAM/FAO/UNCTAD, pp. 85–92.

Meidinger, Errol (2006) 'The Administrative Law of Global Private–Public Regulation: the case of forestry', *European Journal of International Law* 17(1): 47–87.

National Organic Standards Board (2004) Accessed online on 3 March 2004 at: www.ams.usda.gov/nosb/index.html.

Pollan, Michael (2001) 'Naturally', *The New York Times Magazine*, 31 May 2001.

Robinson, Barbara (2004) *Value through Verification: USDA National Organic Program*. Accessed online on 8 November 2004 at: www.ams.usda.gov/nop/NOPPresentation/Introduction.html.

Sahota, Amarjit (2004) 'Overview of the Global Market for Organic Food and Drink', in Helga Willer and Minou Yussefi (eds) *The World of Organic Agriculture: Statistics and Emerging Trends 2004*, Bonn: IFOAM, pp. 21–27.

Schmid, Otto (2003) 'Comparison of EU Regulation 2092/91, Codex Alimentarius Guidelines for Organically Produced Food 1999/2001, and IFOAM Basic Standards 2000', in Christina Westermayer and Berward Geier (eds) *The Organic Guarantee System: The Need and Strategy for Harmonisation and Equivalence*, Tholey-Theley: IFOAM/FAO/UNCTAD, pp. 41–51.

Simmons, Robert (2003) 'Bridging Obstacles to International Trade', in Christina Westermayer and Berward Geier (eds) *The Organic Guarantee System: The Need and Strategy for Harmonisation and Equivalence*, Tholey-Theley: IFOAM/FAO/UNCTAD, pp. 100–102.

Storz, Christina D., Timothy G. Taylor and Gary F. Fairchild (2004) *A Primer on Exporting to Canada*. Accessed online on 8 November 2004 at: www.agbuscenter.ifas.ufl.edu/exprt/revised%20primers/CANADA2004.pdf.

Tomlinson, John (1999) *Globalization and Culture*, Chicago: University of Chicago Press.

Twarog, Sophia and René Vossenaar (2003) 'Obstacles Facing Developing Country Exports of Organic Products to Developed Country Markets', in Christina Westermayer and Berward Geier (eds) *The Organic Guarantee System: The Need and Strategy for Harmonisation and Equivalence*, Tholey-Theley: IFOAM/FAO/UNCTAD, pp. 122–128.

Willer, Helga and Minou Yussefi (eds) (2004) *The World of Organic Agriculture: Statistics and Emerging Trends 2004*, Bonn: IFOAM.

Yussefi, Minou (2004) 'Development and State of Organic Agriculture Worldwide', in Helga Willer and Minou Yussefi (eds) *The World of Organic Agriculture: Statistics and Emerging Trends 2004*, Bonn: IFOAM, pp. 13–21.

7 Beyond Westphalia

Competitive legalization in emerging transnational regulatory systems

Errol Meidinger

Introduction

Remarkable new supra-governmental, transnational regulatory systems are taking shape around us. Driven primarily by civil society organizations, but also by governments and industry associations, these systems draw on conventional technical standard setting and certification techniques to establish market-leveraged, social and environmental regulatory programmes. They go beyond traditional standard setting, however, in seeking to protect interests not directly involved in the market chain. Moreover, these systems incorporate plural rule-making, adjudication, and enforcement programmes. The programmes constantly compete with, but also mimic and reinforce each other. While the most developed example is in forestry, similar systems are also present in agriculture, fisheries, apparel, and mining, among other sectors. They share the assumptions that enterprises around the world should be held to common standards and that compliance with those standards can be assured through use of formally independent expert auditors. The various standards, procedures, and roles of the actors are generally defined in terms of formalized rules, rights, and duties based on normative criteria in ways very similar to those of state-based legal systems.

This paper examines forestry regulation as a central case but also draws parallels to the other sectors mentioned above. 'Regulation' here means simply a purposive, organized and sustained effort to establish a general and consistent order in a field of human activity (e.g. Black 2002). Since it typically centres on rules defined in terms of rights and duties, with differentiated official roles and normative justifications, regulation is a form of law, but one that is characterized by a reliance on credentialed experts who are expected to manage a field and to learn and adapt based on experience.

This paper first describes the forest certification regulatory system and the process by which it has been established, next discusses its relationship to state governance systems, makes some comparisons to other sectors, and finally considers the impacts and possible broader implications for law and society of certification-centred transnational regulatory systems. Overall, it describes a set of multi-centred, competitive regulatory systems that are increasingly rule-permeated and changeable at the same time. The paper closes with a brief discussion of whether these systems might be sketching the outlines of new forms of trans-national democracy.

Forest certification

Forest certification was instituted by a loose-knit group of extra-governmental regulatory entrepreneurs (see Meidinger 1985) in response to the failure of the Westphalian system to curb rapid tropical forest destruction, a process that came to be understood as reaching crisis dimensions in the 1980s (Humphreys 1996; Gale 1998). While there are multiple reasons for tropical deforestation, a major one has been the burgeoning importation of tropical timber by developed countries wanting cheap wood (Brown 2001).

Exasperated with the failure of intergovernmental negotiations to effectively address the problems of tropical ecosystem destruction and biodiversity loss, some Northern environmental groups pursued a tropical timber boycott, but dropped it when its potentially perverse consequences of hurting proper tropical forest management and possibly speeding agricultural conversion because of the decreased economic value of forests became apparent. As an alternative, they tried to get the intergovernmental system, via the International Tropical Timber Organization (ITTO), to establish a system for certifying sustainably produced timber so that it could be distinguished and rewarded in international markets. The idea was to convert the rapidly growing global timber market into an engine of forest preservation, rather than destruction. The ITTO, which consists of approximately 40 of the largest tropical timber exporting and importing countries, refused to establish such a system. Several Southern exporting countries evidently saw it as a potential non-tariff barrier to trade in that northern environmental groups might call for boycotts of non-certified timber.

As early as 1989 the non-profit US-based Rainforest Alliance established its own programme for certifying sustainable tropical timber – 'SmartWood'. While many of the larger environmental groups continued to pursue intergovernmental regulatory solutions, they also began laying plans for what they saw as the distinctly inferior option of establishing a free-standing non-governmental forest certification system. After the 1992 UN Conference on Environment and Development (UNCED) in Rio failed to achieve a binding forest convention these plans were put into motion with the 1993 founding of the Forest Steward-ship Council.

The FSC

Although discussions of creating an umbrella forest certification system went back at least to 1990, the FSC faced a daunting set of challenges. As suggested above, the FSC was founded by a small progressive coalition of transnational environmental NGOs – primarily the Worldwide Fund for Nature (WWF) and Greenpeace – together with some high end wood buyers, progressive foresters, and social activists. Most of the major powers in forestry at the time were absent and many were hostile. Moreover, nothing like a global system for certifying forest management practices had ever been attempted. On the other hand, the standard institutional methods of technical standard setting and certification were available. So too were a professional forestry credo laying out the basic elements of proper forestry and an emerging discourse of sustainable development stressing the interdependence of economic development, environmental protection and social justice and the importance of using participatory policy mechanisms. Moreover, forestry had long been a relatively self-governing industry and had developed reasonably effective methods of imposing 'sustained yield' forestry in most developed countries, although these had recently been shown to leave out key environmental and social concerns in many cases.

Standard setting

The FSC is constituted as a global, non-governmental, multi-stakeholder organization, reflecting the ascendant canon that effective organizations must incorporate the voices of all interests relevant to their missions. It is governed by a 'General Assembly' organized in three chambers – environmental, social, and economic – each with equal voting power (see generally FSC 2006). The chambers are further subdivided into 'Northern' and 'Southern' sub-chambers, again with equal voting power, to counterbalance the relative overrepresentation of northern interests. Day-to-day management is delegated to an Executive Director who works in close collaboration with a nine-member elected Board of Directors. Membership of the FSC is open to all organizations and individuals who subscribe to FSC's mission (providing responsible management of the world's forests) and who are endorsed by two existing members.

Shortly after its founding the FSC promulgated a set of 'principles and criteria' (P&C) intended to govern proper forest management worldwide. Bringing together tenets from forestry, environmental, and human rights discourses, the P&C require compliance with applicable laws and treaties, clear and adequate property rights, protection of indigenous, community, and worker rights, full and efficient use of forest resources, and fairly stringent environmental protection, among other things. These requirements have been revised in limited ways over time and are given further place-appropriate content in national and regional standard-setting processes.

Certification and accreditation

Much of the FSC's early work focused on accrediting and overseeing the certification organizations whose job it is to ascertain and publicly verify that certified companies in fact comply with the P&C as well as any applicable national or regional standards. While certification organizations are formally independent of the FSC, the quality of their work and their public credibility are crucial to the success of the FSC programme. A typical FSC certification process includes, among other things: (1) an intensive site visit by a team of certifiers possessing forest management, environmental, and social expertise and seeking to ascertain compliance with the full array of applicable standards (but with latitude to grant certification despite minor shortcomings); (2) consultations with local stakeholders; (3) preparation of a draft report which is subjected to peer review by two or three external experts; (4) discussion of possible terms of the certification with the applicant, including possible pre-conditions or corrective actions to be taken within a specified amount of time; (5) an official certification decision including final preconditions or corrective action requirements; (6) a public summary of the decision containing 'sufficient information to make clear the correlation between the specific results of the certification assessment and FSC principles'; (7) annual audits; and (8) a full review for possible renewal every five years.

Certifiers thus combine the traditional public law functions of administrative inspection and adjudication, but their services are paid for by the applicants for certification. The risks of corruption posed by this arrangement do not seem to have been a major concern of the FSC system early on, evidently because of the faith in professionalism that characterizes the forestry sector and the assumption that, if anything, certifiers were likely to be too tough in doing the bidding of what was perceived to be a zealous certification programme. Nonetheless, the FSC set up a system for auditing certification decisions and has suspended the accreditation of certifiers on a few occasions. Over time the accreditation and auditing programme has become more formalized, and it was recently made financially independent of the FSC.

Labelling

The FSC also developed standards for certifying the 'chain of custody' of certified products. The original goal was to be able to prove that the wood in any product carrying the FSC logo actually came from a certified forest. This can be quite complicated in the highly differentiated, multi-supplier, long distance, high volume, and low margin markets that characterize the modern forestry sector. Over time the FSC-certified content requirements have become considerably looser, allowing certain products to carry the logo based on a set percentage of FSC content.

Enforcement

While the FSC certification programme was initially scorned or ignored by most established forestry powers, it soon came to be perceived as a force to be reckoned with. One of the most important reasons was a series of campaigns by environmental activists to pressure major wood product retailers to commit to buying FSC certified wood. British do-it-yourself retailer B&Q quickly welcomed the FSC as a way of responding to activist criticisms of its purchasing policies that predated the FSC's founding. American retailer Home Depot joined after several hundred well publicized actions by the Rainforest Action Network (RAN) in its parking lots and stores threatening to associate the Home Depot brand with rainforest destruction (e.g. Sasser 2002). By thus focusing on key retailer links in the extended global forest product chain, activist groups were able to use market relationships to leverage the FSC into an important new role in forest governance. Leveraging market chains has become a primary enforcement mechanism, although the official mechanisms include unannounced inspections, random auditing, and potential loss of certificates.

Industry-based programmes

Although surprised and often offended by the rise of the FSC, many traditional forestry interests responded quickly. North American industry groups in particular were already worried about their declining public image and promptly decided to establish their own forest certification programmes, the Sustainable Forestry Initiative (SFI) in the US and the Canadian Standards Association (CSA) Forest Management Standard in Canada (see generally Cashore *et al.* 2003). Programme details and histories are too complex to be recounted here, but the broad outlines are clear. Both initiatives sought to develop programmes that were acceptable to the public but minimally onerous to industry. The SFI was established by the largest forest products association in the US, the American Forest & Paper Association (AF&PA), on its own motion. The CSA was established by the Canadian national technical standard-setting body in cooperation with the Canadian forest products industry.

Management systems

Although there were many differences between the programmes, they both favoured the 'environmental management system' (EMS) approach that had recently been developed by the International Organization for Standardization (ISO) in its ISO 14000 series of standards (ISO 2006). This approach relies on 'installing' an EMS in the firm which provides mechanisms to (1) assess the environmental aspects of the firm's operations; (2) plan which ones to improve and how; (3) set measurable goals for improvement; and (4) assign responsibilities for implementing, monitoring, correcting failures, and revising plans to specific individuals. In addition, flowing from the 'total quality management' movement of the 1980s, the EMS approach requires 'continuous improvement' in the management system. Its stress on fully assessing the environmental aspects of the firm's activities expands upon the 'environmental impact assessment' concept originally developed for public environmental management, and may be particularly important for firms operating in unfamiliar environments, as is often the case for global corporations.

The EMS approach differs from the 'performance standard' approach adopted by the FSC in that the firm, rather than the external standard setting organization, is primarily responsible for setting its goals. Moreover, what is audited is the presence of management programmes to pursue those goals rather than their achievement. The management systems themselves seem to involve an intensification of internal rules, since auditors generally look for documentation of procedures and responsibilities, and for documentary evidence that they are being carried out.

Federation

Industry-based programmes were also established in a variety of other countries, including the major exporters of Malaysia, Brazil and Indonesia. With the partial exception of the Indonesian programme, which is coordinated with the FSC, they all tended to see themselves in opposition to the FSC, which they perceived as too environmentalist-dominated and stringent. In 1998–1999 a Europe-wide federation of forest certification programmes was established. The Pan-European Forest Certification Council (PEFC) defined itself not as promulgating a single standard to be deployed world-wide, but rather as providing a common framework for the mutual recognition of nationally based certification programmes operating to verify the sustainable forest management practices that were believed already to exist in most European countries. Institutionally and conceptually, it drew heavily on the experiences of the existing certification programmes as well as criteria and indicators that had been produced by intergovernmental processes such as a series of Ministerial Conferences on the Protection of Forests in Europe that started in 1990 and continue to the present.

In 2003, PEFC went global, renaming itself the Programme for the Endorsement of Forest Certification. It currently includes 32 nationally based programmes, of which 22 have been officially endorsed (PEFC 2006). Although they vary considerably, PEFC programmes tend to be more lenient than FSC ones, not only in terms of standards, but also in terms of inspection and chain of custody requirements. They thus tend to be less expensive to participate in and appeal particularly to smaller land owners.

Convergence, competition and recentred governance

The field of forest certification thus centres around two primary alliances. On one side is the FSC with its orientation to relatively uniform performance standards, including environmental and social concerns, providing for low discretion on the part of firms and certifiers and a high degree of multi-stakeholder control. On the other is the PEFC alliance, with its preference for procedurally oriented management system standards, focused primarily on locally defined best forestry practices, high discretion, and a high degree of landowner and business control. And yet, the systems have also developed a growing number of similarities over time.

Standards

There have been numerous and almost continuous changes in standards, particularly in the PEFC programmes as they seek to compete more effectively in the broader field of certification. Thus, the categories and language of standards have converged in numerous ways. While much of this change has involved gradual 'ratcheting up' (Fung *et al.* 2001; Overdevest 2004) by PEFC members of their environmental standards and occasional addition of social ones, a certain amount has also involved concessions by the FSC to make its programme more workable in the face of market challenges. A good example is the adoption of the 'percentage claims' policy discussed above. The FSC is also working on streamlined standards for 'small and low intensity forests' (SLIMFS) to reduce costs for small and low income enterprises.

While their standards have come to resemble each other more closely, the different programmes are still locked in debates and contests regarding appropriate standards for a number of controversial issues, such as allowable levels of clear cutting, use of pesticides and genetically modified organisms, duties to communities and workers, and the availability of certification information to the public. These are manifested through their contending systems of rules and procedures.

Procedures and roles

There has also been considerable convergence on appropriate practices and procedures among the programmes. Indeed, since they are essentially extra-governmental regulatory systems, it is not surprising that they have focused a great deal on administrative law questions – i.e. general rules for rule making, adjudication, and information gathering and sharing (see generally, Meidinger 2006). On the whole, the programmes have concentrated on their standard-setting processes, gradually making them more transparent and participatory. Today they all appear to follow notice and comment procedures similar to administrative agencies in most modern states. Certification programmes also increasingly acknowledge duties to respond to public comments and to explain their policies in reasoned ways. Additionally, all of the programmes are trying to demonstrate participation by diverse interests in their deliberations. The FSC has gone much farther in this regard than most industry programmes, which typically seek to maintain industry control over policy making, but even the industry programmes acknowledge a need for broad-based stakeholder participation and seek to foster it in various ways.

Similarly, much effort has gone into defining appropriate standards, procedures, and accountability structures for certifiers. The programmes differ on how certifiers ought to be accredited (with most PEFC programmes relying on generalized ISO accreditation agencies and the FSC relying on a programme it originally created and later spun off), but they all stress the professionalism and ostensible independence of certifiers and increasingly seek to provide formal auditing systems for certifier decisions. Moreover, following the FSC, the programmes are beginning to require that certifiers publish public summaries of their findings, thereby subjecting administrative adjudications as well as rulemakings to public scrutiny. The FSC also requires stakeholder consultations as part of the certification process; the PEFC programmes sometimes do, but not always. Hence, while the certification programmes stress the importance of defined roles and procedures, they have also blurred the social boundaries between administrators and the public by providing for increased participation, transparency, and responsiveness in rulemaking and adjudication procedures. They thus manifest the dual reliance on expertise and participation that characterizes many Western state regulatory programmes today but in variable mixes.

Equally importantly, forest certification programmes have blurred the boundaries between regulatory programmes and firms, both by giving firms a larger official role in defining regulatory standards and by using internal control systems (EMSs) to harness the firms to regulatory goals. This approach no longer treats the firm as a black box responsible simply for producing certain outputs, but rather as part of the regulatory programme, with its own organizational and technological resources that can be committed to defining, implementing, and revising regulatory goals (Coglianese and Nash 2001; Parker 2000; Potoski and Prakash 2005; Vandenbergh 2005). In practice, the EMS approach also seems to have the effect of further 'legalizing' forest management operations internally, since certifiers demand to see detailed documentation of planning, implementation, monitoring and correction processes and responsibilities.

Network organization

Together, the forest certification programmes have consolidated extensive transnational alliances into complex interconnected networks of market participants, environmental and social activists, forestry and certification professionals, and many others (including government officials, as discussed in the next section). These networks have been growing over time and also contending with each other about questions such as the appropriate level of centralization and the nature and role of nodes.

The FSC arguably initiated this process by bringing environmental, labour, human and indigenous rights groups and others into what had originally been a rather closed circle of professional foresters and landowners or managers. It continues to try to expand its network through strategies such as attempting to appeal to more small landholders and small enterprises through programme changes and trying to strengthen its alliances with similar interests in other economic sectors. One of the most important steps in this latter process has been its participation in the International Social and Environmental Accreditation and Labelling Alliance, which also includes low wage labour, organic agriculture, fisheries, and other labelling programmes.

Overall, the establishment of the nationally federated PEFC together with the growing reach and complexity of the FSC have prompted the FSC to move towards decentralization. It has established regional offices and is increasingly focusing on national programmes as its fundamental elements (although this strategy remains subject to debate by those who think that the FSC should represent an emerging transnational public, rather than agglomeration of national ones). At the same time, the FSC increasingly sees itself not as a free-standing programme, but rather as part of the larger emerging global forest certification and governance system. Its executive director describes FSC's role as being 'a global pacesetter for development of standards and certification' (Liedeker 2002a).

In sum, while competition among the alternative certification programmes originally seemed to imply the fragmentation, and possibly the disintegration of forest certification, that has not occurred. The programmes have moved into various kinds of complex linkages as a part of their competition. Formerly hostile groups, particularly professional foresters and land owners, have been turned from outright opponents of forest certification, to proponents, but of their own programmes. This inevitably put them in dialogue and mutual surveillance with the FSC programme, and seems to have begun a process of investing them in the forest certification system as a whole. Most participants in the certification system seem to be aware that they have developed a considerable amount of mutual interdependence. They all have an investment in the value and validity of certification, and they understand that they will realize some of their goals through their competitors. The proliferation of forest certification has thus helped to consolidate a multi-interest global network engaged in discussions, debates, and institutional competition over appropriate standards and methods for forestry regulation. If this network persists it may constitute an important new type of global regulatory community over time.

Legalization

As the above sections make clear, the field of forest certification is strikingly 'legalized'.This term has several salient features here. The first is a heavy reliance on formal rules and definitions of roles. Important issues are routinely resolved and memorialized in rules and decisions. Participants almost universally seek to draw on principles, standards, and rules to define the rights and duties of different kinds of actors, organize their behaviour as a whole, and resolve disputes. Most rules and policies are enunciated in formalized procedures and justified in normative terms. Much debate takes place in terms of what constitutes good forest management and a proper allocation of authority, but this debate takes place in the form of contending, heavily legalized regulatory systems. Certification programmes have increasingly differentiated legislative, adjudicative, and administrative authorities, and give increasing care to how those authorities are defined, exercised, monitored and revised. As noted above, the process of legalization is producing a system-wide body of public law stressing public notice and comment proceedings, publicly accessible policies and decisions, participatory procedures and structures, and reasoned explanation. At the same time, it is also producing an extensive body of 'private' law inside forest management firms and trading networks, detailing multiple plans, procedures, duties, etc., and linking them back to external requirements, although, as noted above, there is a tug of war between external and internal legalization.

Why legal forms are being so broadly and rapidly extended is unclear. It could be partly a kind of institutional isomorphism. Since other regulatory and certification programmes typically take these forms, forest certification programmes simply choose to do the same. Or it could be more functional. It is possible that legalization is the best way to achieve the goals of maintaining transnational markets while protecting environmental and social values. Moreover, it could be desirable in part because other programmes with this form are seen as legitimate, thus helping to legitimate the new ones (Szablowski 2006). What is clear is that the process is widespread and probably accelerating.

The concept of legalization as used thus far is similar to that of Abbott *et al.* (2000), except that it is more dynamic and contested. Legalization is not simply a set pattern of institutional characteristics, but also a process of contestation. Here it is helpful to note a further, largely taken-for-granted dimension of legalization in this field – which is that the transnational certification system draws many activities that were previously understood as discretionary, or otherwise outside law, into in the realm of law. Thus, although there are plural legal systems and considerable debate and competition about which rules and whose rules will apply to any given activity, rules will indeed apply. These rules will in turn continue to be elaborated while serving as resources for political contestation. Legalization can thus be understood as a strategy for gaining governance capacity.

Finally, it is important to note two additional characteristics of legalization in this field. First, it is very broad and deep, seeking to integrate environmental, economic, and social goals and to link local, national, and transnational domains, as well as civil society, industry, and state organizations. Thus, although there are plural, competing legal systems, together they have great ambitions and increasing reach. Second, the emerging systems are not inherently separate or distinct from state-based law. In fact, as the next section indicates, they are becoming increasingly intertwined with state law.

Relationships to state governance

Just as environmentalist-oriented and industry-oriented certification programmes appear to be growing together into a larger system, so too does forest certification seem to be growing together with state regulatory and management programmes, albeit more slowly and sporadically. The FSC programme, although formally independent of states, has as its first principle that forest management operations 'shall respect all applicable laws of the country in which they occur, and international treaties and agreements to which the country is a signatory'. Thus, forest certification can be seen as a way of both bolstering state-based legal systems and also drawing upon their legitimacy.

Proprietary activities

Forest certification has received various kinds of direct resource support from governments. The FSC, for example, received early funding from Austria and later from the Netherlands and several other EU countries (most recently rent-free offices in Bonn for 25 years). Several European countries and numerous municipalities have adopted green procurement policies roughly tracking FSC requirements (Tarasofsky *et al.* 2005). These have prompted the PEFC to change some requirements to make its products eligible for government purchase. So popular and controversial are these procurement programmes that the EU is currently working on a policy regarding appropriate rules for government forest products procurement.

Interestingly, a growing number of states, provinces, and municipalities (ranging from Poland to Minnesota to Freiburg, Germany) have had their own forests certified. In most cases they do this not in response to allegations that the state forests are failing to meet legal requirements, but rather to demonstrate that government-run forests meet the highest public standards, implicitly acknowledging that governments no longer claim to be the sole arbiters of public duties and legitimacy (see also Scott 2002).

Regulatory activities

Some governments are also taking advantage of certification programmes in regulating non-state entities. A few (e.g. Guatemala for the Maya Bioreserve) have made certification a requirement of conducting forestry in their jurisdictions. Others (e.g. Bolivia and Estonia) have adopted substantive requirements that are essentially identical to those of certification programmes. Typically, this seems to have occurred because the public deliberations on certification standards have directly influenced contemporaneous public deliberations on state standards. When standards are identical or even very similar, it is apparent that certification of a firm can be seen as tantamount to compliance with law. This would also be the case when a certification standard is stricter, but requires compliance with state law and treaties, as is the case with the FSC. Some countries have officially adopted the position that certification of a firm creates a presumption of legal compliance. Given the costs of conducting inspections, it seems likely that other countries will follow it implicitly (see generally, Meidinger, forthcoming).

Certification programmes are also trying to position themselves to shape state regulatory requirements in the future. International trade law requires WTO members to use recognized international standards in adopting internal technical regulations and standards applicable to internationally traded goods.[1] Over time it seems likely that international trade law will promote the absorption of certification standards into state legal systems.

Certification standards are also likely to be pulled into state legal systems indirectly through such channels as tort standards for reasonable care and administrative expectations of best practices as interpreted by inspectors. These are slow, and sometimes empirically intricate processes, however, and no substantial research seems to have addressed them to date.

Finally, certification programmes are closely interconnected with a recent intergovernmental initiative to fight illegal logging in tropical countries. Spurred by a 1998 G-8 Summit calling for governments to join forces in dealing with the problem, the Forest Law Enforcement, Governance and Trade Action Plan (FLEGT – a European programme), and other similar regional and bilateral programmes, seek to eliminate access to developed markets of illegally produced timber. Thus timber imported from threatened forests must be certified as legal, and existing forest certification programmes offer a way of both providing such certification and possibly leveraging improved forest management generally.

At a broad scale, it is arguable that the certification programmes are giving shape to a new transnational forest regulatory and governance regime, one that is centred in the competition among certification programmes, but also involves continuing monitoring and participation by governments, corporations, and NGOs at the transnational, national, and local levels. The emerging regime centres on plural and competing, yet interconnected, systems of rules and duties, draws in and yet requires changes in state legal systems, and thus both strengthens and threatens to displace them, depending on the particular situation.

Other sectors

The analysis thus far has concentrated on forestry, begging the question whether the competitive legalization that it describes is exceptional or more general. This question is not easy to answer at this stage, both because developments in every sector are highly complex and because relatively little research along the lines outlined above has been carried out. This paper therefore makes some tentative comparisons with other sectors that are necessarily subject to great elaboration and revision in the future.

Organic agriculture

Organic agriculture certification was a direct precursor of forest certification, since some of the FSC founders had prior experience with organic certification. Like the FSC, the organic agriculture movement had its roots in efforts to reform natural resource management – in this case stopping the use of chemical pesticides, herbicides, and fertilizers, avoiding monocultures, protecting ecological systems, and generally keeping people and animals healthier (Conford 2001). Unlike forest certification, however, this movement was premised on a belief that adherence to its principles would directly benefit end consumers, since organically grown foods were believed to be healthier and safer. Thus, it fitted better with traditional standard setting and certification processes, which are also premised on the belief that certified products will perform better than uncertified ones. Still, it was partly a moral and ethical movement aimed at defining a right way of living and minimizing harm to ecosystems.

While the history of organic agriculture is far too complicated to summarize here, it can be roughly sketched in several phases. In the first half of the twentieth century, reformers developed the rationale for organic agriculture and founded various model farms and communities. In the 1960s and 1970s these foundations combined with several chemical scares and the environmental movement to catalyse the first organic certification movement. Interestingly, although a German programme dated from the 1920s (Coleman and Reed, this volume), most non-governmental certification programmes were founded almost simultaneously at the state and international levels. Thus, organic certification programmes in California, Oregon and Washington were immediately complemented by the International Federation of Organic Agriculture Movements (IFOAM), although IFOAM only managed to promulgate its first standards in 1980 (Bolster 2006).

Organic certification in the US has long been a competitive field, and practices evidently have varied greatly among certifiers and jurisdictions. IFOAM finally launched an accreditation programme in 1992, but by this time many certifiers had established businesses and chose not to seek IFOAM accreditation. Certification schemes and organizations proliferated, creating an increasingly complex and inconsistent patchwork that came to be understood as a significant problem.

This 'tower of Babel' paved the way for the US Organic Foods Production Act (OFPA) in 1990.[2] While mandating national standards for organic agriculture certification, the OFPA failed to define 'organic', leaving it to the US Department of Agriculture (USDA) working with a non-governmental advisory committee, the National Organic Standards Board (NOSB). The Act also requires that any food carrying the label 'organic' be certified as such by an organization that has undergone accreditation by a division of the USDA, rather than the IFOAM-affiliated International Organic Accreditation Service. Most of the accredited certifiers are private organizations, although some are states and some are based in foreign countries (Coleman and Reed, this volume).

Overall, the standards promulgated through the US regulatory system tend to be lenient. The USDA has sided with large-scale agriculture and overridden a number of NOSB recommendations by allowing the use of genetically engineered crops, application of sewage sludge to crops, and use of irradiation in producing foods that can be labeled 'organic' (Bolster 2006). Moreover, the US standard does not require ecological practices beyond limitations on ingredients and entirely ignores concerns about the treatment of animals.

Perhaps the most portentous effect of the federal programme is to preemptively define the meaning of 'organic' in US commerce – including for imported foods – at a relatively low level. Farmers are free to exceed the standard if they wish, and states or other programmes may set stricter standards, but they are forced to use additional labels or information to communicate that fact. Similar patterns are evident internationally, where a number of major national governments have largely ignored central elements of the IFOAM standards, and even those of countries they trade with, in promulgating their own. IFOAM is currently working on a major revision of its standard, with the hope that it can shape the development of future governmental and other standards by leading the way in defining core principles and concepts. It will be an interesting test of the transnational regulatory system to see whether and how well governments respond to this IFOAM initiative and to each other's standards. International trade law may provide at least some positive incentive to do so, since it prohibits technical requirements for internationally traded products that are 'unnecessary obstacles to trade' or 'more trade-restrictive than necessary to fulfill a legitimate objective' and also enjoins governments to use recognized international standards when possible.[3]

Fisheries

Although fisheries comprise a large part of the earth's surface, the social world of fisheries regulation appears smaller than that of agriculture regulation. Most ocean fisheries have long been in decline due to heavy fishing pressure and deteriorating environmental conditions. In 1997 WWF joined with Unilever, one of the world's largest buyers of fish, to establish the Marine Stewardship Council (MSC). Modelled in large part on the FSC, the MSC defines itself as 'an independent, global, non-profit organization whose role is to recognize, via a certification programme, well-managed fisheries and to harness consumer preference for seafood products bearing the MSC label of approval'. The MSC standards are largely environmental and operational, omitting social issues. The MSC has accredited a small group of certification organizations, some of which concentrate on fisheries and others on market chains carrying certified fish. Approximately eighteen fisheries have been certified to date, with a similar number under consideration.

In certifying whole fisheries the MSC is in part certifying governments, since their cooperation and effective enforcement is essential to curbing the tragedy of the commons that typically affects fisheries. Although it provides for public comment and participation in standard setting and certification processes, the MSC has a much more limited stakeholder structure than either the FSC or IFOAM, and seems to operate on a more technocratic basis. Its influence on world fisheries governance is more preliminary and unclear as well. But at this point it seems plausible that the MSC process could eventually stimulate the production of relatively widely accepted standards and procedures for certifying sustainable fisheries – provided of course that certified fisheries do in fact prove sustainable.

Apparel

Global apparel markets have long been seen both as exacerbating mistreatment of third-world workers and as offering a possible way to improve their conditions by making revenues contingent on proper treatment of workers. The 1980s brought a flurry of corporate codes of conduct by branded companies in response to highly publicized cases of worker abuse tied to their brands. These were often linked to actual or threatened consumer boycotts. In the late 1990s three separate apparel certification programmes were founded, mainly with the goal of improving the consistency and implementation of codes of conduct. Two of them, Social Accountability International (SAI) and the Fair Labor Association (FLA), were primarily the offspring of NGOS and governments, while the third, Worldwide Responsible Apparel Production (WRAP), was founded by the industry (Bartley 2003). SAI and WRAP certify individual factories, whereas FLA certifies entire supply chains. Competition among the programmes has been intense and contentious at times.

The apparel certification programmes have been able to draw on labour standards developed by governments and intergovernmental organizations, mainly the UN-based International Labor Organization (ILO). Still, a high level of contention about proper standards persists. As in organic certification, there is considerable disagreement among governments, and between governments and certification programmes. Most governments of third world countries have been anxious not to be seen as havens for labour abuse, but also not to be forced into strict labour standards that might reduce their comparative advantage in this highly price-competitive and volatile industry. These complexities combined with the inherent difficulty of regulating labour conditions in far-flung and rapidly rotating factories make it clear that achieving effective global governance over labour conditions in apparel production will be enormously difficult. While the certification programmes have led to notable improvements in particular cases, it is difficult to document widespread effects. Nonetheless, one school of thought strongly argues that the presence of certification programmes has helped to 'ratchet up' worldwide labour standards generally, and it does seem plausible that the overall labour situation would be even worse without apparel certification programmes (Fung *et al.* 2001).

Mining

Mining is one of the most intriguing sectors in which regulation by certification has been attempted. Particularly in developing countries, the mining industry has a reputation for being exploitative in the fullest sense of the word. And yet, this dubious reputation has also been a source of regulatory leverage in the global market, as mining companies seek to avoid campaigns like the recent one against 'blood' or 'conflict' diamonds. Mining certification began in the African diamond industry, after several NGOs demonstrated that rebel groups were using revenues from diamond mines to fuel brutal civil wars in Sierra Leone, Angola, and Congo (Campbell 2002). In the 'Kimberley Process' they were able to cooperate with business interests (mainly the virtual monopolist, DeBeers) and governments to establish a programme for certifying diamonds as not having helped to finance civil wars. The process took about three years and seems to have produced a well functioning certification programme. DeBeers used its virtually unique expertise to work out many of the operational details of the programme and the main NGO involved (Global Watch) was able to successfully push for external auditing (Kantz 2006). The governments directly affected were very supportive of the programme because it helped reduce rebel activity and challenges to their authority.

Since the Kimberly Process Certification Programme was created to address a specific, relatively narrow problem, the question remains as to whether certification programmes can be instituted to address the larger challenges of environmental and community protection posed by mining. At present the sector involves a hodgepodge of individual company codes of conduct (e.g. Newmont Mining 2006), limited subsector initiatives (e.g. CJRP 2006), and proposals for sector-wide certification programmes (e.g. MCEP 2006). The most important of the sector-wide proposals, the WWF-supported Mining Certification Evaluation Project (MCEP 2006), concludes that there is enough convergence in the various initiatives to support the establishment of an industry-wide third-party certification programme involving broad stakeholder participation and covering environmental, human rights, worker health and safety and community issues, among others. Whether such a programme is created remains to be seen, but if it is, it may be a quite remarkable extension on all that has come before it.

Impacts

The first question commonly raised about regulatory systems like the ones described above is how effective they can be. They rely primarily on 'soft' law rules and quasi-voluntary implementation structures, meaning that states play a relatively small role in making and enforcing the rules. Thus, if certification-centered regulation is effective, the primary mechanisms are not likely to be those associated with state-based legal systems. While it is too early to draw strong conclusions on the question of efficacy, there is a growing body of research suggesting that certification has significant effects on management practices as well as larger governance structures, certainly in the case of forestry (Bass et al. 2001; Cashore et al. 2006), probably in the cases of organic agriculture (e.g. Allen and Kovach 2000; Greer 2002; Marshall and Standifird 2005) and apparel (Elliott and Freeman 2003; Fichter and Sydow 2002), and likely in the future case of mining certification (MCEP 2006).

The largest amount of research has been done in the field of forest certification. A recent set of systematic studies of FSC certification in 16 developing and transitioning countries found a host of effects on forest management and local governance institutions (Cashore et al. 2006). Most cases indicated that the adoption of forest certification had led to improved environmental management practices in the industry, including better inventorying and planning, silvicultural practices, biodiversity protection, environmental monitoring, and training. In addition, certification has sometimes stimulated the introduction of entirely new concepts, such as the Estonian 'spring truce', a time during which forestry is curtailed so as to avoid disturbing reproduction patterns of forest fauna. FSC certification has also led to improved labour conditions in many cases, ranging from the provision of protective clothing and shielded tools to better training and sanitary conditions.

Equally importantly, the introduction of FSC certification has led to various 'network effects' in local governance structures. In some countries with relatively closed governance structures, the introduction of forest certification has led to the inclusion of previously excluded groups (typically environmental, labour and community groups) and seems also in some cases to have rebalanced power away from government officials and industry. The amount of change varies greatly among cases, however, and it is impossible to know at this stage how persistent these changes will be.

To date, the effectiveness of certification programmes in forestry as well as other sectors has depended heavily on the ability of activist regulatory entrepreneurs to use market chains to both pressure and monitor changes in forestry practices. Their capacity to do so is unlikely to continue indefinitely. Moreover, although perhaps to a lesser extent in the case of agriculture, global inequalities are an important part of programme effectiveness. Thus, forest, apparel, and mining certification affect practices in developing countries because failure to achieve certification portends potentially serious losses of revenues from developed countries. If international income inequalities decline over time, domestic demand for certified products in developing countries will have to rise to maintain market pressure and support for certification requirements, unless they have already been incorporated in a broader set of regulatory structures.

The mechanisms of certification's efficacy go well beyond market pressure and surveillance; it seems clear that they must operate through the general process of institutionalization, wherein changed practices become routine and taken-for-granted over time, ultimately shifting cultural understandings of appropriate behaviour. While it is apparent from the general literature on institutionalization (e.g. DiMaggio and Powell 1983; Colyvas and Powell 2006) that this process is likely to occur, there has been little research to date documenting its dynamics in certification-based regulatory systems. It seems reasonable to expect that institutionalization will operate through a variety of pathways, including routine interactions within firms and among wood producers, processors and buyers as well as changing assumptions in professional education. It will be important to try to understand how the tendency toward legalization – i.e. the formal expression of rights, duties and expectations together with the development of increasingly elaborate justificatory rationales and implementation institutions – affects institutionalization. The same goes for the effect of mutually reinforcing legal orders slowly bringing extra-governmental orders into alignment with governmental ones. Ultimately, if some critics of ostensibly technocratic standard-setting processes are correct, the effects should be visible as changes in the very identities of the participants in the regulatory systems (Wood 2004).

Finally, to say that certification systems have significantly affected resource management and governance structures and that they are expanding and linking up with each other and with state systems is not to say that they are adequate to handle the problems they seek to address. Each of the certification-centred regulatory systems discussed in this paper has been vehemently criticized as inadequate to the task at hand. Some critics even argue that they are counterproductive, since they may give the impression of offering solutions without the reality, thus diverting attention and resources from 'real' solutions (e.g. Latin 2005). These criticisms and the underlying questions they pose cannot be firmly answered at this stage, since the systems are still in formative stages and have not been carefully studied. Furthermore, the question of adequacy demands a referent – adequate in relation to what? And here there is a huge problem, because the perfect 'hard' regulatory systems do not exist and appear to have no prospect of coming into being in the near term. Even so, however, eventually this question will have to be addressed head on: has the turn toward certification-based regulatory systems been an effective move, or a fundamental mistake? Fortunately or unfortunately, that time has not yet arrived. Moreover, part of the answer will undoubtedly depend on questions beyond simple effectiveness.

Broader implications

While the regulatory systems described in this paper employ conventional standard setting and certification techniques, they simultaneously constitute new institutional arrangements with potentially significant implications for law, society, and their changing relationship.

Law

The argument of this paper is that emerging certification-based regulatory systems entail a particular and somewhat novel kind of law making. Even prior to certification programmes, the emergence of global markets typically generates legal pluralism on its own, since different parts of the expanded social space delimited by the market are subject to different territorially based legal regimes. At the same time, actors in one part of the market are both implicated and increasingly understood as having interests in actions in other parts, as the results of their transactions have effects there. Global certification programmes are efforts by self-appointed non-state officials to bring these interests and effects into a common legal regime.

Yet in the cases discussed above, the creation of one certification regime typically provokes establishment of at least one other, and often significant developments in state regulation as well, all of them with increasingly transnational reach. Thus, at any given point in the global market chains discussed above there are likely to be at least three operative legal orders, an NGO-oriented one, an industry-oriented one, and probably a state one as well.

These orders are neither independent of each other nor static. Instead, they interact and compete, generating a larger governance structure and associated legal system that grow increasingly dense and yet unsettled at the same time, at least in the short run. To some extent, as discussed above, the competing systems may tend toward convergent standards and institutions, but the evidence for this proposition is not persuasive at this point. The case of organic agriculture, for example, suggests persistent and possibly expanding divergence among regimes, and this despite the pressures of expanding international trade for harmonization. Thus, at least in the near term there is continued plurality and contestation. While there may be 'more' and more detailed law, and while it may permeate more social spaces, it is also deeply contingent and contested. So much so, that it seems likely to engage more and more actors in each sector in the process of defining and redefining the rules, and to face them with repeated choices about which rules to accommodate.

Just as the spread of certification may bring those who would traditionally have been low-level legal functionaries or addressees into active law making roles, so also it may turn those who would have been primarily lawmakers into legal entrepreneurs. The executive director of the FSC, for example, sees the FSC as fundamentally a change agent, rather than a certifier of good practice. To him the critical challenge facing the FSC is that of 'finding new objectives for the future' (Liedeker 2002b). Leaders of industry-based certification organizations portray their programmes in similar ways. Virtually in unison, they talk about the importance of continuous improvement, expanding public participation, and building new relationships across constituencies. Law making as it has been described here is very much an entrepreneurial activity.

Much work remains to be done in describing the dynamics of these emergent legal systems. As suggested above, it is possible that they represent a distinctive form of law, one in which competition and change have taken on new importance while stability and consistency have receded. The traditional legal forms of (1) defining rights and duties through rules (2) made through increasingly participatory, transparent, and regularized procedures (3) implemented by specialized officials and (4) justified in terms of normative principles, are retained. Yet, change is built into the system through both traditional processes of legislation and adjudication and new ones of competition and contestation before a public that remains amorphous, segmented, and very much under construction.

Society

If the above depiction of emerging legal systems is at all accurate, it poses many important questions about what kind of society they will foster and support. One of the most obvious is the very definition of society. The Westphalian system of international law presumes national societies whose governments negotiate relationships with each other and promulgate international rules through treaties, conventions, mutually accepted customs, and the like. Clearly, however, global markets place pressure on that conception, since growing numbers of people are in more regular contact with 'foreigners' than with many people in their own countries, may have more in common with those foreigners, and often work out rules to organize their interactions without significant state involvement. Moreover, the vision of national societies has always been problematic in many states because they contain distinct communities with different, often inconsistent legal traditions, most of which have been suppressed.

Some certification-based regulatory systems seem more sensitive to such differences than are traditional national and international legal systems. They appear to incorporate normative discourses such as human and community rights and environmental protection more readily than the Westphalian system, and they officially value community protection and participation. Moreover, their very existence as alternative legal orders is a powerful indicator of the fact that people in the modern world participate in and negotiate their way through multiple legal communities.

Yet certification-based regulatory systems may also have widespread homogenizing effects over time. Their competition to define common standards seems to have centralizing tendencies. While it is also tempered by a competition to fit local circumstances, those local circumstances are for the most part filtered through 'practical realities' defined by the global economy. Pressures to accommodate the global market make many traditional modes of existence less feasible by the day, and certification systems seem to facilitate that trend, with their emphasis on standard methods of operation, management systems, audited accountability, and so on.

The problem is not purely an anthropological one, however; the question is not simply whether traditional societies can be 'preserved'. Rather, it is whether they can participate in global commerce in ways that sustain their capacity to define important terms of their own lives. If certification-based regulatory systems are indeed sufficiently responsive to diverse communities to facilitate this process, they may help over time to construct a world society that both preserves spaces for distinctive communities and provides forums for interaction and negotiation among them.

At present, transnational society is organized along several different lines, including economic sectors, states, and communities and peoples. The interaction among these contending organizational orders is disjointed at best. Whether one sees the emerging system as a heterarchy (e.g. Ehrenreich *et al.* 1995) or a polyarchy (e.g. Dahl 2003; Cohen and Sabel 1997) or something else, the nature of the interaction among the orders is amenable to many alternatives and carries many possible normative implications.

Perhaps the most vexing normative implication is the thorny problem of democracy. The emerging regulatory systems are not representational in any traditional sense of the concept. Rather, they rely on various procedural devices such as transparency, expanded participation, and reasoned explanation as substitutes, together with relatively open interactions among the plural social ordering structures noted above. The problem is, what kind of democracy, if any, is possible in these circumstances? The response up to this point seems to be a conceptual hodgepodge, with discursive and structural elements linking in multiple and shifting forms. A particularly notable feature on the discursive side is the reliance by many certification programmes on adumbrating concepts tied to what some commentators have described as 'high moral authority' (Keck and Sikkink 1998; Wapner 1996). Concepts such as human rights and ecosystem health provide powerful reference points that help to orient the systems, even as they remain subject to continuing elaboration and contestation through economic, governmental, and civil society ordering systems (e.g. Baxi 2005).

Whether the emerging regulatory ensembles will learn to perform in ways that compose a global democracy will depend on simultaneous development of new theoretical and empirical understandings that inform and drive each other forward. Perhaps they will learn to implement new forms of cosmopolitan democracy (Held 2004), and perhaps they will find areas of 'overlapping consensus' among peoples by settling on 'reasonable pluralism' (Rawls 2001). Or perhaps they will converge around quite different governance structures that may or may not qualify as 'government by the people'. No doubt we will engage in many debates on this question in years to come.

Notes

1 E.g. Article 2.2, Technical Barriers to Trade (TBT) Agreement.
2 Food, Agriculture, Conservation and Trade Act of 1990, Pub.L. No. 101-624, Title XXI, Organic Food Production Act, 104 Stat. 3359, 3937 (1990), 7 U.S.C. § 6501–6523.
3 Article 2.2, TBT Agreement.

References

Abbott, K.W., Keohane, R.O., Moravcsik, A., Slaughter, A.-M. and Snidal, D. (2000) 'The Concept of Legalization', *International Organization*, 54(3): 401–419.

Allen, P. and Kovach, M. (2000) 'The Capitalist Composition of Organic: The Potential of Markets in Fulfilling the Promise of Organic Agriculture', *Agriculture and Human Values*, 17: 221–233.

Bartley, T. (2003) 'Certifying Forests and Factories: States, Social Movements, and the Rise of Private Regulation in the Apparel and Forest Products Fields', *Politics and Society* 31(3): 433–464.

Bass, S., Thornber, K., Markopoulos, M., Roberts, S. and Grieg-Gran, M. (2001) *Certification's Impacts on Forests, Stakeholders, and Supply Chains*. London: International Institute for Environment and Development.

Baxi, U. (2005) 'Market Fundamentalisms: Business Ethics at the Altar of Human Rights', *Human Rights Law Review*, 5(1): 1–26.

Black, J. (2002) 'Regulatory Conversations', *Journal of Law and Society*, 29: 163–196.

Bolster, T. (2006) 'Governing Organic', Independent Study, SUNY Buffalo Law School, 23 January 2006 (Copy on file with author).

Brown, K. (2001) 'Cut and Run? Evolving Institutions for Global Forest Governance', *Journal of International Development*, 13: 893–905.

Campbell, G. (2002) *Blood Diamonds: Tracing the Deadly Path of the World's Most Precious Stones*. Boulder: Westview Press.

Cashore, B., Auld, G. and Newsom, D. (2003) 'The United States' Race to Certify Sustainable Forestry: Non-State Environmental Governance and the Competition for Policy-Making Authority', *Business and Politics*, 5: 219–259.

Cashore, B., Gale, F., Meidinger, E. and Newsom, D. (eds) (2006) *Confronting Sustainability: Forest Certification in Developing and Transitioning Countries*. New Haven: Yale Forestry School.

CJRP (2006) Council for Responsible Jewelry Practices: What We Stand For. Online, available at: www.responsiblejewellery.com/what.html.

Coglianese, C. and Nash, J. (eds) (2001) *Regulating from the Inside: Can Environmental Management Systems Achieve Policy Goals?* Washington, DC: Resources for the Future.

Cohen, J. and Sabel, C. (1997) 'Directly-Deliberative Polyarchy', European Law Journal, 3: 313–342.

Colyvas, J. and Powell, W.W. (2006) 'Roads to Institutionalization,' in B. Staw (ed.) Research in Organizational Behavior, 01/06. Online, available at: www.stanford.edu/group/song/papers/colyvas_powell.pdf.

Conford, P. (2001) *The Origins of the Organic Movement*. Edinburgh: Floris Books.

Dahl, R.A. (2003) 'Can International Organizations be Democratic? A Skeptic's View', in D. Held and A. McGrew (eds) *The Global Transformations Reader: An Introduction to the Globalization Debate*. London: Polity Press.

DiMaggio, P. and Powell, W.W. (1983) 'The Iron Cage Revisited: Institutional Isomorphism and Collective Rationality in Organizational Fields', *American Sociological Review* 48(2): 147–160.

Ehrenreich, R.M., Crumley, C.L. and Levy, J.E. (eds) (1995) *Heterarchy and the Analysis of Complex Societies*. Arlington, Va.: American Anthropological Association.

Elliott, K. and Freeman, R. (2003) *Can Labor Standards Improve Under Globalization?* Washington: Institute for International Economics.

Fichter, M. and Sydow, J. (2002) 'Using Networks Towards Global Labor Standards? Organizing Social Responsibility in Global Production Chains', *Industrielle Beziehungen*, 9(4): 357–380.

FSC (2006) 'Forest Stewardship Council Governance'. Online, available at: www.fsc.org/en/about/governance.

Fung, A. O'Rourke, D. and Sabel, C. (2001) *Can We Put an End to Sweatshops?* Boston: Beacon Press.

Gale, F. (1998) *The Tropical Timber Trade Regime*. New York: St. Martins.

Greer, A. (2002) 'Policy Networks and Policy Change in Organic Agriculture: A Comparative Analysis of the UK and Ireland', *Public Administration*, 80(3): 453–474.

Held, D. (2004) *Global Covenant: The Social Democratic Alternative to the Washington Consensus*. Cambridge, UK/Malden, MA: Polity Press.

Humphreys, D. (1996) *Forest Politics: The Evolution of International Cooperation*. London: Earthscan.

International Organization for Standardization (ISO) (2006) 'ISO 9000 and 14000 – in brief'. Online, available at: www.iso.org/iso/en/iso9000-14000/understand/inbrief. html.

Kantz, C. (2006) 'Public-Private Partnerships in the South: The Case of the Kimberley Process', paper presented to the International Studies Association, San Diego, 25 March 2006. Online, available at: convention2.allacademic.com/index.php?cmd= Download+Document&key=unpublished_manuscript&file_index=1&pop_up=true&n o_click_key=true&attachment_style=attachment&PHPSESSID=2bc3bd8e41a6526b4d 34b2815ca240f3.

Keck, M.E. and Sikkink, K. (1998) *Activists Beyond Borders: Advocacy Networks in International Politics*. Ithaca: Cornell University Press.

Kimberly Process (2006) Online, available at: www.kimberleyprocess.com:8080/site/.

Latin, H. (2005) 'Is FSC Helping or Hurting Forest Conservation', email to the envlaw-professors list serve, John Bonine, moderator, University of Oregon. Message dated 29 June 2005 (Copy on file with author).

Liedeker, H. (2002a) Executive Director's Comments to the General Assembly, Forest Stewardship Council, Oaxaca, Mexico, 22 November 2002.

Liedeker, H. (2002b) Interview with the Author, 16 October 2002.

Marshall, R.S. and Standifird, S.S. (2005) 'Organizational Resource Bundles and Institutional Change in the U.S. Organic Food and Agricultural Certification Sector', *Organization and Environment*, 18(3): 265–286.

MCEP (2006) Mining Certification Evaluation Project Final Report. Online, available at: www.minerals.csiro.au/sd/Certification/MCEP_Final_Report_Jan2006.pdf.

Meidinger, E. (forthcoming) 'Multi-Interest Self-Governance through Global Product Certification Programs', in O. Dilling, M. Herberg and G. Winter (eds) *Responsible Business? Self-Governance in Transnational Economic Transactions*.

Meidinger, E. (2006) 'The Administrative Law of Global Private-Public Regulation: the Case of Forestry', *European Journal of International Law*, 17: 47–87.

Meidinger, E. (1985) 'On Explaining the Development of "Emissions Trading" in US Air Pollution Regulation', *Law and Policy*, 7(4): 447–479.

MSC (2006) Marine Stewardship Council, Fisheries. Online, available at: www.msc.org/html/content_463.htm.

Newmont Mining (2006) Five Star Management Program. Online, available at: www.newmont.com/en/social/fivestar/management/index.asp.

Overdevest, C. (2004) 'Codes of Conduct and Standard Setting in the Forest Sector: Constructing Markets for Democracy?' *Industrial Relations*, 59: 172–195.

Parker, C. (2000) 'Reinventing Regulation Within the Corporation: Compliance-Oriented Regulatory Innovation', *Administration and Society* 32(5): 529–565.

PEFC (2006) PEFC Members and Schemes. Online, available at: www.pefc.org/internet/html/members_schemes/4_1120_59.htm.

Potoski, M. and Prakash, A. (2005) 'Covenants with Weak Swords: ISO 14001 and Facilities' Environmental Performance', *Journal of Policy Analysis and Management*, 24(4): 745–769.

Rawls, J. (2001) *The Law of Peoples*. Cambridge: Harvard University Press.

Sasser, E. (2002) 'Gaining Leverage: NGO Influence on Certification Institutions in the Forest Products Sector', in L. Teeter, B. Cashore and D. Zhang (eds) *Forest Policy for Private Forestry*, Oxford: CABI Press.

Scott, C. (2002) 'Private Regulation of the Public Sector: A Neglected Facet of Contemporary Governance', *Journal of Law and Society*, 29: 56–76.

Szablowski, D. (2006) 'Of Models and Mimics: Legitimation Strategies and the Constitution of Transnational Legal Authority', Paper presented at the International Studies Association Conference, San Diego, 22–25 March 2006.

Szablowski, D. (2004) Legitimacy and Regulation in the Global Economy: Legal Mediation of conflicts Between Communities and Transnational Mining Companies. Ph.D. Dissertation in Law, York University, Toronto, Ontario.

Tarasofsky, R.G., Mechel, F. and Sprang, P. (2005) 'Public Procurement and Forest Certification: Assessing the Implications for Policy, Law, and International Trade', Draft report to Chatham House and Ecologic. Online, available at: www.ecologic.de/download/briefe/2006/933_brief_procurement_forest.pdf.

Vandenbergh, M. (2005) 'The Private Life of Public Law', *Columbia Law Review*, 105: 2029–2096.

Wapner, P. (1996) *Environmental Activism and Worlds Civic Politics*. Albany: State University of New York Press.

Wood, S. (2004) 'Three Questions About Corporate Codes: Problematizations, Authorizations and the Public/Private Divide', in W. Cragg (ed.) *Ethics Codes: The Regulatory Norms of a Global Society?* Aldershot, UK: Edward Elgar, pp. 245–288.

8 Beyond legalization?

How global standards work

Bas Arts and Dieter Kerwer

Introduction

Since the 1990s, there has been a highly visible trend towards managing transborder problems by global rules. These emerging regimes of 'global regulation' (Braithwaite and Drahos 2000) have transformed the way in which rule-making at the global level works. One of the major changes identified is a trend towards 'legalization' (Abbott *et al.* 2000). There has developed a rich array of 'law-like' arrangements in the international system, which varies according to the degree of bindingness of the rules as well as the type of actors involved and the role they play in setting and enforcing those rules (Brütsch and Lehmkuhl in this volume). Furthermore, these rules are now increasingly enforced by bodies that come close to autonomous international courts, for example the dispute settlement system of the WTO. However, this process of 'legalization' is characteristic only of parts of global rule-making. Global regulators also increasingly resort to voluntary rules, soft law, or standards in order to tackle public policy problems. So far, this form of global regulation has received less attention than legalized global rule. The present chapter seeks to redress this imbalance.

Voluntary rules – 'standards' in the terminology of this chapter – have become increasingly popular as an alternative to multilateral treaties that issue binding directives for their members. They can address all kinds of public policy issues. Examples of such voluntary rules are the International Standards Organization's quality management standard ISO 9000 or its environmental management standard ISO 14000, the International Labour Organization's core labour standards, the International Monetary Fund's financial reporting standards for its member states, and the International Migration Organization's standard on immigration policies.

Why global regulators such as international organizations use voluntary standards is a formidable puzzle. Why should sovereign states or powerful transnational companies follow them? Why should standards be an adequate answer in cases in which binding regulation by law fails? What makes such standards work? This paper seeks to address these questions to show that standards are indeed a feasible and potentially successful mode of regulation. We argue that in some instances standards are surprisingly successful in influencing the behaviour of firms or states. By providing an explanation of this phenomenon, we want to identify strengths and weaknesses of such international standards and show how they could be remedied.

In order to enhance our understanding of how standards work, we shall analyse two different cases, the standards of the Basel Committee for Banking Supervision (BCBS) designed to prevent bank failures and the standards of the Forest Stewardship Council (FSC) seeking to promote sustainable timber production. The major aim of the comparison is to get a better understanding of how standards work in each case. There are numerous similar aspects which will contribute to our understanding of how standards work. However, there are also important differences. The standards are not equally successful in these two different issue-areas. Their penetration into financial affairs is much more profound than into environmental ones. This gives the opportunity to search for factors determining the success or failure of standards.

Conceptualizing standards

Standardizing can be defined as a form of regulation based on the attempt to influence others by voluntary rules. For standards to be successful they need other actors who use standards. If no users exist, a standard setter will sooner or later cease its activities. If standards are voluntary rules, the question arises: why should autonomous actors follow? The literature on standardization is highly fragmented; it is organized mostly around different types of standards and offers few general treatments (but see Nadvi and Wältring 2004). Nevertheless, two alternative concepts of standardization can be distinguished which offer different explanations of how standards work.

The most common approach is to understand standards as rules that facilitate co-ordination. This is especially important in the market place, where autonomous actors interact. For example, a product standard defining the properties of an electric plug makes sure that any plug bought will fit into an appropriate type of socket. Such a standard is typically set by a specific standard-setting organization. Co-ordination standards are much more effective as product standards than as process standards (Werle 1995). The simple reason is that a standard that improves a product (e.g. by making it compatible with other components) appeals to the self-interested actor, while a standard improving the process by which a product is made (e.g. by reducing environmental degradation during its production) does not do so. Co-ordination standards regulating processes are only self-enforcing to the extent that consumers with altruistic preferences (e.g. for a cleaner environment) exist.[1] As a consequence, if process standards want to be as successful as product standards, they will need to be formulated as directives rather than standards; they need to be set by the state.

The concept of co-ordination standards is not a useful starting point for the present chapter, since in both instances, regulators seek to redress how markets work and thus cannot appeal to a trivial material self-interest of autonomous actors (see below). A better alternative is an understanding of standards as a form of regulation based on voluntary rules. Regulatory standards give 'advice to many' (Brunsson 1999). In this perspective, standards are not limited to specific issues (e.g. technical compatibility), but can address any kind of problem. Furthermore, there are no inherent limits as to who plays the roles of the standardization game. Thus, standard-setting is not limited to a specific standard-setting body; any actor – public or private – can set standards. Also, standards can be addressed to anyone, for example not only firms but also states. In fact, our cases are examples of standards which are public policy prescriptions.

How standards regulate

If a standard is a voluntary rule, yet addresses any kind of issue that could also be the object of regulation by binding directives at the same time, the following question is raised: how do they motivate actors to follow them? As has been shown above, such standards cannot be self-enforcing or enforced by the market, at least not to the same extent. But they still exist. There is an explanatory gap here that needs to be filled. One way of filling this gap is suggested by organization theory (Brunsson and Jacobsson 2000). Standards can become legitimate when they incorporate credible expertise and are built on elaborate enforcement structures.

Expertise

For standards to be useful to a potential group of users, they need to incorporate expertise with a high reputation among peers and in other relevant communities. Only credible expertise allows users to solve their cognitive and normative problems. It can be relied on as a guide to effective problem-solving, and it thus reduces the search costs that a custom-made solution would imply. Also, if a user is able to refer to an established standard to justify his conduct, it is in a strong position, even when the user is held accountable for his conduct. If a standard does not define widely established practice, users referring to it are more likely to be challenged by counter expertise.

Expertise as the basis of authority of standards is what distinguishes standards from other types of rules, namely directives (which rely on the formal hierarchical legitimacy plus sanctions) and norms (which are taken for granted because they are based on accepted values) (Brunsson 1999). From this, one could conclude that the proliferation of standards is actually a sign of a shift to a technocratic rule, in which an expert elite increasingly decides on matters that have been associated with the political process (Loya and Boli 1999). But this is contradicted by the fact that global standard setting is often a politicized process in which states and non-state actors compete to promote their own interests in the standard setting process (Mattli and Büthe 2003). Arguing that standards are based on expertise does not need to deny that the process of standard setting can be politicized. The argument is merely that the politicization of standard setting is limited by the relevant expertise. A voluntary standard that is just the expression of a dominant interest, but does not convince users that it presents a solution to the problem they address, will hardly be used. The importance of expertise is shown by some common characteristics of standard-setting processes.

1   Standards are usually formulated by a limited group of experts sharing a similar professional background. Compared to the number of potential users, only few participate.
2   Decision making is exclusive, rather than inclusive. Admittedly, there are attempts to incorporate important potential users into the standard-setting process (Hallström 2004). However, probably the frequent discussions on the issue of 'user participation' are not a sign for a trend towards broader participation but rather for the difficulty of making standard-setting more inclusive.

Standard-setting processes are framed as expert-driven arguing rather than political bargaining. Gag rules seem to prohibit a mere expression of a partisan interest, be it a firm or a state. Rather, special interests have to be translated into the language of expertise. Where this is not possible, they will be irrelevant. To the extent that these observations are true, a political economy view of standard setting will be a highly selective view that risks neglecting important dimensions of the problem.

Enforcement mechanisms

The basic standardization model consisting of the interaction between standard setters and standard users can become more complex by different enforcement mechanisms. First, other standards can recommend or incorporate a certain standard. This is probably rather effective when standards form webs of mutual support. Second, standards can be institutionalized in the sense of becoming '*infuse[d] with value* beyond the technical requirements of the task at hand' (Selznick 1957: 17, emphasis in the original). This in effect turns standards into norms. This will be a very effective way of bolstering a standard, but is rather difficult to achieve because autonomous actors need to go through a long process of socialization in order that they take the validity of a rule for granted. Third, a directive can turn a formerly voluntary standard into a compulsory standard. This should be a rather effective way of enforcing standards.

In the case of norms and directives, external enforcement might give the impression that standardization itself is not important anymore, because standards have actually become either norms or directives themselves. Such a transformation of standards into other rules is possible. When standard-setting activities stop, then such a transformation has probably taken place. However, whenever standard setting continues, standards do not get transformed but rather form the core of a complex rule system. A good example is the Basel Capital Adequacy Standard. While external enforcement is important, standard-setting activities constitute the core of this rule-system.

A different possibility of enforcing standards does not concern the rule-making itself, but the institutional setting in which rule-making takes place. The basic model assumes that the standard setter, the standard user and the enforcement agents are autonomous organizations. But this need not necessarily be the case. Standard-setting activities also often occur within meta-organizations (Ahrne and Brunsson 2004). Meta-organizations are associations of autonomous organizations. For example, international organizations are meta-organizations in that they consist of autonomous, 'sovereign' member states. Most meta-organization have the competency to make rules for their members. As such, meta-organizations are similar to any type of organization. However, while organizations are effective hierarchies that permit the top to set directives for the bottom tiers, meta-organizations are much less so, because their members are themselves autonomous rule-makers. Therefore, meta-organizations are likely to resort to standards, rather than to directives. Still, compared to a mere organizational field of autonomous organizations, in meta-organizations, standard setting can be much more effective. When the standard setter is a meta-organization, it can selectively use organizational elements to impose standards on members. Also, it is easier to create a monopoly for one standard. Thus, members of a meta-organization are more likely to follow standards than non-members.

The different mechanisms by which standards can be enforced can be activated in various ways. The first way is by deliberate strategies of the standard setter himself. Standard setters can seek to enhance the effectiveness of the rules not only by bolstering their expertise. They can also seek to formulate them in such a way that certain enforcement mechanisms will be put to work. However, various enforcement mechanisms can also be activated by 'third party enforcement' meaning here simply that other actors promote standards by endorsing them.[2]

First, there are private firms, which, by auditing and certifying compliance with a certain standard, act as a deliberately designed monitoring structure (Power 1997). Second, some market players will demand that certain standards be obeyed before they agree to enter into a transaction. For example, institutional investors will only consider investing in firms that obey certain minimal standards of corporate governance. Third, another important category of actors are non-governmental organizations (NGOs). These often play an important role as watchdogs, which, by using various strategies, such as 'naming and shaming' or by provoking consumer boycotts, can force firms and even states to observe certain social and environmental standards. Fourth, a meta-organization might take over a standard in order to make it (more) mandatory for its member. Finally, another way in which standards can be enforced by third parties is through endorsement by states or other regulators who have the power to set directives. For example, in Germany technical standards are set by a private body, the most important being the Deutsche Institut für Normung, which is mostly staffed by technical experts. These private standards acquire quasi legal status because they are referred to in laws (Voelzkow 1996). Similarly, in the

European Union, standard-setting bodies produce uniform rules to reduce barriers to trade, which are then enforced by European framework directives and national law (Joerges *et al.* 1999). All of these types of third party enforcement can add up to complex, unplanned control structures, which make standards much more compelling.

Hypotheses

The literature on regulatory standards identifies the following sets of mechanisms, which can account for how standards work. These can be classified into internal and external. The internal mechanism is logically prior to the external mechanism. Only if the internal mechanisms enforce standards can they also be amplified by external enforcement mechanisms.

1 Internal preconditions for compelling standards
   Standard setting
   – Standards work if they are endowed with legitimacy. Standards acquire substantive legitimacy by expertise.
2 External preconditions for compelling standards
   Governance structure
   – Standard use is amplified if the standard setter is a meta-organization formulating rules for its members.
   Endorsement
   – Standard use is amplified by recommendation of important actors.
   – Standard use is amplified by certification, i.e. if the correct use by one actor is signalled to other actors.
   – Standard use is amplified by endorsement within other rules. Standards can be incorporated in all types of basic rules, other standards, norms, or directives.

Below, these hypotheses as well as the structure of their presentation are used to analyse and compare the two case studies.

Standards in action

How regulatory standards actually work has rarely been explored beyond single cases and sectors. As a modest start we would like to analyse two rather prominent examples of regulatory standards. The first example is the standard on sustainable banking defined by the Basel Committee for Banking Supervision (BCBS). The second example is the standard on sustainable forestry as defined by the Forest Stewardship Council (FSC). Each case already figures rather prominently in the literature. They are both examples of regulatory standards in that they are voluntary rules that address market externalities. Banking standards seek to avoid that banks engage in reckless lending and in case they fail cause other banks to fail in a chain reaction. The aim of forest standards is to prevent forest owners and timber companies from logging in such a way as to cause environmental damage. In this section, in each case the question is raised: how successful were they and why? In the next section, we compare the two cases to establish similarities and differences. Given the heterogeneity of the cases, the findings could well be valid beyond the single cases analysed.[3]

Standards for safe banking: the Basel Committee Banking Supervision (BCBS)

Any financial transaction, be it an investor buying a share or a bank lending money, is characterized by a fundamental uncertainty about the future pay-off of a present investment. Time and again investors are tempted to transform this uncertainty into risk, not by carefully calculating possible future pay-offs, but rather by estimating how others will evaluate it. If such speculation occurs on a grand scale, manias are followed by panics and crashes – with adverse economic and social consequences. But such adverse consequences are only possible if a large crowd of investors behaves that way. Banks are even more dangerous. A single bank that engages in risky lending and goes bankrupt can trigger an attempt on the part of the investors to take out their deposits. If such bank runs pass a certain threshold, they can undermine the confidence in the entire national banking system. Over time, advanced industrial states have successfully developed different regulatory systems to prevent such systemic risks (Kaufman 1995).

Deposit insurance, capital reserve requirements, and banking supervision have been designed to prevent systemic risks from materializing. This national regulation of banking and financial markets on the whole has been rather successful and has contributed to the development of financial markets and banks. However, the gradual liberalization of financial markets since the beginning of the 1970s has undermined the effectiveness of financial markets. Banks can escape national regulators by shifting risky transactions out of a demanding jurisdiction or by re-locating to the least demanding jurisdiction and, by so doing, triggering a race to the bottom in regulatory standards. At the same time that national regulation becomes less effective, the problem of bank runs becomes more severe: the possibilities of such global repercussions have become much larger with the liberalization of capital markets and the increasing number of global banking operations. In 1974, a couple of spectacular bank failures revealed some of the weaknesses of a regulatory system based on nation states in an increasingly global financial system. The most spectacular was the failure of Bankhaus Herstatt. Its failure disrupted the settlement of a large number of foreign exchange contracts, which, for its part, had prolonged repercussions (Herring and Litan 1995).

As a reaction to the problem of bank failures, concerned governments founded an international organization. In 1974, a club of states established the Basel Committee on Banking Supervision. The main mission of the Committee is to prevent the risk of bank failures and the resulting risk for financial systems of possible bank runs. This was supposed to be achieved by co-ordinating the individual national risk mitigation policies towards banks. The members of this new Committee are all states with an internationally active banking sector: Belgium, Canada, France, Germany, Italy, Japan, Luxembourg, the Netherlands, Spain, Sweden, Switzerland, the United Kingdom and the United States. Each country is represented by a member of its central bank and by a member of the banking supervisory authority. The present chairman of the Basel Banking Committee is the Governor of the Bank of Spain, Jaime Caruana, who succeeded William McDonough, President of the Federal Reserve Bank of New York, in May 2003.[4]

Standard setting

From the start, the Basel Committee was not designed to be a forum in which to negotiate legally binding international treaties on banking regulation. The Basel Committee is not a classical multilateral organization because it operates outside international law. It has no founding treaty, and it does not issue binding regulation. Its main function is to act as an informal forum to find policy solutions and to promulgate best practice standards. The fact that the Basel Committee is not in the business of issuing binding directives is not often acknowledged, but it is an essential part of the self-description of the Committee: 'The Committee does not possess any formal supranational supervisory authority, and its conclusions do not, and were never intended to, have legal force. Rather, it formulates broad supervisory standards and guidelines and recommends statements of best practice in the expectation that individual authorities will take steps to implement them through detailed arrangements – statutory or otherwise – which are best suited to their own national systems. In this way, the Committee encourages convergence towards common approaches and common standards without attempting detailed harmonization of member countries' supervisory techniques' (www.bis.org/bcbs/aboutbcbs.htm).

During its history, the Basel banking committee has issued a host of standards to make banks safer (see e.g. Kapstein 1994). The most important one was the 'Capital Adequacy Standard', issued in 1988. This standard specified the minimum capital reserves that any internationally active bank needed to retain to be safe from short term liquidity stress or even bankruptcy. The rule essentially consisted of a formula showing how to calculate the minimum amount of capital as a ratio of the liabilities of a bank (e.g. loans) and the risk involved in each liability. Banks themselves were responsible for its implementation. Banks in the European Union and in some other member states were obliged by law to follow the capital adequacy standard. Observing this standard was expensive for banks since it forced them to retain some of their capital without putting it to use. A major shortcoming of this rule was that it created an incentive for banks to do business in ways which did not require any increase in reserve capital. This type of regulatory arbitrage was one of the main reasons why the Basel banking committee embarked upon a reform process of this rule in 1999. As a result, the

Committee will abandon the old standard which defined a threshold of minimum capital reserve in favour of a new approach based on standards that give advice on how banks can manage their own risk. However, since the present reform process has not yet come to an end, the present evaluation will concentrate on the period from 1988 to 1999.

Standard usage

Many observers would probably agree that the 1988 Basel Accord has been a success story of global rule making. With over 100 countries having subscribed to it, it has far surpassed the original ten members of the BCBS that initially developed the standard (Quillin 2002). A World Bank survey found that about 90 per cent of all respondent countries report to be adhering to the Basel capital adequacy standard, with non-compliant states like Burundi, Kenya, and the Philippines – hardly important international banking centres (Ho 2002). Probably most of the banks which are internationally active are now subject to the rule. Furthermore, countries have often extended the standard to all banks, not just the ones that are internationally active. Given the difficulties of international co-operation in general and the specific problem that needed to be overcome in the case of banking regulation, this was a considerable achievement.

Admittedly, it is difficult to be sure about the effect of the Basel standard, because many additional factors impinge on the behaviour of banks. Also, in the case of the Basel accord, these difficulties are even more pronounced because of the type of data used. Studies focus on aggregate data of bank's capital reserves and neglect specific cases of reaction to the standard (Quillin 2002). This said, the picture that emerges is that the Basel standard has been rather effective in influencing banks. Judging from their balance sheets, banks did in fact increase their capital reserves. Furthermore, there has been (some) global convergence of the capital reserves of banks. However, compliance with the standard has been undermined to a certain extent by regulatory arbitrage: in order to reduce the amount of required reserve capital, banks have shifted some of their activities off the balance sheet. This was counter productive, since it actually increased the level of risk banks incurred. The evidence presented in the literature leads one to conclude that the exact nature of the effect of the Basel standard leaves some doubt, but not the effect as such.

One of the primary factors in BCBS's standards gaining such wide recognition is the quality of its expertise. The definition, specification and reform of the global banking standard is primarily the task of experts on banking and finance. The legitimacy of the rule is based on the fact that the standard is the best way to make international banks safer. The primacy of financial expertise in the rule making is shown by how standard setting works. First, experts are dominant in all phases of standard setting. Studies and drafts of new rules are prepared in numerous sub-committees staffed by experts from the public and the private sector. The final decision is then taken by the Basel Committee on banking Supervision, which consists of representatives of the national banking regulators from the member states. Thus, they are not diplomats negotiating the national interest on behalf of their governments, but rather public servants proposing rules to the world public on how banking could be made safer. Second, the output itself shows the high level of expertise involved in the rules. The rules do not read like a legal text but rather like a work of consultancy in a highly complex technical area. Also, the rules are not binding, signalling that the Basel standards were not devised under the authority of governments and are not intended to be implemented by ratification (Basel Committee 2006). Third, many of the Basel proposals are widely discussed among regulatory and academic experts, showing not only the degree of expertise involved but also the impeccable reputation the Basel Banking Committee enjoys.[5] The high reputation is also underlined by the fact that there are no serious competitors in standard setting for banks. The Basel banking committee holds an undisputed monopoly in this area.

Governance structure

Decision-making within the BCBS is organized as a rather exclusive club. Although the BCBS standards have a global outreach, only a very limited number of countries are members. The Committee consists of representatives from the member state's banking watchdogs, i.e. mostly financial regulators and central banks. Experts from these institutions work in numerous technical sub-committees to draft the standards. These standards are adopted by the Committee, once the consensus of all members has been reached (voting or bargaining do not play a role). The common ground for the members is the expertise underlying the standard. Typically, the national interest has to be formulated in the language of the expertise underlying the standard. In the case of the capital adequacy rules for banks, national delegations typically do not seek 'derogations', i.e. amendments that alleviate hardship, but rather they argue that a standard needs to be modified to do justice to specific national circumstances. This is shown by the German experience. German representatives felt that the obligations of the standard in its original version were harmful to its banking sector and the economy at large. However, to obtain corrections, the German representatives in the Committee had to argue that the standard was not adapted to the specific German situation and should be improved to define the capital reserves more appropriately. The obligation to argue for changes in the language of expertise, in contrast to simply demanding derogations to prevent national disadvantages, effectively excluded some of the demands voiced by the German banking industry (interview, Federal Financial Supervisory Authority (2001)).

Endorsement

The enforcement structure of the Basel standard is rather well documented. The major enforcement mode is the implementation of the Basel Accord by national bank regulators. At present, there are over 100 countries in which banking regulators have made the observation of capital reserve requirements as defined by the Basel banking committee compulsory (Ho 2002). The standard can be transposed into law (EU), or the law can directly refer to the standard (e.g. Korea). Often, enforcement by national regulators goes beyond the minimum requirements of the standards. One study examining the degree of implementation of the Basel accord finds that in a sample of 26 countries, a large majority of 23 imposed a stricter standard than the accord calls for (Quillin 2002). For example, all banks registered in a member state of the EU have to observe the Basel standard, not just the internationally active banks, for which the standard was originally designed. Another enforcement mechanism at work is the IMF's policy of conditional lending. In the aftermath of the financial crisis of the 1990s, the IMF often granted large loans to countries for stabilization purposes. However, according to a long-standing policy, these loans are granted only if reform measures were adopted. An increasingly important IMF demand was that global standards for financial markets be observed by the country in difficulty. In the case of Korea, the IMF insisted that banks should shore up their capital reserves as demanded by the Basel Accord. Finally, financial market information intermediaries play a role. Credit rating agencies evaluating the creditworthiness of banks or of states assign a lower rating if the Basel standard is not observed. This in turn leads to higher borrowing costs on the capital market.

Standards for sustainable forest management: the Forest Stewardship Council

Regulatory standards appear in different forms and fields. In order to expand our findings beyond the BCBS case, we selected a second one from another field and in a different form: the Forest Stewardship Council (FSC). But before going into the characteristics of the FSC standards, their origin will be shortly elucidated.

The issue of deforestation hit the international political agenda in the early 1980s (Humphreys 1996). At that time it became clear that for several reasons – commercial logging, cultivation of agrarian lands, mining activities, building of infrastructure, large-scale burning, unjust land rights, etc. – huge areas of forests had disappeared. Special attention was drawn to the tropical forests, and the region of Amazonia in Brazil in particular. Figures – although always contested – pointed at an area of forests of the size of the Benelux which disappeared in this region each year (Kolk 1996). Later on, deforestation in other countries (Canada, Ivory Coast, Russia) and other types of 'endangered' forests (boreal forests, ancient forests in general) became part of the agenda. In addition, it became clear that forest regulation at national level, particularly in developing countries, was weak or side-stepped by illegal practices. Even at the international level, hardly any governance structure for 'good' forest management was present at that time. As a consequence, forestry in many areas of the world resembled a sort of 'wild west' economy, where legality and sustainability considerations were more or less absent.

These problems led to a number of responses. First, NGOs like Greenpeace,

WWF and the World Rainforest Movement started world-wide campaigns to stop these practices. Second, timber importing and exporting countries established the International Timber Trade Organization (ITTO) in 1986, to deal with trade problems as well as environmental issues, and launched the voluntary ITTO 2000 target. This target aimed at basing the entire global timber trade on sustainable forestry principles in the year 2000, but it obviously failed (Kern *et al.* 2001). In addition, attempts of NGOs to collaborate with the ITTO, for example on a forest certification programme, were not successful either, as this intergovernmental organization was reluctant to co-operate with NGOs. And third, governments in the United Nations decided that a global forest treaty to enhance conservation and sustainable management should be decided upon. However, this initiative also became a failure, due to fierce contradictions between developed and developing countries, the former emphasizing the need to conserve (tropical) forests, the latter the need to exploit them for economic reasons (Humphreys 1996).

In the meantime, given these regulatory failures, several environmental organizations had expressed their wish to do business with industry on sustainable forestry themselves. As one NGO-leader said: 'You cannot just sit back and wait for governments to agree, because this could take forever' (Bendel and Murphy 2000: 69). For example WWF started a dialogue with industry under the slogan *Forests are your business* in the UK in 1991 (Bendel 2000). At the global level, similar developments – dialogues between NGOs and industry – took place. In 1993, 150 organizations from the business sector, the environmental sector and the human rights movement founded the Forest Stewardship Council (FSC) in Toronto (Kern *et al.* 2001; Meidinger 2002). Today, its headquarters are in Bonn, Germany. The main merit of the council is the design of a forest certification programme, based on general values, guidelines and criteria, on national standards as well as on a trademark.

Standard setting

The overall aim of the FSC is to stop large-scale deforestation and unsustainable forestry around the world by defining and certifying those management practices which enhance the conservation and sustainable use of forests (Meidinger 2002). The FSC system is based on ten principles: forest management; property rights; rights of the local community; labour rights; sustainability; ecology and biodiversity; planning; control of adverse social and ecological effects; conservation of forests with high ecological value; and plantation. These principles are elaborated upon in a number of more practical criteria. After certification, forest owners and timber producers may use the FSC trademark, so that wood processors, retailers and consumers can recognize this timber. With that, the FSC promotes sustainable forestry through the market mechanism.

It should be realized that the FSC *itself* is not a standard. In fact, it is an accreditation organization, which endorses national standards for sustainable forest management in cases where these match the FSC principles and criteria.

These national standards are then used to certify forest owners and companies in the country concerned. FSC standardization can follow two routes, the local or the global (Kern *et al.* 2001). Either national sustainable forestry standards can be developed, e.g. by national NGOs and businesses (and eventually in co-operation with governments), which at a later stage apply for FSC accreditation, or national standardization groups immediately take the global FSC principles and guidelines as the starting point to formulate their own standard, adapted to national circumstances. Besides the accreditation of national initiatives and standards, the FSC also operates as an accreditation organization for certifiers and verifiers (Cashore 2002; Kern *et al.* 2001). In order to gain credibility, an independent certification and verification system has been set up by the FSC. This means that monitoring of compliance is undertaken by independent private organizations. So far, the council has accredited 13 independent bodies, from KPMG in Canada, SKAL in the Netherlands to Smart Wood in the USA (source: www.fsc.org).

Standard usage

As Kern *et al.* (2001: 38–39) note: 'The FSC has emerged as a considerable force in the world-wide diffusion of forest certification. [. . .] From a global perspective, the certification result can be seen as a success.' The global diffusion process has been especially accelerated since 1995. It started in Mexico in 1991, where a forest area of nearly 90,000 ha. was certified by Smartwood, which was brought under the label of the FSC after its foundation in 1995. Similar practices took place in the USA and Costa Rica in 1992. In the period from 1995 to 1997, just after the establishment of the FSC, several European countries acted as pioneers in this field: the Netherlands, Poland, Sweden, Italy and the UK. Since then, the FSC has diffused world-wide. Today, about 500 forest areas in 55 countries have been certified, in total 37 million ha., which is eight times the size of the Netherlands (source: www.fsc.org). In some countries, the forest area certified exceeds the size of 25 per cent of the total area (e.g. Sweden, Poland and UK). At the same time, about 3,500 companies were certified world-wide. And to give an impression of its growth potential in Western Europe: about 4 per cent of the Dutch market in wood and timber, both primary and secondary products, was FSC certified in 1999. This figure rose to 8 per cent in 2003.

Yet one should not exaggerate the FSC's success. First of all, a market share below 10 per cent in all countries involved (and below 1 per cent in most of these) still implies a marginal economic position of FSC-labelled products. Second, many forests which have been certified are maintained under Western forest management practices, which were already rather sustainable, as in Sweden. Consequently, FSC certification did not add much to common practice, so that the 'depth' of the standard can be doubted. Third, FSC finds difficulty in widely diffusing in developing countries, where problems of deforestation are the most severe. In most Third World countries, certified forest areas do not generally exceed 1 per cent of the total area (with an exception of Costa Rica).

Fourth, (western) consumers have difficulty in finding their way to FSC labelled products, because they lack knowledge of the FSC trademark or are confronted with shortage of supply. Also, the higher prices of such products do not, of course, stimulate consumers to buy these. Finally, the FSC standard has been challenged by other forest standards. One example is the Sustainable Forestry Initiative (SFI) of the American Forest and Chapter Association (Cashore 2002). Another is the Programme for the Endorsement of Forest Certification Schemes (PEFC), initiated by European forest owners and companies and designed in the context of the inter-governmental Pan-European Helsinki process (Meidinger 2002). In total, some 15 certification programmes have been established worldwide.

It is obvious that the usage, diffusion and (relative) success of the FSC cannot be understood from the perspective of market co-ordination standards. After all, it is hard to understand why producers and consumers would follow the FSC, given their self-interests. Producers would be confronted with higher production costs, given all requirements for responsible forest management, and consumers would not get better products in terms of quality and price, as a FSC-labelled wooden chair is qualitatively similar to a non-labelled one, whereas prices are generally much higher. Therefore, the FSC cannot be considered a co-ordination standard. Instead, we need to conceptualize it as a regulatory production chain standard, addressing the quality of production processes.

As was outlined in the above, the usage of regulatory standards can, according to organization theory, best be understood from a legitimacy perspective. Regulatory standards will be used in case these are considered legitimate by the target groups (and wider audiences). Credible expertise is the main source of such legitimacy (see also Auld and Bull 2003; Cashore 2002; Meidinger 2002). It is beyond doubt that the FSC certification programme is built on much expertise. The council brings together technical knowledge from the business sector, environmental knowledge from the NGO community and social as well as local knowledge from human rights and indigenous people's groups. As Meidinger (2002: 18) notes: 'The field is at least as powerfully shaped by the professional view of foresters and ecologists as are state-based regulatory systems – perhaps more so'. Also, practice has shown that FSC standards deliver: timber can be produced according to the FSC principles and guidelines and, moreover, in a profitable, environmentally sound and socially desirable way.

Yet, the quality of the expertise of the FSC has been contested from the very beginning. Mainstream industry has challenged the appropriateness and cognitive legitimacy of the FSC standard for forest management (Auld and Bull 2003). The reason was that the FSC has been regarded as an NGO (read WWF) initiative by most forest industries. From their perspective, the programme has been based on environmental and social ethics rather than on expertise with regard to economically viable forestry. As a consequence, FSC standards have been challenged by other business-type standards, which claim to be closer to the reality of mainstream forestry business and, hence, are thought to incorporate more relevant and practical knowledge. Examples were mentioned in the above (SFI and PEFC).[6]

Governance structure

The FSC exhibits a unique democratic governance structure (Auld and Bull 2003; Meidinger 2002). The core decision-making body is the General Assembly, with three chambers – economic, social, environment – and with a Northern and Southern section in each of these. All these chambers and sections have equal voting rights. As far as membership is concerned, all interested and concerned organizations and individuals are eligible (in principle). With that, the FSC functions as a multi-stakeholder organization, which sets rules for sustainable forestry. The standards themselves, though, are set by national associations and, subsequently, endorsed (or not) by the General Assembly. Consequently, the system comes close to a multi-level governance system, or federalism, with central review, national standard-setting and regional harmonization as its central elements (Hooghe and Marks 2001; Meidinger 2002).

Whereas policy-making is covered by the General Assembly and standard-setting by national associations, policy implementation and standard enforcement is covered by other bodies, or so-called third parties. In order to be able to monitor and enforce compliance with FSC rules in a credible and trustworthy way, an independent system has been set up. As was already noted in the above, certification and verification are undertaken by independent private organizations, accredited by the FSC. These check and monitor whether users of the standards and trademark – forest owners and timber producers – meet, and continue to meet, the principles, guidelines and criteria. If not, their certification may be withdrawn. All in all, the governance structure of the FSC contributes to the overall legitimacy of the certification programme, which is the ultimate reason why producers and consumers are prepared to follow its rules.

Endorsement

The certifying and auditing bodies comprise the main enforcement structure of the FSC standard. However, that is only one side of the story. The other consists of (some) governments, 'buyers' groups and environmental NGOs who endorse the use of the FSC standard (Boström 2003; Cashore 2002; Kern *et al.* 2001). Several governments, for example, have adopted the 2000 target of the International Timber Trade Organization (ITTO). True, this target has not been achieved at all, but it has made governments more sensitive towards the issue. Also, governments as forest owners have adopted FSC rules themselves in a number of cases (e.g. in Mexico and Switzerland). Some even go as far as to prepare legislation which binds importers of timber and wood to inform consumers about the sustainability of its products, the Netherlands being one example. And some governments have become directly involved in the national FSC standardization processes themselves, Indonesia and Sweden being two examples (Boström 2003; Cashore 2002). Besides governments, NGOs have promoted the label, although through different mechanisms and by tactics other than states. For example, environmental groups like Greenpeace, Friends of the

Earth and WWF have pressured forest owners and companies to adopt the FSC standard. They have also put pressure on retailers and shops to take up FSC wood and FSC-labelled products in their assortments, so that consumers can actually buy those goods. All these examples of external endorsement have contributed to the (relative) success and legitimacy of the FSC.

Comparing standardization strategies

At first sight, a comparison of the FSC's forest management standards and the BCBS's standard for risk management of banks seemed to be far-fetched. Yet, there are a number of important similarities (see Table 1). First of all, both standards are regulative standards: although making use of the market mechanism, they are not market co-ordination standards with in-built incentives for users. Therefore both standard-setters rely on a number of different mechanisms that make them compelling. Both the BCBS as well as the FSC take great care to safeguard the integrity of the expertise and actively promote third party enforcement. Second, and thanks to these mechanisms, both standards have a considerable group of users, in spite of being formulated as voluntary rules. Almost all internationally-active banks as well many firms in the timber supply chain now adhere to the global standards addressed to them. Hence, both standards are rather successful (although to a different degree, see below). Third, both standard-setters have set rules because global regulation by binding law failed for various reasons. The BCBS was designed as a forum which would allow the harmonization of national banking supervision. The FSC originated from NGO campaigns against deforestation and was an explicit attempt to create rules where states failed.

At the same time, we should acknowledge the differences between the two standards as well. For example, whereas the BCBS standard was designed by

Table 1 Comparison of BCBS and FSC standards

Standards	BCBS	FSC
Type	Regulation standards; organizational management standards; no logo and trademark	Regulation standards; production chain standards; include a logo and trademark
Setting	Standards are set by the BCBS, it functions as a meta-organization	Standards are set by local organizations; FSC functions as an accreditation organization
Usage	>100 countries; international *and* national banks; legitimacy through expertise	>500 forest areas; about 37 m. ha.; about 3,500 companies; 55 countries; legitimacy through expertise and moral authority
Governance structure	Exclusive standard-setting; professional elitism	Inclusive standard-setting; pluralism; federalism
Endorsement	National and internal law; third parties (governments, IMF, rating agencies)	Certification programme; third parties (NGOs, buyer's groups, governments)

experts from member states' administrations alone (with input and endorsement of governments and industry), the FSC certification programme and its national standards have been designed by alliances of NGOs and business organizations. Here the input of civil society has been huge. In addition, the BCBS standard applies to financial management processes in banks, whereas the FSC standards apply to the environmental and social quality of the timber production chain. Also, BCBS as a standard does not include a logo nor a trademark, which is the case for the FSC. With that, FSC also addresses individual consumers. Finally, the governance structures differ substantially. Whereas the BCBS is a meta-organization characterized by exclusive, elitist standard-setting, the FSC exhibits characteristics of more inclusive, pluralist and federalist forms of governance.

Explaining performance

The success of the two standards is surprising, since both standards are not co-ordination standards. Nevertheless, in comparison, the BCBS is much more successful than the FSC. This is revealed by the figures on the geographic spread presented in the previous section. While 90 per cent of the countries around the globe adhere to the BCBS standard, less than one third acknowledge the FSC. Moreover, the BCBS standard is often applied to all banking activities in a country, whereas the FSC is just an option, in addition to non-certification or competing standards.

Given the structural similarities between the FSC and the BCBS, what explains their performance differences? As shown in the theoretical section, organization theory identifies two key sets of variables as success factors for standardization. The expertise base of standards and the way they are enforced are considered essential. The higher the quality of expertise and the more elaborate the enforcement structure, the higher the probability that standards will be followed. Taking these factors into consideration, a comparison seems to lead to the conclusion that the BCBS is superior to the FSC on both accounts. Not only has the BCBS formulated standards of best practice for the risk management of banks that have gone unchallenged, these standards have also been enforced by its member states through law and compulsory rules of regulatory agencies. The FSC, by contrast, has neither formulated undisputed standards nor has it been enforced by states with similar rigor. Thus, the BCBS seems to be clearly superior to the FSC in these respects.

However, a closer look reveals that this conclusion might be premature. Regarding the enforcement structure, the differences between the FSC and the BCBS are easily exaggerated. On the one hand it is important to note that BCBS standards have only partially been enforced by states. Often enforcement is restricted to internationally active banks. In addition, there is a second group that was under no legal obligation to adopt the Basel banking standard, and did so anyway. Here the structure of third party enforcement is similar to that of the FSC. For example, institutional investors and rating agencies put these banks under pressure to adhere to the safety standard. The same holds true for NGOs that pressured all types of agents in the timber production chain to adhere to the FSC standard. On the other hand, the FSC was also partially endorsed by states (although admittedly not to the same extent). Thus, the differences regarding the enforcement of standards are smaller than a superficial impression suggests. Yet these nonetheless exist and may partly explain the level of success.

However, the main difference between the two modes of standardization does not exist with respect to enforcement, but rather with respect to expertise and legitimacy. Whereas the BCBS has uncontested authority in setting banks' safety standards, the FSC has not yet acquired comparable authority. In fact, whereas there is only one safety standard for banks, there are several standards for sustainable forest management. This leads to a comparatively weaker authority base for the FSC. In order to compensate for this, the FSC has to actively engage in other sources of legitimacy as well as in building other enforcement structures, especially to muster the support of NGOs. This in turn creates a dilemma: the standard cannot be designed to maximize the number of firms adhering to the scheme, without jeopardizing the support of the NGOs (see Cashore 2002). This is shown by attempts to build coalitions of FSC standards with other standards. For example in Switzerland, the FSC label has been fused with the industry's 'Q-label' (Kern *et al.* 2001). By so watering down its standard, the FSC risks alienating the support of some NGOs.

Conclusion

This chapter started with the observation that regulators – public and private – increasingly resort to standards. The increasing use of voluntary rules raises important questions: 'Why should sovereign states or powerful transnational companies follow them?' and 'Why should standards be an adequate answer in cases in which binding regulation by law fails?' In order to provide answers to these questions, the chapter then subsequently develops a framework and designs a number of hypotheses to explain how standards work. The focus is on regulatory standards, i.e. voluntary rules that address all kinds of public policy issues. The framework is subsequently used to analyse two different sets of standards, the BCBS's risk management standards for banks and the FSC's sustainable forest management standards.

First and foremost, the analysis shows that – although both cases analysed are regulatory standards and are therefore not self-enforcing – they have had considerable effects. Due to the expertise-based nature of the rules and the elaborate enforcement structure they have become rather compelling. Both the BCBS and the FSC are built on high quality expertise as well as on elaborated systems of third-party enforcement. With that, the cases show how standards can be a significant form of regulation beyond the rather narrow issue of co-ordination. This suggests that standards should be taken seriously. They are a viable form of regulation in their own right.

Second, the framework and the subsequent analysis have mainly pointed at the importance of sound expertise for the success of regulatory standards.

Probably the main reason for the success of the risk management standard for banks has been its undisputed expertise. In contrast, the case of the forest management standard shows that, although it is built on expertise as well, it lacks credibility for several potential users, particularly mainstream industry. In our view, the success of standards mainly depends on the reputation of the experts in the standard-setting body.

Furthermore, it also depends on the number of standard setting bodies. The smaller the number of standards produced that address the same problem, the higher the probability of their use. This is not a trivial condition, as there is often a multitude of bodies producing standards in the same issue area. This can be an advantage to circumvent decision-making deadlocks (Genschel 1997; Princen 2006). However, as the number of standards increases, firms will become less enthusiastic about using them. A high number of different standards regarding the same problem reduces the guidance standards offer and the normative support for following a specific standard. This is exactly the case for FSC, with about 15 competing standards in the field. In contrast, the BCBS is the only one standard in its issue area.

If the above analysis is correct, two implications for reforming standard-based governance follow. As a remedy to supposedly ineffective voluntary standards, it is frequently proposed that they should be turned into binding laws instead. An example in this respect is the plan to convert the UN's voluntary global compact into global directives (source: *Financial Times*, 12 August 2003). From the perspective of the results of our case study, this is not necessarily a good strategy, since regulators often choose voluntary standards precisely because of anticipated or real problems with directives. This is most obvious in the case of forest management. The FSC came on the scene precisely because it grew impatient with the regulatory failure in the UN (as well as in the ITTO). Our results suggest that a better alternative would be to strengthen standards instead, either by improving the expertise upon which they are based or third party enforcement.

The analysis presented also has theoretical implications. First, the importance of expertise contradicts views of regulatory standards as primarily enforced by market processes. Instead, they suggest that market enforcement is a secondary mechanism that has at its basis the primary mechanism of expertise. Also, they point at functional equivalents to market enforcement, i.e. various forms of endorsement by other regulators (among them in compulsory legal provisions). The importance of expertise also puts into question a political economy view of standards that sees standard setting as a political game only (Mattli and Büthe 2003). This is not to deny that in the process of standard setting interests play a role. Yet, an outright politicization would probably thoroughly undermine the effectiveness of regulatory standards.

Second, and more importantly in the context of this volume, the findings raise the question, whether the rationalist 'legalization approach' is fruitful for conceptualizing global regulation by voluntary rules (see also Finnemore and Toope 2001). The 'legalization approach' mainly identifies a trend towards law-like rule-making and enforcement by courts (Abbott and Snidal 2000) and conceptualizes standards as a softer kind of international law, which might be less precise, carries lower formal obligations and has a less developed judicial enforcement structure. This conceptual strategy of assimilating soft law to hard law can be problematic. In the cases analysed, 'soft law' follows a different logic of rule-making than hard law. They show that voluntary rules are based on authority and enforcement mechanisms which are different to law. It would therefore be better to identify law and standards as different types of global rule-making rather than subsuming the former under the latter.

The analysis thus corroborates the criticism that the 'legalization approach' neglects the 'differentiation of legal and law-like arrangements' (Brütsch and Lehmkuhl in Chapter 2 of this volume). Furthermore, it has offered a conceptual framework for analysing some of the 'law-like arrangements' of the real world. In this chapter, we have employed what could be called a 'regulation approach' consisting of different categories of transnational rules. Additional variation is introduced by different enforcement mechanisms of these rules. We hope that this approach possesses the requisite variety to deal with the bewildering complexity of rule-making beyond the state (see Koenig-Archibugi 2002).

Notes

1 We want to thank Sebastiaan Princen for having clarified this point.
2 We borrow the term 'third party enforcement' from Barzel (2000), but disregard its roots in contract theory.
3 It goes without saying that due to the heterogeneous nature of the cases these statements will be hypothesis only.
4 See the website of the Bank for International Settlements at www.bis.org.
5 For the impact of the Basel Committee rules see professional journals for financial analysts such as *The Financial Regulator* or the German *Risikomanager*.
6 It should be acknowledged that besides an assumed lack of expertise, other arguments have played a role in the mainstream forest industry's desire to develop its own alternative standards. On the one hand, it has realized that it should do something to tackle the forest crisis and to please the critical consumer in the West. On the other hand, it has considered the FSC standard far too strict, demanding too much organizational change, especially regarding forest management practices in the Third World, thus limiting 'easy' profit-making from forestry.

References

Abbott, K.W. and Snidal, D. (2000) 'Hard and Soft Law in International Governance', *International Organization*, 54: 421–456.
Abbott, W.A., Keohane, R.O., Moravcsik, A., Slaughter, A.-M. and Snidal, D. (2000) 'The Concept of Legalization', *International Organization*, 54, 401–419.
Ahrne, G. and Brunsson, N. (2004) 'Soft Regulation from an Organizational Perspective', in: U. Mörth (ed.) *Soft Law in Governance and Regulation: An Interdisciplinary Analysis*, Cheltenham: Edward Elgar.
Auld, G. and Bull, G.Q. (2003) 'The Institutional Design of Forest Certification Standards Initiatives and its Influence on the Role of Science: The Case of Forest Genetic Resources', *Journal of Environmental Management*, 69: 47–62.

Barzel, Y. (2000) 'The State and the Diversity of Third-Party Enforcers', in: C. Ménard (ed.) *Institutions, Contracts and Organizations. Perspectives from the New Institutional Economics*, Cheltenham: Edward Elgar.

Basel Committee on Banking Supervision (BCBS) (2006) *International Convergence of Capital Measurement and Capital Standards: A Revized Framework – Comprehensive Version*, Basel: Bank for International Settlements www.bis.org/publ/bcbs128.pdf).

Bendel, J. and Murphy, D. (2000) 'Planting the Seeds of Change: Business–NGO Relations on Tropical Deforestation', in: J. Bendel (ed.) *Terms of Endearment: Business, NGOs and Sustainable Development*, Sheffield: Greenleafe Publications.

Bendel, J. (ed.) (2000) *Terms of Endearment: Business, NGOs and Sustainable Development*, Sheffield: Greenleafe Publications.

Boström, M. (2003) 'How state-dependent is a non-state-driven rule-making project? The case of forest certification in Sweden', *Journal of Environmental Policy and Planning*, 5: 165–180.

Braithwaite, J. and Drahos, P. (2000) *Global Business Regulation*, Cambridge: Cambridge University Press.

Brunsson, N. and Jacobsson, B. (2000) *A World of Standards*, Oxford: Oxford University Press.

Brunsson, N. (1999) 'Standardization as Organization', in: M. Egeberg and P. Laegreid (eds) *Organizing Political Institutions: Essays for Johan P. Olsen*, Oslo: Scandinavian University Press.

Cashore, B. (2002) 'Legitimacy and the Privatization of Environmental Governance: How Non-State Market-Driven (NSMD) Governance Systems Gain Rule-making Authority', *Governance*, 15: 503–529.

Federal Finanacial Supervisory Authority (2001) Interview, Bonn, Germany, May 2001.

Financial Times (2003) 'UN aims to scrutinise multinationals', 12 August 2003.

Finnemore, M. and Toope, S. (2001) 'Alternatives to "Legalization": Richer Views of Law and Politics', *International Organization*, 55: 743–758.

Genschel, Ph. (1997) 'How Fragmentation Can Improve Co-ordination: Setting Standards in International Telecommunications', *Organization Studies*, 18: 603–622.

Hallström, K.T. (2004) *Organizing International Standardization: ISO and the IASC in Quest of Authority*, Cheltenham: Edward Elgar.

Herring, R.J. and Litan, R.E. (1995) *Financial Regulation in the Global Economy*, Washington D.C.: Brookings Institution.

Ho, D.E. (2002): 'Compliance and International Soft Law: Why Do Countries Implement the Basle Accord?' *Journal of International Economic Law*, 5: 647–688.

Hooghe, L. and Marks, G. (2001) *Multi-level Governance and European Integration*, Lanham: Rowman and Littlefield.

Humphreys, D. (1996) *Forest Politics: The Evolution of International Cooperation*, London: Earthscan.

Joerges, Ch., Schepel, H. and Vos, E. (1999) *The Law's Problem with the Involvement of Non-Governmental Actors in Europe's Legislative Processes: The Case of Standardization Under the 'New Approach'*, Florence: European University Institute.

Kapstein, E.B. (1994) *Governing the Global Economy: International Finance and the State*, Cambridge, MA: Harvard University Press.

Kaufman, G.G. (ed.) (1995), *Banking, Financial Markets, and Systemic Risk*, Greenwich: JAI Publishers.

Koenig-Archibugi, M. (2002) 'Mapping Global Governance', in: D. Held and A.

McGrew (eds) *Governing Globalization: Power, Authority and Global Governance*, Cambridge, Cambridge University Press.

Kern, K., Kissling-Näf, I., Landmann, U. and Mauch, C. (2001) *Policy Convergence and Policy Diffusion by Governmental and Non-Governmental Institutions – An International Comparison of Eco-Labeling Systems*, Berlin: WZB Discussion Paper.

Kolk, A. (1996) *Forests in International Environmental Politics*, Utrecht: International Books.

Loya, Th.A. and Boli, J. (1999) 'Standardization in the World Polity: Technical Rationality Over Power', in: J. Boli and G.M. Thomas (eds) *Constructing World Culture: International Nongovernmental Organizations since 1875*, Stanford: Stanford University Press.

Mattli, W. and Büthe, T. (2003) 'Setting International Standards: Technological Rationality or Primacy of Power?' *World Politics*, 56: 1–42.

Meidinger, E.E. (2002) *Law Making by Global Civil Society: The Forest Certification Prototype*, Revised Paper Prepared for the International Conference on Social and Political Dimensions of Forest Certification, University of Freiburg, Germany, June 2001.

Nadvi, K. and Wältring, F. (2004) 'Making Sense of Global Standards', in: H. Schmitz (ed.) *Local Enterprises in the Global Economy*, Cheltenham: Edward Elgar.

Power, M. (1997) *The Audit Society: Rituals of Verification*, Oxford: Oxford University Press.

Princen, S. (2006) 'Governing through Multiple Forums: The Global Safety Regulation of Genetically Modified Crops and Foods, in: M. Koenig-Archibugi and M. Zürn (eds) *New Modes of Governance in the Global System: Exploring Publicness, Delegation and Inclusiveness*, Houndmills: Palgrave.

Quillin, B. (2002) *Understanding Degrees of Compliance with the 1988 Basel Accord*, Paper Prepared for Presentation to the 2002 UK Political Studies Association Annual Conference, London: London School of Economics.

Selznick, Ph. (1957) *Leadership in Administration: A Sociological Interpretation*, Evanston: Row, Peterson and Company.

Voelzkow, H. (1996) Private Regierungen in der Techniksteuerung: Eine Sozialwissenschaftliche Analyse der technischen Normung, Frankfurt: Campus Verlag.

Werle, R. (1995) 'Staat und Standards', in: R. Mayntz and F.W. Scharpf (eds) *Gesellschaftliche Selbstregelung und Politische Steuerung*, Frankfurt: Campus Verlag.

9 International standards

Functions and links to law[1]

Erich Schanze

Introduction

In the famous article on the basic design of legal rules, Calabresi and Melamed refer to Monet's cycle of paintings of the Cathedral of Rouen.[2] The circumspection of a monumental object in the turn of the sunlight displays the whole cosmos of forms and colours. For the equally famous 18 haystacks, Monet is quoted to have intended 'to fix a genuine impression of a certain aspect of nature'. The 'nature' of the relation of law and the associated extra-legal norms such as standards or codified practices is rather vague. An exploration by circumspection may be an adequate approach in this matter.

I will first try to explore a number of views concerning the relevance of extra-legal norms for law. Then I will describe a variety of 'linkage mechanisms' between law and extra-legal norms which can be found in a number of technical contexts of law – so-called 'reference norms'.[3] All reference norms are styled from a legal centrist perspective, that of a judge who has to determine whether and to what extent a specific extra-legal norm can be 'included' in the legal considerations for reaching an equitable result in a given conflict. The legal centrist perspective starts from the premise that extra-legal norms are relevant only to the extent a legal norm provides for them to be 'included' in the legal system. This perspective is essentially a backward-looking one, taking both legal and extra-legal norms for granted and using legal norms to determine their reciprocal relevance. At this point, I will try to expand the path of circumspection to a radically different viewpoint. I will argue that we might gain new insights into the relation of law and extra-legal norms by looking at it from a drafting perspective.[4] In what light do draftspersons develop and use extra-legal norms such as standards, guidelines or codes of practice? What are the working tools and building blocks? Where and to what extent do they consider limitations of their production? This perspective swaps the backward-looking view for a forward-looking perspective, largely uncommon to Continental European legal systems.[5] To be sure, the legal centrist view and the drafting view do not exclude each other. They are complementary perspectives of a complex relationship in the present system of economic governance, both of which merit our attention.

Some current views on the relationship between law and standards

The analysis of the relation of standards and law is perplexing because there is little consensus about the province of both modalities of ordering.[6] I will list three views, and then turn to a fourth perspective, that of a draftsperson concerned with a regime design of international transactions. To illustrate the choices, I will look at 'neighbouring' governance structures – hoping that the affinity will produce some insights as to why and how standards are 'produced' and 'used' and how conflicts with the legal order (in a narrower sense) are aligned there.

Lawyers usually assume that they operate with clear cut definitions of law. However, once they reach the area of complex economic regulation (what Europeans term 'economic law') they realize a need for surprising extensions of a legal centrist position.

The 'realist' economic law perspective

Obviously, a textbook on 'economic law' needs a definition of its subject matter. Looking at the conventional sources of law making, including parliamentary legislation, constitutionally delegated law making by government authorities on various levels etc. did not capture what 'courts do in fact'[7] in the area of economic regulation. Therefore, Mertens/Kirchner/Schanze turned the issue from the 'sources of law' aspect to a 'law-in-action' analysis.[8] The latter concerns the exploration of all rules relevant for decision making. What would a judge or a regulator consider to be relevant for decisions in individual cases? Realistically, she or he would not only look at those rules which are 'official sources of law' but also at the extra-legal norms which structure the relevant transactions. Thus we arrived at a 'pragmatic' extension of classical law including, inter alia, the 'relevant' practices, guidelines and technical standards. Hence we considered 'standards' as a part of 'economic law'.[9] Relevance alone, however, may lead into a full circle. Obviously, an inclusion mechanism has to be named that 'legitimizes' the reference.

The international governance perspective

Whereas our definition starts from the centrist ('constitutional') national law view by stretching it to include the 'relevant' aspects of social ordering, the influential analysis of Abbot and Snidal[10] starts from the other end by defining standards broadly as 'guides for behaviour or for judging behaviour'. Naturally, they have no problem including the important instance of standard setting. This would be trivial where a standard is 'incorporated' by legislation or other forms of legitimate recognition in the classical concept of law, be it national law or public international law.

Abbot and Snidal share, in part, Ellickson's basic notion that 'law' is largely inoperative, if it is separated from – what Ellickson calls – the 'social norms'.[11] A related concept may be found in Eric Posner's recent 'Law and Social Norms', where he broadly refers to social norms as behavioural regularities which actors observe in order to show that they are desirable partners of cooperative endeavours.[12] In a world of transacting, 'compliance' with 'standards' signals that these conditions are met. However, it is noteworthy that 'standards' or 'social norms' are of relevance in this concept, not because of their very substance but because of the credibility players gain by incurring the costs of observing these norms. Later, I will also return to the issue of 'compliance' as a general norm of legitimizing extra-legal norms and will put it in the centre of my analysis.

Obviously, an approach starting from the 'social norm' side is less interested in a clear-cut definition of law and extra-legal norms, and it does not provide a complete answer as to why decision-makers resort to extra-legal norms. The emphasis is, as Abbott and Snidal state, on the general problem of internalizing externalities by appropriate governance structures, be they technically 'legal' or 'non-legal'.

The new institutional economics perspective

The aforementioned international transaction perspective is related to the analysis of the function of institutions by the neo-institutional school of economics. In their standard text, Richter and Furubotn[13] stress that markets do not work as abstractions; rather, they operate in a complex setting of 'elementary operational rules and prescriptions'. In this view, opposing the neo-classical perspective, a set of institutions is not only a 'second-best' surrogate for the price mechanism of the market, but the very foundation of it. These preconditions of transacting in an economy based on property rights not only include the stipulation of the property rights themselves for the transaction partners but also a long list of further preconditions, including language and writing; ethical values; the numerical system; measures and weights; time and its units; money; means of communication and transport; legal norms, plus the mini-rules of technical market order concerning the variety of goods and services at the various locations. In the list, a number of preconditions may qualify as 'standards', although their origin and relevance may not fully comply with the procedural elements stressed by Abbot and Snidal. The institutional economics perspective is concerned with all facilitating and restraining factors (and their 'economics'). They are eligible or unavoidable 'frames' for real market choices influencing the outcomes significantly ('institutions matter'). In essence, this spectrum of market framing norms deals, in a normative sense, with the general problem of internalizing externalities, or even more broadly, the institutional settings serve as devices reducing the pervasive presence of uncertainty.[14]

A drafting perspective

The three views on the relationship of law and standards are guided by different motivations. As our original 'economic law' perspective tries to capture the relevant rules for legal decision making in the economic sphere, the Abbot and Snidal view is oriented towards the functioning of standards in their variety in relation to other guides of behaviour in the international system.[15] The neo-institutional view tries to remedy the myopia of the neo-classical explanation of the functioning of markets.

Without denying the usefulness and relevance of these approaches, I will advance, for purposes of analysis, a different perspective which I call a 'drafting perspective'. My questions are as follows: Under what circumstances will a professional draftsperson refer to 'law,' and when will she/he refer to extra-legal norms such as standards? How do standards, practices and guidelines operate in the drafting process?

No doubt, this is primarily an issue of the individual case. However, I expect some general observations, which may shed some light on the structures of international governance including its complex relation between 'law' and 'extra-legal norms'. Draftspersons are primarily interested in the functioning of the regime which they are designing, be it a contract, a hybrid arrangement or a corporate charter with its by-laws.

In all instances there is the basic objective of designing a valid transactional vehicle. Moreover, the regime has to be workable. Therefore, it should be immune against charges of lawlessness. Draftspersons care for the 'legitimacy' of the used regimes. 'Legitimacy' is, indeed, one of the preconditions of the success of private ordering. Neglecting the rare and costly case of self-enforcing arrangements or the abstraction of a complete incentive compatible arrangement, the draftsperson will typically resort to those legally enforceable solutions, which are not only provided by the law but which will also include lawful references to extra-legal norms and procedures. 'Law' in this perspective is a modification of Holmes's 'realistic' definition ('what courts will do in fact'). From the viewpoint of the drafting profession, 'law' is what professional consultants cautiously assume courts and regulators 'will do in fact' (and enforce).

The legitimacy of a transactional design is frequently discovered in a trial-and-error process of the drafting practice.[16] One of the most successful strategies here is the use of 'off-the-rack' solutions. These might not account for all idiosyncratic features of the transaction to be handled, but they save the high transaction costs of 'tailored' solutions. In a way, the written and judge-made facilitating law (what is called 'dispositive law' on the Continent or 'defaults' in the US) is 'off-the-rack' by definition.[17] It is a standardized system of ordering between the parties in a legitimate context. The interesting part is that 'dispositive' law may be found in both the acclaimed legal text and in the 'legitimate' private practice. Nevertheless, the choice of a facilitating regime is complex. The real choices are sometimes difficult to explain. Take the example of the choice of an incorporation jurisdiction in the United States. New York lawyers mainly select Delaware law. Some attribute this to Delaware allegedly offering the least-demanding preconditions, Delaware being the winner of a 'race to the bottom' of the preconditions for corporate chartering. The original claim by Cary is reduced to laxness toward managers.[18] The mainstream literature today points out that New York lawyers select Delaware because it is a specialized jurisdiction, which offers particularly useful and predictable regimes. They claim that Delaware has won the 'race to the top'.[19] The most convincing argument seems to me to be that Delaware is, indeed, a specialized jurisdiction and that the choice of the professionals has to do with the fact that Delaware offers, by and large, the most standardized services in this field. The incorporation business and the corporate litigation in Delaware are more 'convenient', because the interplay between the profession and this jurisdiction is best known. It is the 'standard', and it is considered to be legitimate. In this sense, it comes closest to the ideal of being a jurisdiction which is completely 'off-the-rack'. Successful standards, practices and guidelines have almost the same properties: they can typically also be taken 'off-the-rack'.

Linking social norms, especially standards to law: the need for reference norms

If the task is a pure description of social practice, the borderline between 'social norms' and 'legal norms' is irrelevant. If non-legal norms, however, become relevant as 'guiding criteria' for legal decisions, we need 'linkage mechanisms' which 'authorize' the 'inclusion' of relevant norms in the 'official' rules. This need for and the use of reference norms is well-known in a number of technical settings of all legal orders. I will browse through some conventional situations where the existing law is extended or changed by the 'application' of 'foreign' law or 'external' norms.

Conflict-of-laws-methodology

The most elaborate system of 'inclusion', of 'linking' external 'rules' with the internal legitimate order is private international law. The 'foreign rule' is included if an internal conflicts rule contains an authorization for the application. The debate about the underlying reasons why courts 'include' 'foreign laws' in their deliberations of a case has become less urgent with the comprehensive positive statutory or judge-made regulation of this complex set of rules.

However, for understanding the mechanism of 'choice-of-law' we should note that two relevant basic arguments are advanced. They should be of interest for a theory of 'inclusion of social norms'. The first is the classical argument of 'comity'.[20] It says, in essence, that the courts will recognize a foreign rule in cases with a foreign element because the 'friendly relations' between the nations require reciprocity of recognition of rules. This view is based, by and large, on the notion that the foreign legal norm is, albeit 'foreign', a legal one and therefore generally well-suited for inclusion by the domestic legal system. The more rigid, even unfriendly, argument was advanced by Brainerd Currie. He denies, in essence, the viability of 'friendly recognition' of a foreign rule if the state has expressed its regulatory interest in the subject matter. Only an issue in which the state is disinterested could then be decided with reference to a 'foreign' rule.[21]

If we transfer both conceptions to the recognition of standards: do we recognize them for reasons of 'friendliness' or because we are 'disinterested'? It may be that 'disinterest of the state' is frequently a valid rationale for the increasing use of standards.

Private autonomy as a link

The next, even more significant, 'inclusion rule' for non-legal norms in structures of private governance is the constitutional principle of private autonomy.[22] It comprises both freedom of contracting (i.e. freely stipulating terms in contracts and organizational charters) and the choice of the applicable law for contracts. This authorization for designing private transactions is an important avenue of 'including' extra legal standards because the parties are authorized by the principle to refer to 'outside' norms as part of their 'legitimate', binding private arrangement. Indeed, many contracts and charters contain explicit or implicit references to standards. Size and quality aspects are typically backed up by such reference.

The most elaborate scheme of 'including' private norms is the system of control developed for 'adhesion contracts' or 'standard terms'.[23] In essence, it is a negative system of 'avoiding' illegal components of private legislation. It is hidden in the theory that generally standard terms are considered part of the private agreement between the parties. This is a fairly far-fetched concept because it neglects the very fact that 'standard terms' used in a multitude of transactions resemble much more abstract norms than concrete private arrangements, but it operates within its limits. It is based on a hypothetical bargain which is used as a method of comparing the boiler plate clause to a 'fair' hypothetical agreement. In essence, a deviation from reasonable expectation puts the private legislation under the pressure of justification.

Standards as trade usages

A third relevant mechanism including extra legal standards is the reference to 'trade usages' (cf. Section 346 German Commercial Code). There are many standards that could be classed as parts of trade usages.

The concept of trade usages is theoretically interesting in that it contains an explicit set of legitimizing criteria for 'inclusion':[24]

1   factual exercise of the practice;
2   a certain duration of the practice;
3   a consent of the participating business community;
4   the definiteness of the practice as a matter of fact.

Looking at examples, one usually refers to the highly standardized INCO-terms, which are, so to speak, 'frozen trade usages'. However, in this case, many commentators (adhering to the prevalent view of 'standard terms') assume that they are not incorporated by the methodology of inclusion under Art. 346 German Commercial Code but are rather short-hand stipulations under the inclusion rule of private autonomy.

Customary international law as a standard?

For the sake of completeness, reference should be made to the inclusion mechanism used in public international law referring to customary international law. It resembles the inclusion technique used for the trade usages. The affiliation of customary international law to the issue at stake can be illustrated best by consideration of the fact that here also, a controversial debate exists about the source of its binding nature, which is typically sketched by the keywords of 'state practice' and 'opinio iuris'.[25]

Structural lessons

What can we learn from the various patterns linking extra-legal norms to law? First of all, we understand that local law is obviously interested in a number of situations to 'apply' extra-legal norms. The second point is that law is concerned about the 'inclusion' and establishes some limitations. This does not contradict the sociological/neo-institutional observation that legal norms do not operate in a vacuum but relate to established social practices, and that, under some circumstances, law is more a retreat rather than a system of containing the societal order.

In terms of the structure of all discussed mechanisms that link law to certain extra-legal norms, it is apparent that they are defined from the viewpoint of the judge. There is no problem if the norms do not challenge the validity and scope of application of the local legal order. The most telling example is private international law. Brainerd Currie makes the convincing point that – from a democratic constitutional perspective – foreign law can only be applied if a state is disinterested. The remaining question is, however, to define – in a legally-predictable fashion – under what circumstances the judge can declare the state to be disinterested. Driven to the extreme, a state court would have no jurisdiction in this case. In most cases, some 'concerns' can be established. The same may be true for the problem of regulating a context by standards or guidelines.

Once we start from the assumption of a comprehensive legal order and a system of remedies monopolized by the state, we can hardly claim, in important matters of regulation, a disinterest of the legal system or a lack of concern for these norms. There is no 'principle of subsidiarity' between law and extra-legal rules. Is there a general system of testing extra-legal norms from a legal centrist perspective? Could we conceive of a committee of the parliament or a regulatory agency which would 'screen' all extra-legal norms in a procedure and declare them eventually 'applicable'?[26]

If we look at the available mechanisms, by and large, we find a system of traditional screening on a case-by-case basis, resembling the system of determining the validity of standard term contracts. It is interesting that for standard terms, all legal systems have developed complex testing schemes which guide decision making. For consumer contracts, the scheme has even entered a 'harmonized' state by using directives which have been transformed into the various national laws in the European Union.[27] As has been mentioned earlier, the basic concept of reference here is the 'fair' hypothetical bargain. From a legal centrist perspective this is probably the most viable approach for 'admitting' extra-legal rules.[28]

A current puzzle in German law is the nature and the quality of the new 'corporate governance codex', which is attached to section 161 of the Aktiengesetz.[29] Naturally, it would be very hard to say what a 'fair hypothetical bargain' would mean in this context of an institutional arrangement (the corporation), which, at least from a neo-institutional perspective, seems to evade the picture of a 'fair' contractual transaction. Here, the legislator declares explicitly that the rules of the codex are not binding legal norms but rules describing the desirable practice. The problem may have to do with the hybrid nature of this sort of 'codification'. The draftspersons may have felt that codification of textbook aspirations for good management might eventually lead to legal entropy.

If we cannot establish fairness of the use of extra-legal norms by reference to a fair hypothetical bargain, we might be inclined to be more modest from the outset. If we ought to formulate minimal rules, we would probably be able to define at least a borderline from a legal centrist perspective, which would be consistent with the following two basic rules.[30]

1   Extra-legal norms should not contradict the legal rules in 'relevant' legal orders (a rule that is largely identical with a control criterion developed for contracts under the rule of private autonomy). In the case of 'off-the-rack' solutions (like 'standard terms') this includes not only compatibility with the non-fungible norms (*ius cogens*) but also adherence to those default rules that belong to the 'core' of the balancing of interests envisioned by the legislator (see Section 307 of the German Civil Code).
2   Extra-legal norms should be 'incentive compatible' in that they encourage actors to operate in a cost effective, friction-avoiding way, which also ensures a maximum of internalization of possible externalities of the given transaction.

Producing and using standardized regimes

Reasons

Let us now turn to a perspective of 'regime production' and 'regime use' of standardized non-legal regimes. I will first discuss reasons why private actors who are interested in the functioning of transactions produce these regimes.

There are three reasons which relate to the limits of legislation and the legislative process.

Lack of generality

One of the central features of law is general applicability. A legal rule is – by definition – applicable to a large set of cases including the characteristic of equal application. We observe that general laws, which would comply with these conditions, become increasingly dysfunctional in view of the increasing specificity. In Continental European private law, this process typically ends in delegations to judges, especially by using general clauses or broad formulations. Courts then develop a closely knit case law for dealing with the specifics of the situations. A good example is the law on unfair trade practices, where case law uses the legal norms in the statute mainly as a reference system. The same is true for tort law, where few general norms cover a huge field of highly specified legal practice.

Political deadlocks

The second problem relates to the increasing inability of legislators to settle issues in the legislative process. Political deadlocks lead to escape strategies. A well-known example is either leaving the issue for settlement in a high court, particularly the constitutional court, or to referring it to the comitology process in EC law. However, an important escape strategy is also to 'privatize' the issue and to refer it to a non-legal rule-making body. Thus, there is – at first glance – a somewhat odd interaction between the legal system and private activity: in fields traditionally considered to be a domain of private action, i.e. the price mechanism of the market, there is increasing state intervention (as in the case of consumer contracts) while the making of general rules is, at least in the field of economic law, no longer a prerogative of the state but also open to private institutions.

Mobility of the issue

A third reason for leaving the system of constitutional law making is the inherent mobility of the issue. If goods or services or other factors are fungible, a national regulation may simply lead to avoidance of this jurisdiction. A comprehensive transnational regulation is frequently unavailable. Hence, legislators try to stimulate 'private' or 'quasi-public' norm-producing bodies in the hope that they can influence this process indirectly by measures that they are able to control locally. The banking regulation in the Basel I and II processes may be partly explained in the shortcomings of a possible national legislation.[31] Another example for a 'mobile' issue was the case of currency adjustments at the introduction of the Euro. It was obvious that this problem could not be settled by the governments in technical and consistent legal rules. Here, the major banks of Europe agreed on certain practices which they codified privately. The President of the European Monetary Institute declared that he approved of the practice suggested.[32]

Cost of legislation

There are cases in which rule-making in the legislative process is too costly, particularly if information costs are fully included. This especially happens in the grey area between legislation and standard terms formulated by the industry. Take industry-specific rules for insurance, banking, or most recently, the internet.[33] An interesting aspect in developing fields such as the internet is the sequential nature of private rule-making. What first seems to be a rather negligible area, developed and used by a few academics, may establish itself incrementally, developing and stabilizing the necessary rule sets, which are then tolerated or even expressly acclaimed by the constitutionally legitimized bodies. In these new areas, general legislation may then operate more as a repair shop than as an independent, legitimate source of rules.[34]

Private entrepreneurship for extra-legal norm-making

Standards and privately codified practices are sometimes developed by persons or organizations who detect a market for private norms. It is not only technological necessity, as in the case of the original industrial standards, that may be a motivation for this kind of entrepreneurship. Once a rudimentary system is established, the standardizing organization discovers new potential markets for standardization services. The current extensions of the ISO-process can be explained in these terms.[35] The success of standardization in the old industrial fields led to extensions to numerous new service areas. In lucrative areas, the classical standardizing agencies compete with market entrants. Sometimes new organizations promoting standards are developed by a clientele that is dissatisfied with the traditional set-up. The competition between industrial standards (e.g. TV, media standards and computer systems) are fascinating examples of fights between leading groups in the industries in a competitive international market.[36] Entrepreneurship and lobbying activities may then convince the legislators to formally include a standard or codified practice in the current law. There may be a consensus between the legislator and the business circles about the desirability of private law-making in specific cases.

Functions of standardized non-legal regimes in contract drafting

From the perspective of drafting a transaction, standards serve three main 'facilitating' functions: They are 'definers', 'monitors' and 'ex-post-references' of a given transaction.

In many cases, contracts cannot be understood without a reference to a standard. Standards are, in this sense, shorthand descriptions of a performance schedule. A simple example would be the order and delivery of a widget with a reference to a DIN- or ISO-standard. Increasingly, we also see services being marketed with a reference to a standard, not only to emphasize quality aspects but also the 'content' of the service.[37]

The references to standards may control the transaction throughout its duration from the pre-contractual to the post-contractual stage. Standards may serve as patterns of information. They have an orientation function in the contracting phase.[38] They may enter into the contract as part of the definition of a performance. Hence, they serve a stipulation function. In the devolution phase of a contract, performances deviating from existing standards may be considered as inadequate or defective. Hence, standards also serve as references for a better understanding of the performance modalities if the stipulation of the term is unclear. This may be called an interpretation function or even a gap-filling function of standards. In the performance process, standards may be used for monitoring by specifying quality aspects of goods and services including disclosure and liability issues. Finally, if the contract fails, remedies may be specified by reference to standards, e.g. the monetary damage resulting from the non-availability of a certain good at a certain time may be determined by reference to generally accepted private data sheets about customary leasing rates for that good.

Standards as indicators of a shift from personal to professional transaction practices

The increasing and pervasive 'production' and use of standards and private codes signals a secular 'code shifting'. The former classical transactional code referred to vocational business networks. In this system, characterized by stylized individuals, such as 'the merchant', 'the entrepreneur', 'the banker'; business practices and ethical codes were internalized as behavioral codes specific for the membership in the individual trade. These codes were acquired by personal in-house training in apprenticeship procedures.

The massive arrival of standards signals a form of abstraction and specialization. The new, written standards and codes are taught in general teaching systems such as universities; they are exercised by a class of professionals outside the old trading patterns. In this system, the use of standards reflects both a standardization and an abstraction of personal modes of trading with implicit business codes. Business codes are made explicit and exercised by specialists.[39]

The shift from vocational networks to the recruitment of professionals is, on the other hand, associated with a breakdown of the traditional unwritten codes of business ethics. The informal codes are thus substituted by an array of written codes, which are administered and interpreted by 'norm specialists'. Thus, the rise of professional standards is part of the long-lasting transformation of business relations from close-knit groups with personal elements to anonymous transactions in which the 'terms of the trade' are the only tie between the parties.[40]

An interesting extension of this phenomenon of code shifting and specialization is the arrival of administrative specialists for standardized practices.

Large law firms, for example, have created 'knowledge management' systems, which collect computerized knowledge and constantly upgrade the documentation of deals.[41] This used to be a matter of personal knowledge of specialist partners of law firms who would 'remember' their experience from earlier transactions. Standardized written codes of practice instead of conventional vocational knowledge are especially visible in the area of corporate governance, accounting, credit rating and related areas.

A vital problem of this shift from vocational training to systems of knowledge management should be mentioned: documentation of routines and routine enforcement of these new codes may eventually lead to a petrification of practices and standards.

Professional demand for off-the-rack regimes

Tailored solutions as modifications of ready-made solutions

Let us now review the production technology of draftspersons. Typically, an individual contract or charter is a modification of an earlier draft relating to similar problems. In terms of fashion design draftspersons 'customize' regimes. They develop a fitting solution by variation of a standardized arrangement. Most standardized regimes have ready-made properties, which may fit in tailored solutions.

In the architecture of complex contracting, we find mixes of standardized clauses which are kept stable, and incremental variations of specific arrangements.[42] There are a number of ways in which new institutional design is developed in this area; copying is the main exercise. In a contracting world, there is a vivid exchange of contractual documentation simply driven by the fact that parties and their legal agents exchange contracts. In some cases, workable arrangements are transported by the draftspersons from one industry to the other. There are cases where the in-house lawyers address external collaborators in a transaction in order to get access to an innovative institutional design. Moreover, there is a constant proliferation of institutional design patterns through fluctuations on the job market for professionals. For the improvement of the international drafting practices, it is fortunate that contract design is typically a free intellectual good which cannot be protected by the copyright system. Of course, the relevant consulting firms with specialties have ways and means to protect valuable 'shelved' regime products.

The relation of shelved regime products and standards

Draftspersons gain reputation by referring to the workability of a drafted arrangement over time. Workability establishes itself mainly in trial-and-error procedures. Error can be avoided by using a tried, ready-made regime that has worked well in earlier comparable contexts. Standardization organizations as institutionalist specialists offer, on the market for regimes, those off-the-rack institutions which are consented and used by the relevant industries. This leads to an important trait of standard setting as part of the regime production process. Standard setting organizations not only care for the workability of design and the consent of the parties affected by the contract; rather, they look for a broader consensus of the potentially relevant users.[43] Thus we find, in increasing scale and scope, forms of involvement of the relevant business circles in a quasi-democratic process.[44] Some observers assume that this 'democratization process' is a necessary item for the viability of standards.[45]

Reconsidering 'links to law' from a drafting perspective

Conflict avoidance as a legitimating strategy

From a legal centrist perspective, the application of extra-legal norms needs a positive legal rule for 'legitimizing' the inclusion for linking standards to law. Viewed from a drafting perspective, a negative strategy may be sufficient. A draftsperson can avoid a conflict between law and extra-legal norms. As mentioned, a draftsperson will see to it that an extra-legal component of a transaction regime will not contradict the positive legal orders affected by the transaction. This process of clearing the 'legal compliance' is typically the most time consuming exercise of legal consultants.

The exceptional case of circumvention

In a limited set of cases, consultants will advise their clients to try a 'circumvention' of the given rule set of the affected positive law. This, however, will typically be associated with strong other equities. The risk of living with a possibly void transaction – a situation which may amount to a Knightean uncertainty, and thus requires the assessment of worst case outcomes – has to be evaluated in the light of the overall efficiency of the transaction. I have shown elsewhere that judges and regulators will ratify such circumventions if strong attributes of a new Pareto superior regime can be demonstrated.[46]

The circle of transactional hermeneutics

The most salient international transactional regimes are composed of legal and extra-legal components. Think, for example, of international franchise regimes, systems of exclusive dealerships, of production networks, umbrella agreements, international finance consortia, money clearing schemes, international joint ventures, or mergers and acquisitions of firms. Even if – in relatively rare cases – the basic agreements in these instances are distanced from local court intervention, e.g. by agreeing on a national dispute settlement under a national law,[47] they still would have to comply with a massive remaining set of 'local' legal prerequisites.

For making the transaction viable, draftspersons regularly enter in a screening

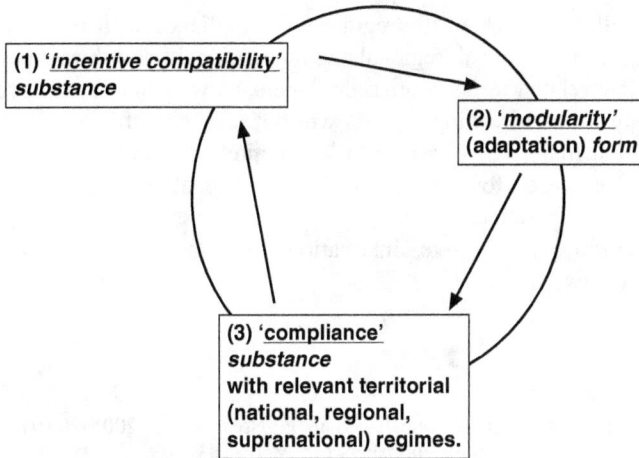

Figure 9 The hermeneutic circle.

process of substantive and formal elements, which are interrelated, and which I suggest to analyse as follows.

The current transactional practice is reflected in three theoretical elements, which are contained in a circle of transactional hermeneutics:

Incentive compatibility

Draftspersons will, first, ensure that the regime is incentive compatible. In legal usage, this is frequently expressed as accommodating the 'interests' of the parties. However, 'interest accommodation' includes overarching elements such as functioning of the arrangement during its life span, from the negotiation stage to the post-contractual phase. Thus, compatibility also includes aspects of accommodating externalities because visible externalities endanger the execution of the transaction. Third parties might rightfully intervene, backed by the local courts. A highly relevant example for cautionary externality control by the draftspersons is the screening of antitrust concerns of arrangements.

Modularity

Draftspersons will, second, verify that the regime contains viable, 'tried' regime components, which operate like 'modules' put into mainframes of electronic systems. Hence, I term them institutional modules. Modules are standardized regimes which can be 'plugged' into the draft with the assurance that they 'function' whenever the contingency arises. In this sense, draftspersons must be interested in a high content of modularity in every regime. Some commentators allude to this phenomenon by using the unfortunate term of '*lex mercatoria*'. Modules are neither '*leges*' nor are they used by 'merchants'.

Compliance

Draftspersons will, third, screen the regime for compliance with regard to the relevant 'territorial' i.e. national, regional and international 'lawful' regimes.

If all three interrelated tests are met, draftspersons will endorse the regime. Professional care in the screening process will not only be enforced by professional liability, but mainly by considerable reputation sanctions. This assures a high degree of legitimacy for the inclusion of extra-legal regime components, such as standards and practices.

From this drafting perspective, international standards and practices are strongly linked to law.

Notes

1 The contribution was originally pubslished in P. Nobel (ed.) (2005) *International Standards and The Law*, Stämpfli Publishers Ltd: Berne, 83–103.
2 Calabresi and Melamed 1972: 85.
3 German term: 'Verweisungsnorm'.
4 See Gilson 1984: 94.
5 See for a comparison of the 'logic of antecedents' with the 'logic of consequences': Posner 2003; for a broadening of the fact sets in a 'constructive jurisprudence' see: Ackermann 1984: 72 ff.; Schanze 1993: 149; Mnookin *et al.* 2000.
6 See for the main definitions of 'standards': Schreiber 2005.
7 Holmes 1897: 10.
8 Mertens, Kirchner and Schanze 1982: 125: '... die Rechtsordnung [kann] als Inbegriff von Normen, als Inbegriff aller rechtlichen Entscheidungen und als Inbegriff aller entscheidungsleitenden Gesichtspunkte verstanden werden.'
9 Ibid.: 140.
10 Abbott and Snidal 2001: 8.
11 Ellickson 1991.
12 Posner 2002: 18–27.
13 Richter and Furubotn 2003: 316.
14 Callon 1998: 244 [250]; see generally: Dawes 1988.
15 Abbott and Snidal 2001: 8.
16 Schanze 1996: 61; Schanze 1995: 151; Schanze 1993: 149.
17 See for a general discussion: Ayres and Gertner 1989: 99.
18 Bebchuk and Ferrell 2001: 87 with references.
19 Romano 2002; but see Roe 2003: 117.
20 Kegel and Schurig 2004: 6.
21 Currie 1963; on this, Joerges 2004: 339.
22 Mertens, Kirchner and Schanze 1982: 133.
23 On contract regulation see Collins 1999: 256; Trebilcock 1993: 250.
24 See for a full account of the German doctrine: Schmidt 1999: 23.
25 See Kokott 2005; Roberts 2001: 95; Stephan 1999: 70; Koh 1997: 106.
26 See for the 'constitutional' dimension of standard setting in the area of accounting: Kirchner and Schmidt 2005; and for the associated 'political' and 'technical' deadlocks: Wüstemann and Kierzek in this volume.
27 See Schulze and Schulte-Nölke 1999.
28 Mertens *et al.* 1982: 134.
29 See Ulmer 2002: 166; Kley 2003: 4; generally Gilson 2001: 49.
30 Schanze 1999: 195.

31 Nobel 2005; Simmons 2001: 55; see also for the massive extension of competencies of regulatory agencies: Zaring 1998: 33; Choi and Pritchard 2003: 56.
32 European Monetary Institute 1997: 'The EMI welcomes and supports the initiative taken by the associations of the banking and financial industry. It notes that there is broad consensus among market participants on common conventions for the Euro financial markets. Implementation of those conventions will enhance integration of, and ensure more transparency in, the Euro financial markets.'
33 von Bernstorff 2004: 257.
34 See Herwig 2004: 199.
35 See the homepage of ISO: www.iso.org/iso/en/ISOOnline.frontpage.
36 For media standards see: Lemley 2002: 90; Teece and Sherry 2003: 87.
37 See ISO 9000; 9001.
38 See Deakin and Mitchie 1997: 1.
39 A most visible example is the financial market: Choi and Guzman 1997: 65; Nobel 2005; Nobel 2000: 23; Simmons 2001: 55.
40 See Maine 1894.
41 Schulz and Klugmann 2005: *passim.*
42 For investment agreements see: Schanze 1986; for project finance see: Sester 2004.
43 Axelrod *et al.* 1997: 96.
44 For the standard setting process: Abbott and Snidal 2005; also Austin and Milner 2001: 8; Besen and Farrell 1994: 8.
45 Steffek 2004: 81; Morais 2002: 50; Abbott and Snidal 2005.
46 Schanze 1995: 151.
47 Mertens 1996: 857; Dasser 2001: 189.

References

Abbott, K.W. and Snidal, D. (2001) 'International "Standards" and International Governance', *Journal of European Public Policy* 3: 345–370.
Abbott, K.W. and Snidal, D. (2005) 'The International Standards Process: Setting and Applying Global Business Norms', in: P. Nobel (ed.) *International Standards and the Law*, Bern: Staempfli Publishers, 105–142.
Ackermann, B.A. (1984) *Reconstructing American Law*, Cambridge: Havard University Press.
Austin, M. and Milner, H. (2001) 'Strategies of European Standardization', *Journal of European Public Policy* 8: 411–431.
Axelrod R. (1997) 'Setting Standards, Coalition Formation in Standard-Setting Alliance', in: R. Axelrod (ed.) *The Complexity of Cooperation*, Princeton, NJ: Princeton University Press, 96–120.
Ayres, I. and Gertner, R. (1989) 'Filling Gaps in Incomplete Contracts: An Economic Theory of Default Rules', *Yale Law Journal* 99: 87.
Bebchuk, L. and Ferrell, A. (2001) 'A New Approach to Regulatory Competition in Takeover Law', *Virginia Law Review* 87: 111.
Besen, S. and Farrell, J. (1994) 'Choosing How to Compete: Strategies and Tactics in Standardization', *Journal of Economic Perspectives* 8: 117–131.
Calabresi, G. and Melamed, A.D. (1972) 'Property Rules, Liability Rules, and Inalienability: One View of the Cathedral', *Harvard Law Review* 85: 1089–1128.
Callon, M. (1998) 'An Essay on Framing and Overflowing: Economic Externalities Revisited by Sociology', in: M. Callon (ed.) *The Laws of the Markets*, Oxford: Blackwell, 244–269.
Choi, S. and Guzman, A. (1997) 'National Laws, International Money: Regulation in a Global Capital Market', *Fordham Law Review* 65: 1855.

Choi, S. and Pritchard, A. (2003) 'Behavioral Economics and the SEC', *Stanford Law Review* 56: 1.

Collins, H. (1999) *Regulating Contracts*, Oxford: Oxford University Press.

Currie, B. (1963) *Selected Essays on the Conflict of Laws*, Durham, North Carolina: Duke University Press.

Dasser, F. (2001) 'Lex Mercatoria – Critical Comments on a Tricky Topic', in: R.P. Appelbaum, W.L.F. Felstiner and V. Gessner (eds) *Rules and Networks: The Legal Culture of Global Business Transactions*, Oxford: Hart Pub., 186.

Dawes, R. (1988) *Rational Choice in an Uncertain World*, Thousand Oaks, London, New Delhi: SAGE Publications.

Deakin, S. and Mitchie, J. (1997) 'The Theory and Practice of Contracting', in: S. Deakin and J. Mitchie (eds) *Contracts, Co-Operation, and Competition*, Oxford: Oxford University Press, 1–39.

Ellickson, R.C. (1991) *Order Without Law*, Cambridge: Harvard University Press.

European Monetary Institute (1997) *Joint Statement on Market Conventions for the Euro*, 16 July.

Gilson, R. (1984) 'Value Creation by Business Lawyers: Legal Skills and Asset Pricing', *Yale Law Journal* 94: 239.

Gilson, R. (2001) 'Globalizing Corporate Governance: Convergence of Form or Function', *American Journal of Comparative Law* 49: 329–429.

Herwig, A. (2004) 'Transnational Governance Regimes for Foods Derived from Biotechnology and Their Legitimacy', in: Ch. Joerges, I.-J. Sand and G. Teubner (eds) *Transnational Governance and Constitutionalism*, Oxford: Hart Publishing, 199–223.

Holmes, O.W. (1897) 'The Path of the Law', *Harvard Law Review* 10: 457.

ISO: www.iso.org/iso/en/ISOOnline.frontpage (accessed 1 November 2006).

Joerges, Ch. (2004) 'Constitutionalism and Transnational Governance: Exploring a Magic Triangle', in: Ch. Joerges, I.-J. Sand and G. Teubner (eds) *Transnational Governance and Constitutionalism*, Oxford: Hart Publishing, 339–377.

Kegel, G. and Schurig, K. (2004) *Internationales Privatrecht*, 9th edn, München: Beck.

Kirchner, Ch. and Schmidt, M. (2005) 'Private Law-Making; IFRS – Problems of Hybrid Standard Setting', in: P. Nobel (ed.) *International Standards and the Law*, Bern: Staempfli Publishers, 67–82.

Kley, K.L. (2003) 'Neue Corporate Governance Regeln in den USA und Europa – Mehr Probleme als Lösungen', *Der Konzern in Recht und Wirtschaft* 4: 264–268.

Koh, H. (1997) 'Review Essay: Why Do Nations Obey International Law?', *Yale Law Journal* 106: 2599.

Kokott, J. (2005) 'Soft Law Standards under Public International Law', in: P. Nobel (ed.) *International Standards and the Law*, Bern: Staempfli Publishers, 15–41.

Lemley, M. (2002) 'Intellectual Property Rights and Standard-Setting Organizations', *California Law Review* 90: 1889.

Maine, H.S. (1894) *Ancient Law*, 10th edn, with Introduction and Notes by Sir Frederick Pollock, Boston: Beacon Press, 1963.

Mertens, H.-J. (1996) 'Das lex Mercatoria-Problem', in: R. Böttcher, G. Hueck und B. Jähnke (eds) *Festschrift für Walter Odersky zum 65. Geburtstag*, Berlin: de Gruyter.

Mertens, H.-J., Kirchner, Ch. and Schanze, E. (1982) *Wirtschaftsrecht*, 2nd edn, Opladen: Westdeutscher Verlag.

Mnookin, R., Peppet, S. and Tulumello, A. (2000) *Beyond Winning*, Cambridge: Harvard University Press.

Morais, H. (2002) 'The Quest for International Standards: Global Governance vs. Sovereignty', *Kansas Law Review* 50: 779–821.

Nobel, P. (2000) 'The Concept of Disclosure Within European Financial Institutions', *Fordham International Law Journal* 23: 41–44.

Nobel, P. (2005) 'Globalization and International Standards with an emphasis on Finance Law', in: P. Nobel (ed.) *International Standards and the Law*, Bern: Staempfli Publishers, 43–66.

Posner, E. (2002) *Law and Social Norms*, Cambridge: Harvard University Press.

Posner, R.A. (2003) *Law, Pragmatism, and Democracy*, Cambridge: Harvard University Press.

Richter, R. and Furubotn, E.G. (2003) *Neue Institutionenökonomik*, 3rd edn, Tübingen: Mohr Siebeck.

Roberts, A.E. (2001) 'Traditional and Modern Approaches to Customary International Law', *American Journal of International Law* 95: 757–791.

Roe, M. (2003) 'Delaware's Competition', *Harvard Law Review* 117: 588–646.

Romano, R. (2002) *The Advantage of Competitive Federalism for Securities Regulation*, Washington D.C.: AEI Press.

Schanze, E. (1986) *Investitionsverträge im Internationalen Wirtschaftsrecht*, Frankfurt am Main: Metzner.

Schanze, E. (1993) 'Legalism, Economism, and Professional Attitudes Toward Institutional Design', *Journal of Institutional and Theoretical Economics* 149: 122–140.

Schanze, E. (1995) 'Hare and Hedgehog Revisited: The Regulation of Markets That Have Escaped Regulated Markets', *Journal of Institutional and Theoretical Economics* 151: 162–176.

Schanze, E. (1996) 'New Directions in Contract Research', in: B. Dahl and R. Nielsen (eds) *New Directions in Business Law*, Copenhagen: Verlag, 61–72.

Schanze, E. (1999) 'Die Entwicklung von Institutionen', in: Ch.J. Meier-Schatz (ed.) *Forschungsgespräch der Rechtswissenschaftlichen Abteilung anlässlich des 100-Jahr-Jubiläums der Universität St. Gallen im Juni 1998*, Basel, Genf, München: Bibliothek zur Zeitschrift für Schweizerisches Recht, Beiheft 28 (1999).

Schmidt, K. (1999) *Handelsrecht*, 5th edn, Köln: Heymann.

Schulz, M. and Klugmann, M. (2005) *Wissensmanagement für Anwälte*, Köln: Heymann.

Schulze, R. and Schulte-Nölke, H. (1999) *Europäische Rechtsangleichung und nationale Privatrechte*, Baden-Baden: Nomos.

Schreiber, V. (2005) 'What are International Standards?', in: P. Nobel (ed.) *International Standards and the Law*, Bern: Staempfli Publishers, 1–13.

Sester, P. (2004) *Projektfinanzierungsvereinbarungen als Gestaltungs- und Regulierungsaufgabe*, Köln: Schmidt.

Simmons, B. (2001) 'The International Politics of Harmonization: The Case of Capital Market Regulation', *International Organization* 55: 589–620.

Steffek, J. (2004) 'Sources of Legitimacy Beyond the State: A View from International Relations', in: Ch. Joerges, I.-J. Sand and G. Teubner (eds) *Transnational Governance and Constitutionalism*, Oxford: Hart Publishing, 81–103.

Stephan, P.B. (1999) 'The New International Law – Legitimacy, Accountability, Authority, and Freedom in the New Global Order', *University of Colorado Law Review* 70: 1555.

Teece, D. and Sherry, E. (2003) 'The Interface Between Intellectual Property Law and Antitrust Law: Standard Setting and Antitrust', *Minnesota Law Review* 87: 1913–1994.

Trebilcock, M. (1993) *The Limits of Freedom of Contract*, Cambridge: Harvard University Press.

Ulmer, P. (2002) 'Der Deutsche Corporate Governance Kodex – ein neues Regulierungsinstrument für börsennotierte Aktiengesellschaften', *ZHR* 166: 150–166.

von Bernstorff, J. (2004) 'ICANN as a Global Governance Network: The Rise and Fall of a Governance Experiment', in: Ch. Joerges, I.-J. Sand and G. Teubner (eds) *Transnational Governance and Constitutionalism*, Oxford: Hart Publishing, 257–283.

Zaring, D. (1998) 'International Law by Other Means: The Twilight Existence of International Financial Regulatory Organizations', *Texas International Law Journal* 33: 281.

10 Beyond legalization

Reading the increase, variation and differentiation of legal and law-like arrangements in international relations through world society theory

Mathias Albert

Introduction

As the title of this volume as well as its individual contributions aptly point out, contemporary international relations are characterized by a bewildering multiplicity of legal and 'law-like' arrangements. Traditional forms of inter-state international and supranational law coexist with less formal, 'quasi-legal' regimes, the 'soft' law formed by the customs of international society, and regulatory activities of various international governmental and nongovernmental organizations. In addition, a broad trend in recent research in International Relations and International Law alike has pointed out that international legalization increasingly also takes the form of a closer cooperation and exchange between and a mutual recognition of relevant national legal institutions, particularly courts. Even the seemingly simple issue of counting and mapping the different forms of law and law-like arrangements in international relations today presents an almost impossible task, prone to get stuck in the quagmire of this new-found international legal plurality.

Seen from a legal sociological perspective, this situation hardly comes as a surprise. Law and law-like arrangements in international relations cannot but represent a microcosm of the vast differences of legal orders and forms of law – and indeed the very different basic assumptions about the nature of law behind them – which can be found in the world. As Twining aptly observes: 'if one accepts that there are different levels of legal relations and legal ordering, the phenomena of law are probably too complex to be depicted on a single map or picture' (Twining 2000: 151).

This situation points to a fundamental methodological as well as a theoretical problem confronting the study of law and law-like arrangements in international relations. Both the conceptual 'cores' as well as the conceptual and empirical boundaries of what counts as and constitutes 'law' and 'international relations' are deeply contested. Relating both to each other in a systematic fashion thus generally leaves the analyst with one of two broad analytical strategies: either to 'fix' one or both referent objects, i.e. to subscribe to specific 'ideal types' of what counts as law and what does not, defining 'law-like arrangements' in relation to these ideal types; and/or to adopt a specific view of what 'international relations' entail (thus, for example, excluding non-governmental 'transnational relations'); or to accept the double uncertainty of both referent objects and focus on specific, clearly demarcated empirical cases only.

Both strategies are legitimate and indeed characterize the vast majority of contributions on the subject matter. Yet both are also highly unsatisfactory if the aim is to strive for a higher degree of theoretical synthesis in order to assess the overall contours and prospective impact of the ever-increasing quantity, variation, and differentiation of legal and law-like arrangements in international relations. The present chapter argues that to conceptualize what is usually called 'legalization' as a form of co-evolution of the political and the legal system of world society in the systems-theoretical tradition of Niklas Luhmann offers a promising strategy to synthesize the many facets of international legalization in a theoretically coherent fashion. Such a strategy avoids both the analytical rigidity as well as the implicit eclecticism inherent in the two common strategies just alluded to. It does so by, on the one hand, radically stripping the law from any underlying ontological assumptions about its 'nature' or 'core', focusing instead on its operation as a complex self-referential, 'autopoietic' social system (see Schulte 2003); and, on the other hand, it does so by giving up the assumption that 'international relations' can be treated as an empirically or conceptually isolated realm within world society, giving analytical preference to the internal functional differentiation of that society (into a political system, a legal system, an economic system etc.) instead.

Admittedly, on first sight this does hardly constitute an innovative exercise. The description and analysis of the evolution of a global legal system as a system of world society and its relation to the evolution of other function systems of world society in the Luhmannian tradition has been provided at length by a number of authors, most prominently by Gunther Teubner (see particularly 1993). Regrettably, however, this has led neither to a systematic reception of this approach by the literature on legalization in international relations, nor, for that matter, a systematic reception and contextualization of this literature by the systems theorists. What follows is thus less an attempt of conceptual innovation, but rather one of conceptual translation. It will first seek to introduce the basic tenets of world society theory and its conceptualization of the (co-)evolution of law, politics, and other function systems of world society, and it will then try to interpret and locate some major trends in international legalization as identified in this volume and beyond in the light of this theory.

The aim of this exercise is not to provide a 'better' theory of international legalization in contrast to existing approaches which aim to analyse specific forms of legalization in international relations. Rather it is to show that much more profitable use of these approaches could be made by interpreting and embedding them in a wider framework of world societal trends, thus strengthening their contribution beyond the relatively narrow disciplinary field of International Relations and International Law.

World society and law

This section will first provide a rough sketch of Niklas Luhmann's theory of world society, including his conceptualization of world society's function systems, before it moves on to visit the current form and function of the legal system in world society as elaborated by a number of scholars in the Luhmannian tradition.

Luhmann's theory of society, which in effect is a combination of a theory of social systems, a theory of differentiation, and a theory of social evolution, basically starts from the observation that society is constituted by communication and by communication alone. Unlike in most classical theories of society, the basic question of such a theory of society is thus not how society is kept together. Rather, it is the question of how communication relates to communication and thus how communication and society continue. It would seem futile to try and summarize such a complex body of theory in the space available here. Thus, for the purpose of the present argument, it may suffice to highlight some basic tenets important to understand its conceptualization of law in particular.[1]

It follows from the main assumption, that society is about communication only, and that since the full discovery of the globe all communication can in principle relate to all other communication, that society knows no societies outside itself and can only be conceived as a world society. This world society is not to be conflated with traditional notions of societies thought of as comprehensive social entities integrated internally and separated from other societies by territorial boundaries. Rather it is simply the totality of all communication and thus cannot be envisaged in any integrated fashion whatsoever. World society is not integrated, but differentiated. One could actually say that it achieves any 'unity' only through its internal differentiation.[2]

World society for Luhmann is differentiated functionally into a political system, a legal system, an economic system etc. Here it is important to note that since society and its function systems are constituted by communication alone, it makes little sense to imagine these different systems as being made up of (different) actors. It is communication which makes up function systems, not actors (and thus it is entirely irrelevant, for example, whether it is a court or a private company which communicates – a company before court or concluding a contract operates in the legal system whereas, for example, a court negotiating the price for new computer equipment operates in the economic system).

The implications of this basic theory design become clear, however, only if Luhmann's systems theory is also taken into account. In contrast to more traditional notions of, for example, cybernetic systems, social systems are conceived as basically autopoietic systems. This means that all of their elements are created within the systems themselves. There is no direct 'input' or 'output' involved here. All communication is generated by the system itself on the basis of self-observation and the observation of its environment. Communication is generated and processed within the system on the basis of a system-specific basal code (such as legal/illegal in the legal system), a system-specific symbolically generalized medium of communication (such as law in the legal system, money in the economic system, power in the political system etc.) and specific programmes on whose basis communication is processed within systems (for example laws, verdicts, contracts within the legal system).

Before the conceptualization of the legal system of society within this theoretical framework is set out in greater detail, it seems worth noting that Luhmann does not provide a legal theory, but a theory about law in society. Particularly when it comes to issues of the 'new' legalities in international relations, the importance of this point can hardly be overstated. In contrast to many approaches to international legalization, such an approach does not treat international politics and law as ontologically distinct realms now increasingly afflicting each other, but as systems operating according to autonomous logics within the same societal context.

As one of society's function systems, law serves a function. In contrast to classical (particularly Parsonian) functionalist theory, however, this function is not to contribute to some kind of a (normative) societal integration, i.e. it is no function performed for an entirety of society. Although systems theory does acknowledge that such a function of normative integration of society forms an important part of the legal system's self-description, most prominently in some of its legal theories, it cannot but determine the legal system's function differently against the background of its theory of society as a society constituted by communication alone (in which the basic question is not how individuals are somehow 'held together' by integration, but how communication can continue). Law's 'function' for a communicatively constituted society is rather to stabilize normative expectations. Against the background of a generally unpredictable future, it provides for a temporal extension of meaning and can thus orient communication towards a certainty of expectation. Law thus underpins a normative style of expectation, where regularly expectations change only slowly if they are disappointed (i.e. for example, a law is not immediately altered simply because it is broken).

Against the background of such an understanding of the legal system, it should hardly come as a surprise that the 'unity' of the legal system is not formed by the sum of legal rules or regulations. As an autopoietic social system, the legal system is constituted by legal communication produced within itself: 'law itself produces all the differentiations and denotations it employs ... the unity of law is nothing else than the fact of this self-reproduction, of "autopoiesis"' (Luhmann 1997a: 30).[3] And irrespective of 'who' communicates, legal communication is always code-oriented communication which refers to the code of 'legal/illegal' (see ibid.: 67). This also implies that from a systems-theoretical perspective the validity of law can only be produced by and within the legal system itself. Although the legal system may describe the reasons for the validity of law to be outside of law, these descriptions are descriptions of the legal system itself. In this sense, the validity of law is not inferred from some extra-legal foundation, but symbolizes the autopoietic closure of the legal system (see ibid.: 98). It is the 'validity of law' (Geltung des Rechts) itself which, in systems-theoretical jargon, is the form through which the legal system observes itself. Yet although validity in this sense is not a meta-norm outside of law, the legal system describes it as such since the validity of law (as the form with which the legal system observes itself) can itself not be coded within the legal system (meaning that the validity of law can itself not be coded as 'legal' or 'illegal'). As Luhmann puts it: 'All law is valid law. Non-valid law is not law. Thus the rule which allows to see validity cannot be one of the valid rules' (ibid.: 102).

Put in simple terms, this continuous 'self-validation' of law leads to paradoxical results in the system's operation whereby a figure is required which operates as a 'stop-gap', a kind of 'tool' for the continuous de-paradoxification of the fact that law finds its validity only through the legal system's observation of itself. Traditionally, this 'stop-gap' is provided by the figure of sovereignty. However, it is important to note that the function of this figure is more important here, rather than the figure itself. On the one hand, what the figure of sovereignty entails varies over time and at any given time within the legal system; on the other hand, there is no logical necessity that the function can only be performed by the figure of sovereignty (see also Albert 2005).

The point of an autopoietic closure and the operative autonomy of social systems also requires to cast the relation between the legal system and other function systems of world society in different terms. The legal system observes and describes parts of its environment and systems in its environment in legal terms. Legal communication is thus always and only happening within the legal system which through this self-referential operation reproduces itself (and in this formal way 'legalization' could be understood as the process in which the legal system describes an increasing part of systems in its environment in legal terms). This absolute operative autonomy of the legal system does not, of course, stipulate a causal independence between different systems, quite to the contrary: 'the separation of systems does not preclude intensive causal relations between them; however, one can only ascertain such causal relations if one is able to distinguish one system from the other' (Luhmann 1997a: 421). However, whatever kind of causal relation between different social systems might exist, these do not disturb the systems' autopoiesis. All elements of the systems are produced within the systems themselves. This seeming quagmire of a causal relationality under the conditions of operative closure is partly addressed by modern systems theory through the figure of 'structural coupling'. Put simply, 'structural coupling' describes the fact that social systems routinize specific descriptions of other systems within their own self-descriptions – and vice versa – thus effecting a close 'connection' between two systems (which does not, however, disturb their operative autonomy).

Gunther Teubner in particular has used the notion of structural coupling in order to describe the emergence of different forms of global law (see, for example, Teubner 2004b; Fischer-Lescano and Teubner 2006). Thus, in contrast to interpretations which read 'globalization' primarily as a challenge to law and politics in the sense that the capabilities for making collectively binding decisions and to provide normative guidance are diminishing in a global context dominated by economic actors, Teubner (2004b) points out that the legal system in fact adjusts to globalization by creating new forms of law all the time. Where others only see a diminishing legal grip on global economic interactions, the systems theoretical perspective would point out that such an observation only refers to the diminishing grip of the law legislated by states. The legal system is capable of producing new forms of law for different systems of society. If this process in fact leads to a strong structural coupling between the legal system and the economic system, leaving out the political system to a considerable extent, it might even be warranted, as Teubner (ibid.) proposes, to talk of an 'economic constitution' of world society – just as, in systems-theoretical jargon, a 'national constitution' usually refers to a structural coupling of the political and the legal system which in this case both use the nation-state as a form of self-description. From this perspective, the question of whether and which such 'constitutions' exist in world society – be it an 'economic constitution', a global 'civil constitution', or any other constitution – is not a theoretical, but an empirical one: the question here is whether the legal system has 'internalized' and 'regularized' the reference to another system in its environment in its operations, i.e. whether it regularly constructs the operation of the other system in legal terms (and vice versa). Of course, there is no 'threshold' here from where on it would be legitimate to speak of such a 'constitution'. In fact, the term might be misleading to a certain extent given that what is described are processes of structural coupling between systems of world society and thus the evolving structures of this world society itself and the question involved is one of degree, not one of kind.

Before it is possible to move ahead and try to engage with the exercise to translate this vocabulary to the analysis of the various emerging 'legalities' in international relations, it is still necessary to point out how the legal system of world society is differentiated and structured internally and how it evolves within society.

First of all, it follows from the idea that the legal system of world society is a functionally differentiated, autopoietic, i.e. operatively closed, yet structurally coupled system of that society, that there is no notion of a 'unity' or a 'homogeneity' of law which could be invoked in this context save the unity provided by the reference to the basal code of the legal system ('legal/illegal'). Although it is the purpose of legal theory to assert some kind of a more substantial (if only processual) commonality of law, from the systems theoretical perspective this is just a part of the self-description of the legal system necessary for reproducing the boundary between system and environment. Thus understood it might indeed be legitimate to assert that the modern systems theory of world society and its account of the legal system is close to various accounts of 'legal pluralism'. However, this similarity is also superficial in the sense that systems theory accounts for the unity-in-diversity of different legal systems within the legal system of world society, whereas legal pluralism usually refers to differences between legal systems. Rather than in legal plurality as such, a systems theoretical perspective would be more interested in the form this plurality takes at any given time and how it evolves through history. In other words, the question here is one of how the legal system of world society is differentiated internally.

At first glance, the legal system seems to share with the political system of world society a primarily segmentary form of internal differentiation (cf. Luhmann 1998). For the political system, this simply means that it describes itself primarily through the form of the territorial state. Likewise, the legal system first and foremost seems to describe itself through the form of national legal systems. This does not mean that no other forms of differentiation would exist within the legal system – quite obviously there are many forms of functional (such as between civil law, criminal law etc.) or hierarchical differentiation (such as between federal and state laws in federal systems, for example) within the legal system itself. But through the doctrine of sovereignty, which serves as the formula through which the legal system asserts the validity of law, a primacy of segmentary differentiation of the system seems to be guaranteed.

It is of course exactly this idea of a primacy of a segmentary internal differentiation of the legal system of world society which becomes questionable as a result of the proliferation of the many legalities in international relations – just as the primacy of a segmentary differentiation can hardly be upheld in relation to the political system with the increasing importance of transnational politics and structures of global governance. Yet before proceeding to more closely inspect not only the empirical contours, but also the theoretical implications of this move away from a primacy of a segmentary differentiation within the legal system, it is important to note what is at stake here: not the evolution of 'new' legal systems (emphasis on the plural), but changing forms of the internal differentiation of the legal system of world society and, closely connected, new structures emerging within this system, particularly also through structural coupling with other social systems. If the notion of 'autopoiesis' is taken seriously and social systems constitute themselves by a distinction from their environment in which all elements of the system are produced within the system itself by reference to a basal code, then there can only be one legal system in world society. There are of course internal differentiations, structural couplings to other social systems, and so on, but no legal systems somehow 'independent' or 'outside' of the legal system of world society. Any distinctiveness of, for example, the international legal system is only achieved through internal differentiations and the according self-descriptions of the legal system of world society. It is thus not a legal 'system' apart from 'national legal systems'.[4]

If the legal system of world society as an autopoietic social system evolves through a change in internal forms of differentiation, through structure-building concomitant to other systems through 'structural coupling', then the main task of the following section would be to translate the many facets and aspects of international legalization and the newly emerging legalities in international relations into such a conceptual framework. However, following the main thrust of a systems theoretical understanding of law, such a translation does not mean that some degree of order or even cohesion is read into this plurality of law and 'legalities' (save the one constituted by reading it in the framework of a theory of society). Quite to the contrary, the main question is whether the legal system can constitute itself as an 'order of disorder' (cf. Willke 2003: 78f.), able to respond to the chaotic and disorderly change of other systems, rather than lose its grip by asserting an 'order of orders' which cannot be upheld in the face of complex change. And there are indeed signs that the legal system of world society changes in such a way: 'What might have sounded daring for the level of the nation-state twenty years ago . . . is nowadays in the centre of a reality which constructs and constitutes legal regimes on the level of global relations at a breathtaking speed. In a relaxed fashion, the development of law goes over doubts that an increasing unstability of normativity could ring in the end of law' (ibid.: 94). It is in this sense that the remainder of this chapter will seek to map some major trends in the evolution and proliferation of 'legalities' in inter-national relations and seek to describe them in terms of a systems-theoretical description of the evolution of the legal system of world society. As has been pointed out before, the claim associated with this exercise is not to provide a 'better' explanation of any particular trend of international legalization or asso-ciated processes. Rather, it is to provide a vocabulary and thus a framework for a more comprehensive understanding of multiple processes in the international legal realm.

Trends in global legalization

As witnessed not least by the contributions to this volume, trends in the increase, variation and differentiation of legal (or 'law-like') arrangements beyond the boundaries of nation-states are now as complex and multi-faceted as the evolu-tion of mature national legal systems – or possibly even more so. Although it is now almost impossible to provide a comprehensive overview over these trends, let alone in the space available here, it seems possible to distil some broad developments which characterize the evolution of world society's legal system in its entirety.[5] These developments comprise:

1   The continuing evolution of international law, including the emergence of more and more elements of supranational law.
2   The emergence of 'new' legal arrangements mostly in the realm of a so-called 'transnational law'.
3   The increasing internationalization of national (and subnational) legal systems.
4   The increasing 'legalization' of various fields of social relations, but particularly also of international political relations.

(1) Although dismissed by some as an archaic body of law in a world less and less characterized by a monopoly or even a primacy of states (see Zumbansen 2001), 'classical' international law is alive and well and constantly evolving. International treaties are being concluded, rulings and opinions of international courts are being handed down, and the 'soft' law emerging out of practice and

academic opinion is constantly evolving.[6] This is of course not to suggest that international law would be the most dynamic sector of legal evolution; nor is such a diagnosis meant to ignore the massive problems stemming from continuing substantial breaches of the law. It is however to assert that since the end of the Second World War international law has developed at an exponential pace and has developed highly stable structures which contribute to its overall robustness. The constant evolution and domestic effectiveness of international human rights law is the case in point most frequently referred to in this context. And against fears that the standards of international human rights law and even the historically antecedent laws of war from the pre-First World War and inter-war periods have been hampered by events surrounding the post-9/11 'War on Terror', and particularly the 2003 invasion of Iraq, two things seem to be particularly noteworthy. First, although severe human rights abuses have occurred in Iraq, these have without exception been brandished and treated as such. They have not led to a delegitimation of the international human rights regime as such, but rather highlighted its claim to universal validity and applicability. Second, one of the most far-reaching recent innovations of international law, namely the installation of an international criminal law under the Rome statute and the resulting founding of International Criminal Court in The Hague, has taken place. Although quite often criticized for being ineffective without the participation of the United States in particular, the remarkable thing here rather seems to be that the ICC came into existence despite massive and active opposition form the US. This may have led to a considerable birth defect of the international criminal law system. Yet what it demonstrates is a remarkable degree of robustness of the international legal system as such, given that it can turn out major structural innovations even without (or, more precisely: even against) the will of major powers.

Although arguably different things in many respects, developments like the establishment of a system of international criminal justice on the one hand and the continuing evolution of European Union law on the other hand together point to a strengthening of different kinds of increasingly supranational legal forms. Together with some of the other developments mentioned below, the increasing supranationality of international law contributes to a growth in an emergent system level of world law which cannot plausibly be reduced to the sum of any underlying 'constituent units' (i.e. the legal systems of sovereign states).

(2) The development probably most intensively discussed at the disciplinary interstices of political science/international politics on the one hand and various branches of the legal sciences on the other has been the emergence of 'new' legal arrangements mostly in the realm of a so-called 'transnational law'. This transnational law today marks a field in which a bewildering variety of actors and regulating activities can be found. By definition, it is however characterized by either the absence or a new kind of state activity in drawing up legal arrangements. While the new '*lex mercatoria*' as the law of trade dispute settlement has long served as the 'showcase' of this new transnational law,[7] a growing body of

literature has pointed out that legal regulation can now be found in a wide array of areas beyond national legal systems and international law. Most notably, transnational legal arrangements are not limited to law-like arrangements between private actors alone. Governments too can choose law-like arrangements with a strong binding power without ever concluding an official international treaty, thus acting as 'quasi-private' law entrepreneurs. The Basle Committee on Banking Supervision or the International Organization of Securities Commissions are good cases in point (see on these Zaring 1998).[8] Other examples, ranging from internet domain name regulation (as part of an emerging '*lex digitalis*') to environmental law making by certification are aptly described in the chapters of this volume.

(3) A major development which only recently has received increased attention in the literature concerns the growing internationalization of national (and, by extension, subnational) legal systems beyond the mandatory recognition of norms of international law. Although, despite in a few cases such as within the European Union's legal system, it seems premature to speak of an extensive 'harmonization' of law between the many different national legal systems in the world, an increasing internationalization is taking place within national legal systems.[9] On the one hand, many legal practices and formulas from other legal systems, such as plea bargaining (see Langer 2004), are copied and applied all over the world. On the other hand, courts and lawmakers alike are increasingly willing to resort to the experiences and rulings of other national or international courts or law-making bodies (see Attanasio 1996). This is, for example, demonstrated by the increasing recognition of foreign legal opinions by the US Supreme Court as a traditionally rather 'inward-oriented' court (and notwithstanding the fact of the sometimes very outspoken criticism of this practice by some of its judges; see Williams 2004). As mentioned already, it may seem premature to read into this increasing recognition of foreign legal practices and standards by national legal systems a trend towards a 'harmonization' or even an 'integration' of law. Yet it does point to a development within the legal system, where the 'globalization' of law which takes place in the fields of international and transnational law and the references by national legal systems to them is supplemented by an increasing 'internationalization' of law in which national legal organizations observe and link with each other.

In *A New World Order*, Anne-Marie Slaughter (2004) has extensively described this dimension of the globalization of law and pointed out that this internationalization of national legal systems is supported not only by an increasing recognition of the laws and rulings in other national legal systems by judges and legislators alike, but also by rather dense networks between parliaments, courts, bar associations, and, perhaps most importantly, the global operation of the big law firms.[10] This points to the fact that indeed all the developments described in this section are accompanied by an increasing density of legal organizations and inter-organizational networks without which the variety of new legal and law-like arrangement in international relations could not have occurred or be sustained.

(4) In recent years the debate within the academic field of international relations in particular has debated trends of 'international legalization' (see Abbott *et al.* 2000; Finnemore and Toope 2001; Zangl and Zürn 2004). Although the subject of sometimes heated controversy regarding its scope and meaning, it seems safe to say that what is usually primarily associated with the term is not any particular of the developments alluded to in the preceding paragraphs, but primarily a new quality of political cooperation between states. Set against the background of regime theory in international relations, the entire debate on legalization can be said to be primarily about the fact that in regulating cooperation of various kinds, states increasingly resort to law or law-like arrangements. Unlike the three developments mentioned before, 'international legalization' is thus not a development of the legal system itself, but more of a 'mirror' development of the international political system (necessitating change in the legal system also, however). It is listed here nonetheless exactly because it is an area which has attracted vast attention in discussions over the evolution of new legalities in international relations without being clearly separated from other developments of the legal system as such. In this respect, it provides a useful entry point for the next section in order to illustrate how the evolution of the legal and the political system conceived as different function systems of world society can be described under the theoretical umbrella provided by a systems-theoretical world society theory which allows for a coherent account of the various developments alluded to in this section, without denying the sometimes vast differences.

World society's legal system: towards constitutionalization

The debate about international legalization provides a suitable example with which it is possible to illustrate the systems-theoretical perspective on the evolution of the legal system of world society. Against the premise of the autopoietic closure and resulting operative autonomy of social systems, 'legalization' first and foremost refers to a process in which the legal system increasingly describes systems in its environment in legal terms. It is not something somehow 'happening to' other systems, but marks an evolution of the legal system itself. Of course, the political system may observe itself as being increasingly bound by law. The question in this case becomes an empirical one about whether this indeed corresponds to descriptions emerging within the legal system – but 'legalization' thus understood can only take place within the legal system. It is a development within and of the legal system which 'legalizes' in the sense that it describes more and more realms of society in its terms. Indeed, bar any of the highly controversial debates on what constitutes or counts as 'law', such an understanding might in fact account for the oscillating meaning seemingly inherent in the differentiation between 'law' and 'law-like' applied within this volume and beyond. 'Law' in this case would be strictly reserved to something observed and described by the legal system as legally binding (in whatever remote and weak sense), whereas 'law-like' would then indicate a property ascribed within another function system without any corresponding development within the legal system.

Such a notion of legalization is quite different from those discussed in the IR literature since it does not primarily point to the legalization of political affairs, but to the evolution of the legal system. Nonetheless, some kind of 'translation' is possible if one takes into account the notion of structural coupling which serves as a theoretical means in systems theory to describe the 'link' between evolutions in different function systems. Grossly oversimplifying the theoretical account for illustrative purposes again, structural couplings represent sedimented or institutionalized observations of systems by other systems. And it may indeed seem to make sense to read the trend of 'international legalization' as a development which indicates specific emerging forms of structural coupling between the legal and the political systems of world society. To reiterate the point, legalization taking the form of a structural coupling between different systems is not specific to the relation between the legal and the political systems of world society. Quite to the contrary, much of the vibrancy of the evolution of the global legal system takes place as a more or less 'spontaneous' law-formation without the involvement of the political system at the interstices of the legal system and various function systems which exhibit an ever-increasing demand for legal regulations in an – in their perception – ever more complex globalized environment. It is in this sense that 'legalization', in relation to the political or other function systems of world society, does not refer to a uniform or ordered process at all; rather, legalization happens as a chaotic process of systems co-evolution (which is not even necessarily synchronized). It is however a process which achieves a dynamic of its own if and when social systems observe this process as such and begin to orient expectations not only towards specific demands for legalization, but towards legalization itself, i.e. when there is a growing expectation that the legal system moulds specific developments in systems in its environment in legal terms.[11] Such an understanding of legalization is broader than that mostly discussed in the field of International Relations, yet in an important sense also narrower than the one mostly employed throughout this volume, which, as Brütsch and Lehmkuhl point out in the introductory chapter, refers to 'legalities' broadly understood as 'social constellations in which individual and organizational behaviour is guided by overt sets of norms and rules'. This definition explicitly does not link 'legalities' to legal norms and rules. From a systems theoretical point of view, however, it only makes sense to speak of 'legalities' when and where communication takes place within the legal system – with reference to the system's basic code of legal/illegal. A reference to any kind of norm- or rule-oriented communication seems far too elusive for providing a reliable benchmark in order to distinguish legal and non-legal communication.[12]

Of course, such a rather 'strict' understanding of legalization processes leads to the question of the quality of these processes, their impact in different social systems, and, most importantly, their structural effects across such systems in world society.

As alluded to briefly already, the strongest such structural effect in world society would seem to be the emergence of various 'constitutions' in world society. The basic idea underlying this diagnosis is that constitutions are in fact societal phenomena of a strong coupling between the legal system and another function system of world society, and are not limited to a structural coupling between the legal and the political system in 'state-centred' constitutions (cf. Teubner 2004a). In addition to a global political constitution, an economic constitution building on the law of a *'lex mercatoria'* and a *'lex digitalis'* has been most widely discussed in this context, although of course not every process of legalization leads to a constitutionalization in this sense. Yet if such constitutionalizing processes can be observed, then indeed it may be warranted to speak of an important, newly emerging structural feature of world society – and one which can barely be seen from the perspective of many other accounts of legalization. However, a cautionary note is in place here. Although there seems to be ample evidence that something like an economic constitution or in fact a number of different economic constitutions are emerging in the field of *lex mercatoria* and the like, these remain constitutions in a weak sense only. In particular it seems questionable whether a significant constitutional discourse can be observed empirically (at least outside of its descriptions within the scientific system). Without denying the existence of some indicators in this direction, and without questioning the theoretical plausibility of such an approach of 'societal constitutionalism' applied to world society via the systems-theoretical notion of structural coupling, it still seems that the political system of world society is the most 'advanced' in terms of producing a constitution through structural coupling with the legal system. According to the reading proposed here, this is exactly what the discourse about 'legalization' in international relations in its entirety is mainly about: an ever-increasing density of politics beyond the nation-state being described by the legal system on the one hand, and a corresponding expectation by the political system on the other hand that new issues arising will be described in legal terms. At first this seems to be a rather nuanced shift in reading processes of international legalization. However, given the usually rather one-sided institutionalist account of legalization as something somehow 'happening to' political relations, it provides a rather substantial change of perspective, relocating the processes of international institutionalization[13] and legalization into the framework of the structural development of a global political constitution.[14] This still may sound rather unspectacular if what is expected under the term is an equivalent to a state-centred constitution. Yet it is far from being a marginal development if read as a main emergent feature of world society – with other constitutionalizing processes possibly following suit.

Such a sceptical diagnosis of constitutionalization in world society (compared to Teubner *et al.*), which for the time being primarily perceives constitutionalization to take place between the political and the legal systems of world society, should however not obscure that legalization does take place in many other forms and varieties as well. Yet only in relation to the structural coupling between the political system and the legal system of world society does the

observation and systemic self-description of this process in terms of 'global governance' seem to have achieved a quality that the criteria referred to above are
met to a significant degree and it thus seems legitimate to refer to a global constitution. Regularities and evolving patterns notwithstanding, no such 'ordering
of disorder' through systemic reflective devices seems to have emerged in structural couplings between the legal and other function systems to warrant extensive talk of 'constitutions' there yet. Legalization here takes place in a much
more chaotic and disorderly fashion.[15]

Any analysis of constitutionalization in world society therefore needs to be
complemented not only by an analysis of other forms of legalization, but also of
course of purely internal evolutions of the legal system of world society.

Beyond legalization

What is 'gained' by enlisting the difficult language of systems theory in the Luhmannian fashion for the analysis of the increase, variation, and differentiation of
legal and law-like agreements in international relations? Very little if one is
happy with adding case after case in a vain search for some emerging regularities. Very much however, if the aim is to bring the many facets of contemporary
legalization in international relations under the umbrella of a conceptual framework which allows them to relate to each other and to a broader societal context
in their diversity. Here, the systems theoretical description of world society provides a powerful tool to put some degree of analytical order to what otherwise
might seem as utter empirical chaos. It does so by starting from the observation
that regularities and orderliness in the global legal system and beyond cannot be
accounted for by reference to any underlying regularity given the kinds of complexity in which self-referential, autopoietic social systems operate. Yet by
building on the notions of operative closure of function systems as well as by
introducing the notion of structural coupling, such an approach is able to
describe the bewildering variety of 'legalities' in a much more systematic
fashion – as developments of the legal system on the one hand, and developments of the legal system in structural coupling with different function systems
on the other hand. A specific understanding of 'constitution' emerges in this
context which points to the fact that beyond various processes of legalization
these can form the basis for emergent structures of world society. The description and analysis of such structures provides a necessary task if one not only
seeks to be alert to changes within existing structures of world politics and law,
but also to the possibility that within social systems genuinely new ('emergent')
phenomena and structures can occur, which can neither be reduced to the sum of
preceding phenomena and structures, nor be properly described with the conceptual vocabulary appropriate for the latter.

Notes

1 The major summary of Luhmann's theory is laid down in Luhmann 1997b; a useful introduction to its analysis of law is provided by Teubner *et al.* 2002.

2 On this conceptualization of world society and its relation to other world society theories, see Albert and Hilkermeier 2004.

3 All translations are my own.

4 The notion of 'international law as an autopoietic system' (D'Amato 2005) can in my view not be upheld; there is no code specific to the international legal system which would enable it to achieve operational closure.

5 For a more comprehensive overview arguing in a similar direction, see Günther and Randeria (2001).

6 See as overviews: Bogdandy 2003; Paech 2004.

7 See Albert 2002 for an extensive review of the literature.

8 'In the absence of world government, sovereign nations do not function within a background legal environment. Thus, they must create their own rules of the game. Lacking a coercive world authority to enforce these rules, sovereigns embed them in governance mechanisms roughly analogous to those used by market actors to structure their relationships' (Tarullo 2000: 485f.).

9 This is not to deny at all that harmonization is taking place (see Wiener 1999); but it is not a process at pace with the overall evolution and proliferation of law.

10 For a critique of Slaughter's position which basically identifies her position as legitimizing a hegemonic approbation of international law by the US legal system, see Alston 1997.

11 These theoretical considerations apart, the empirical analysis of 'legalization' leaves much to be desired. Despite notable attempts during the course of the legalization debate in the field of International Relations in particular, there still seems to be no systematic attempt of stock-taking of international legalization in relation to the political system (and even less so beyond); but see, for example, the attempt to systematically collect the body of law making up the '*lex mercatoria*' under www.transnational-law.de (last accessed 15 June 2006); or the collection of international courts and tribunals under www.pict-pcti.org (last accessed 15 June 2006).

12 Thus understood, it does also seem to make little sense to speak of things like 'extralegal contractual relations' (see Bernstein 1992). The very notion of a 'contract' does refer to its validity as a legally binding norm. For a more fundamental critique of a norm-oriented understanding of law in general, see Willke 2003 and, albeit in the different direction of an 'interactional theory of law' which 'treats bindingness as an internal quality of actors', Brunnée and Toope 2000 (56).

13 Although the notions of 'institution' and 'institutionalization' arguably have no place in the systems-theoretical framwork, in 'IR terms', 'structural coupling' could be described as an extremely 'thick' form of institutionalization with resulting emergent properties within a system which can no longer be reduced to original constitutive units.

14 Another sense in which the notion of 'constitutionalization' could be used is thereby excluded here, namely the possibility to increasingly read charters of international organizations as 'constitutions' of these organizations (see Alvarez 2001), possibly even leading to the emergence of some kind of 'intergovernmental societies' (Allott 2001). Given the rather 'broad' understanding of what constitutes a political constitution in relation to more 'classical' state-centred constitutions, particularly those laid down in constitutional texts, it seems highly implausible that such a global constitution could ever (or already has been – see Fassbender 1998) be laid down in a concentrated written format.

15 And it needs to be emphasized here again that the emerging 'global constitution' as a

structural coupling between the political and the legal system is not characterized by an 'ordering principle'; an order of disorder is only provided by forms of second-order observation by the systems themselves.

References

Abbott, K.W., Keohane, R.O., Moravcsik, A., Slaughter, A.-M. and Snidal, D. (2000) 'The concept of legalization', *International Organization*, 54 (3): 401–419.

Albert, M. (2002) Zur Politik der Weltgesellschaft. Identität und Recht im Kontext globaler Vergesellschaftung, Weilerswist: Velbrück.

Albert, M. (2005) 'Restructuring world society. The contribution of modern systems theory', in E. Grande and L. Pauly (eds) *Reconstituting Political Authority: Complex Sovereignty and the Foundations of Global Governance*, Toronto: University of Toronto Press, pp. 48–67.

Albert, M. and Hilkermeier, L. (2004) *Observing International Relations: Niklas Luhmann and World Politics*, London: Routledge.

Allott, P. (2001) 'Intergovernmental societies and the idea of constitutionalism', in J.-M. Coicaud and V. Heiskanen (eds) *The Legitimacy of International Organizations*, Tokyo: United Nations University Press, pp. 69–103.

Alston, P. (1997) 'The myopia of handmaidens: international lawyers and globalization', *European Journal of International Law*, 8 (3): 435–448.

Alvarez, J.E. (2001) 'Constitutional interpretation in international organizations', in J.-M. Coicaud and V. Heiskanen (eds) *The Legitimacy of International Organizations*, Tokyo: United Nations University Press, pp. 104–154.

Attanasio, J.B. (1996) 'Rapporteur's overview and conclusions: of sovereignty, globalization, and courts', in T. Franck and G. Fox (eds) *International Law Decisions in National Courts*, London: Transaction Publishers, pp. 373–395.

Bernstein, L. (1992) 'Opting out of the legal system: extralegal contractual relations in the diamond industry', *The Journal of Legal Studies*, 21 (1): 115–157.

Bogdandy, A. von (2003) 'Demokratie, Globalisierung, Zukunft des Völkerrechts. Eine Bestandsaufnahme', *Zeitschrift für Ausländisches Öffentliches Recht und Völkerrecht*, 63: 853–877.

Brunnée, J. and Toope, S.J. (2000) 'International law and constructivism: elements of an interactional theory of international law', *Columbia Journal of Transnational Law*, 39 (1): 19–74.

D'Amato, A. (2005) 'International law as an autopoietic system', in R. Wolfrum and V. Rüben (eds) *Developments of International Law in Treaty Making*, Berlin: Springer, pp. 335–399.

Fassbender, B. (1998) 'The United Nations Charter as constitution of the international community', *Columbia Journal of Transnational Law*, 37 (3): 529–619.

Finnemore, M. and Toope, S.J. (2001) 'Alternatives to "legalization": richer views of law and politics', *International Organization*, 55 (3): 743–758.

Fischer-Lescano, A. and Teubner, G. (2004) 'Regime-collisions: the vain search for legal unity in the fragmentation of global law', *Michigan Journal of International Law*, 25 (4): 999–1046.

Fischer-Lescano, A. and Teubner, G. (2006) *Regimekollisionen. Zur Fragmentierung des Globalen Rechts*, Frankfurt/M.: Suhrkamp.

Günther, K. and Randeria, S. (2001) *Recht, Kultur und Gesellschaft im Prozeß der Globalisierung*, Bad Homburg: Werner Reimers Stiftung.

Langer, M. (2004) 'From legal transplants to legal translations: the globalization of plea bargaining and the Americanization thesis in criminal procedure', *Harvard International Law Journal*, 45 (1): 1–64.

Luhmann, N. (1997a) *Das Recht der Gesellschaft*, 2nd edn, Frankfurt/M.: Suhrkamp.

Luhmann, N. (1997b) *Die Gesellschaft der Gesellschaft*, Frankfurt/M.: Suhrkamp (2 vols).

Luhmann, N. (1998) *Die Politik der Gesellschaft*, Frankfurt/M.: Suhrkamp.

Paech, N. (2004) 'Epochenwechsel im Völkerrecht?', *Aus Politik und Zeitgeschichte*, B43: 21–29.

Schulte, M. (2003) 'Begriff und Funktion des Rechts in der Gesellschaft', in M. Aitenza, E. Pattaro and M. Schulte (eds) *Theorie des Rechts und der Gesellschaft*, Berlin: Duncker & Humblot, pp. 767–789.

Slaughter, A.-M. (2004) *A New World Order*, Princeton, NJ: Princeton University Press.

Tarullo, D.K. (2000) 'Norms and institutions in global competition policy', *American Journal of International Law*, 94 (3): 478–504.

Teubner, G. (1993) *Law as Autopoietic System*, Oxford: Basil Blackwell.

Teubner, G. (2004a) 'Societal constitutionalism: alternatives to state-centred constitutional theory?', in C. Joerges, I.-J. Sand and G. Teubner (eds) *Constitutionalism and Transnational Governance*, London: Hart, pp. 3–28.

Teubner, G. (2004b) 'Global private regimes: neo-spontaneous law and dual constitution of autonomous sectors?', in K.-H. Ladeur (ed.) *Public Governance in the Age of Globalization*, Aldershot: Ashgate, pp. 71–87.

Teubner, G., Nobles, R. and Schiff, D. (2002) 'The Autonomy of law: an introduction to legal autopoiesis', in R. Nobles and D. Schiff (eds) *Jurisprudence*, London: Butterworths, pp. 897–954.

Twining, W. (2000) *Globalisation and Legal Theory*, London: Butterworths.

Wiener, J. (1999) Globalization and the Harmonization of Law, London: Pinter.

Williams, D. (2004) 'Courts and Globalization', *Indiana Journal of Global Legal Studies*, 11 (1): 57–70.

Willke, H. (2003) *Atopia*, Frankfurt: Suhrkamp.

Zangl, B. and Zürn, M. (2004) *Verrechtlichung – Baustein für Global Governance?* Bonn: Stiftung Entwicklung und Frieden.

Zaring, D. (1998) 'International law by other means: the twilight existence of international financial regulatory organizations', *Texas International Law Journal*, 33 (2): 281–330.

Zumbansen, P. (2001) 'Die vergangene Zukunft des Völkerrechts', *Kritische Justiz* 34 (1): 46–68.

11 The role of the transnational corporation in the process of legalization

Insights from Economics and Corporate Social Responsibility[1]

Andreas Georg Scherer and Dorothée Baumann

Introduction: transnational corporations as addressees or authors of global rules?

Traditionally, the state has been regarded as the sole actor designing the legal framework that guarantees private rights, political rights and social rights for all members of society (Marshall 1965). In this ideal conception, companies are the addressees of public rules and regulations and the state apparatus enforces companies' compliance to the given legal framework. With globalization, however, the activities of companies go beyond the sphere of national regulations, and transnational corporations (TNCs) are thus no longer subjected to an individual national legal framework. For a functioning market economy though, some rules are indispensable. Therefore, even liberal authors who are very critical of state interventions would agree that some rules need to be in place (Friedman 1962; Nozick 1975; v. Hayek 1945). Yet on a global scale, frameworks that encompass global rules cannot be designed by a centralized governmental institution.

The analysis of global governance processes, referring to rule making and rule enforcement on a global scale, clearly demonstrates that the formulation of rules is no longer a task managed by the state alone (see, e.g. Braithwaite and Drahos 2000; Brozus *et al.* 2003; Günther 2001; Kingsbury 2003; Shelton 2000; Zürn 1998). Rather, in recent years, civil society groups as well as TNCs increasingly participate in the formulation and implementation of rules in policy areas that were once the sole responsibility of the state or international organizations (Matten and Crane 2005). Rule making activities of TNCs and civil society groups include, e.g. protecting human rights (Breining-Kaufmann 2004; Kinley and Tadaki 2004; Campbell and Miller 2004; Cragg 2005), implementing social and environmental standards (Christmann 2004; Scherer and Smid 2000), or involvement in peace-keeping activities (Fort and Schipani 2002). Such activities indicate the shift in global business regulation from state-centric towards new multilateral and non-territorial modes of regulation with non-state actors involved (Braithwaite and Drahos 2000).

In legal studies, however, only recently have scholars given credit to these developments. Some scholars acknowledge the significance of private rule making (Parker and Braithwaite 2003; Teubner 1997) and discuss the responsibility of private firms to implement human rights beyond the scope and territory of national regulation (Campbell and Miller 2004; Kinley and Tadaki 2004; Weissbrodt and Krueger 2003). Cragg (2005: 24) states that there is an 'emerging international consensus, [. . .] that respect for human rights is a basic obligation of multinational corporations operating at home and abroad'. At present, however, neither national nor international law is able sufficiently to regulate the behaviour of multinational firms (Avi-Yonah 2003). In their recent discussion on human rights responsibilities of TNCs, Kinley and Tadaki (2004: 1021) therefore conclude that

> [t]he state-centric framework of international human rights law and attendant institutions is at present ill-equipped to regulate powerful non-state actors like TNCs, which are, by definition, not constrained by notions of territorial sovereignty.

Obviously, the problems of globalization require new conceptions that go beyond traditional approaches in legal studies (see, e.g. Günther 2001; Kingsbury 2003; Parker and Braithwaite 2003). Kingsbury (2003: 295) stresses that an adequate theoretical approach to international law 'must be concerned with participation and with managing inequality'. Günther and Randeria (2001) analyse the transnationalization of the law and they identify international law firms, legal counsels and international organizations as important private actors that play an active role in shaping these processes. TNCs, however, are not yet fully recognized as potential sources of rule-making and enforcement. Too often business firms are mainly considered addressees of national regulation rather than the authors of public rules.

In international relations the situation is quite similar. While the issues of global governance and the contribution of non-state actors are widely discussed in the political sciences, TNCs have not yet come into sharp focus (see e.g. Abbott and Snidal 2000; Risse 2002; Zürn 1998). This is also true when students of political sciences explicitly consider the process of legalization in world politics, i.e. the process of the institutionalization of international rules, and analyse its characteristics. Here the sources of the rules' obligations, the precision of rules as well as their interpretation or enforcement by third parties are discussed extensively, while business firms are still neglected (see e.g. Goldstein *et al.* 2000). In fact, private business firms and their behaviour are rather seen as a problem of global regulatory policy rather than as part of the solution. Therefore, the potential of private business firms to contribute to the process of global legalization has not been acknowledged sufficiently in the political sciences.

The state of the art in theory stands in stark contrast to empirical observations in management practice. The initiatives of TNCs towards private rule-making are manifold and have received various labels: 'Corporate Social Responsibility'

(CSR) (Smith 2003; Snider 2003; Zadek 2004); 'Corporate Sustainability' (Sharma and Starik 2002); 'Corporate Citizenship' (Matten and Crane 2005); 'Corporate Philanthropy' (Porter and Kramer 2002); or 'Business Ethics' (Cavanagh 2004). Many TNCs engage in self-regulation and set up their own 'codes of conduct'. These codes define the humanitarian and environmental standards of their business practices that are implemented within the companies. Often, they are even enforced within their entire area of influence, including contractors and subcontractors (Sethi 2002, 2003; Williams 2000). TNCs also engage in rule-making activities at the industry level (see e.g. the responsible care initiative of the chemical industries) and they cooperate with NGOs and state actors in public–private partnerships to identify and solve problems in various areas of public concern (Argenti 2004; Grimsey and Lewis 2004; Reinicke and Deng 2000; Schneider and Ronit 1999).

The United Nations even wants to explicitly employ this potential of TNCs (Annan 1999; Williams 2004; www.unglobalcompact.com). At the World Economic Forum in 1999, UN secretary general Kofi Annan asked business leaders to join a 'Global Compact' with the goal of fostering nine – now ten – fundamental principles in the areas of human rights, labour and environment worldwide.[2] Annan argues that the involvement of business is necessary because in many Third World countries governments are either unable or unwilling to implement social and environmental standards. Since state sovereignty prevents supranational organizations like the UN or the ILO from intervening, TNCs in many cases remain the only actors that, due to their economic power, can effectively influence conditions. This situation has led some students to argue that business firms have an enlarged responsibility to engage in these issues (see e.g. Santoro 2000; Weissbrodt and Kruger 2003; Young 2004).

The UN Global Compact initiative has advanced as one of the most popular examples of emerging global government structures. Sahlin-Andersson (2004: 134) describes the UN Global Compact as an initiative

> in which new rules, standards and reporting systems are advocated as ways of coordinating or facilitating collaboration and coordination without challenging the sovereignity of individual actors. The Global Compact does emphasize that it is not a regulatory framework. Yet, every group that joins the Global Compact is expected to comply with and actively spread the agreed principles.

As these examples show, new modes of regulation are emerging at a global level. So called 'soft' forms of regulation and network-building have been growing over the last decades (see Mörth 2004) and they 'tend to transcend the regulation-deregulation divide' (Sahlin-Andersson 2004: 135).

Given these developments, how could the rule-making activities of TNCs be integrated in the new emerging theoretical framework of 'legalization' in legal studies and political science? In the following, in order to facilitate interdisciplinary discourse, we will consider what economics and business management contribute to these problems. We are convinced that it is of mutual benefit for the various disciplines (international relations, legal studies, economics, and business management) to learn from each other how to approach the important issues of global governance and legalization and how these problems affect or are affected by transnational business firms.

To give credit to the different theoretical perspectives of this volume, we will use a very broad definition of 'regulation'. The definition is based on the observation that regulation is not confined to law but that there are various sources of regulatory ordering. We agree with Parker and Braithwaite (2003: 136) that 'there exist many forms of formal and informal, legal and non-legal ordering in society and multiple motivations and normative commitments amongst targets of regulation'. On this broad view, 'regulation' stands for influencing the flow of events and as governments increasingly shift their energies to enable other actors to regulate (a development that Braithwaite and Parker call the 'new regulatory state') this broad understanding of 'regulation' comes close to the meaning of 'governance' where not only state organizations but all kinds of actors are involved in rule making.

Transnational corporations as economic actors – insights from economics and the theory of the firm

Economic theory of free trade

Many economists do not recommend business support of the UN Global Compact or other CSR-initiatives (see e.g. Henderson 2001; Krauss 1997; Lal 2003). Irwin (2002: 214) for instance argues:

> Still, the best and most direct way to raise wages and labor standards is to enhance the productivity of the workers through economic development. Trade and investment are important components of that development, and therefore efforts to limit international trade or to shut down the sweatshops are counterproductive.

In economic theory, the dominant perception is that it is only through free trade that worldwide economic development and welfare becomes feasible (Irwin 2002). In past decades this position was very influencial on world politics and has led to a policy of liberalization and the abolition of trade barriers (Hoekman and Kostecki 1995). Economists suggest that market forces are set free so that capital can be optimally allocated and the advantages of specialization and division of labour become effective. It is assumed that only under the conditions of free trade developing countries can employ their (comparative) cost advantages through labour-intensive production.

A policy in favour of a worldwide harmonization of social and environmental standards, or tax rates, as is suggested by some students of legal studies (see e.g. Avi-Yonah 2000, 2003) is harshly convicted by economists (Irwin 2002).

Economists are convinced that the definition of a global level playing field would, by contrast, diminish the cost advantages of developing countries and would be unfavourable for economic development. Standards are regarded as 'non-tariff trade barriers' that only create obstacles to free trade (see e.g. Lal 1998, 2003). This is one of the main reasons why developing countries have in all multilateral meetings, like the WTO or the UNCTAD meetings, voted against the introduction of social and environmental standards or the definition of a 'social clause' (see critically, Lee 1997). From the same perspective, Krauss argues '[t]he way to help poor people abroad is to open our markets to them ... not to force them to adopt human rights standards' (Krauss 1997: 51). According to Barro (1994, 1997) economic development has to come first, leaving aside democratization or social and environmental standards. And even economists from third world countries argue 'a lousy job is better than no job at all' (Martinez-Mont 1996). Therefore, from the economic point of view democratization and social development may be seen as a result of economic development but not as its preconditions.

Economic theory and the social responsibility of the firm

While the comments outlined above are directed towards state policy, some economists also criticize the socially responsible behaviour of private business firms (Henderson 2001; Jensen 2002; Rugman 2000; Sundaram and Inkpen 2004). This was already emphasized by Milton Friedman (1970) in his well-known statement 'the social responsibility of business is to increase its profits'. Friedman has examined initiatives of business firms and managers that were not oriented towards profit-making but towards emphasizing the social responsibility of the company. Friedman (1970) rejects such activities and even claims that they harm the roots of the free society. While he entitles owners of business firms to behave in a socially altruistic way – they can do whatever they want with their money – he harshly criticises managers that are not focusing solely on profits because they are wasting the money of other people. Managers, as agents of the company owners, are obliged to act in the owner's best interest and this interest is usually to increase profits. Today this position has become widely known as the so-called shareholder-value orientation of the corporation. This critical position towards corporate social responsibility also becomes obvious in recent statements of economists. In his examinations of the stakeholder approach, Jensen (2002: 242) rejects the social responsibility of the firm:

> stakeholder theory plays into the hands of self-interested managers allowing them to pursue their own interests at the expense of society and the firm's financial claimants. It allows managers and directors to invest in their favourite projects that destroy firm-value whatever they are (the environment, art, cities, medical research) without having to justify the value destruction.

Profit-orientation, however, is not set absolute, neither in Friedman's nor in Jensen's conception. They both stress that managers have to abide by national and local laws and by common decency. Friedman, for example, refers to 'basic rules in the society, both those embodied in law and those embodied in ethical custom' (Friedman 1970: 218). Profit-orientation is instead justified (in the tradition of Adam Smith) through the increase of public welfare that it generates and of which all members of a society should profit. In the words of Jensen: '... social welfare is maximized when all firms in an economy maximize total firm value' (Jensen 2002: 239). This, however, only works under the precondition that the state sets the rules of the economic game and all members of the society can be forced to comply with these rules. The state produces the public goods that neither the market nor any private actor can supply. In addition, the state attempts to define the rules in a way so that the externalities of market coordination can be internalized.

Therefore, the coordination mechanism of the market only develops in the desired direction if the market is embedded in a politically designed framework of rules and this 'framework' defines the rules that are necessary to achieve the optimal allocation of resources through market processes. The framework then assures that actors can pursue their private interests without considering the desired societal outcome such as economic welfare and peace. As long as certain preconditions are in place, the 'invisible hand' (Adam Smith) of the market will help to achieve these goals.

In this model of the integration of society the design of the regulatory framework is the sole task of the state. This is still a dominant premise in the economic theory of the firm. It also becomes obvious when Sundaram and Inkpen (2004) suggest that managers of corporations should focus on profits only to satisfy the legitimate concerns of shareholders assuming that '[t]he interests of stakeholders such as employees, suppliers, bondholders, communities, and customers are protected by contract law and by regulation' (ibid.: 335). Thus, it is the state that has to define and to enforce the rules according to which economic processes can develop. The liberal model of society is based on a strict separation of the public sphere (state) and the private sphere (economy) (Friedman 1962). The state sets the rules of the game and the companies pursue profits within these rules. Conclusively, in the economic model, firms are considered as economic actors only. While so-called 'political' activities of firms such as lobbying or public relations (Keim 2001) as well as an instrumental understanding of corporate social responsibility are seen as part of the economic role (see e.g. McWilliams and Siegel 2001), an intrinsic political or social responsibility of the firm is rejected.

The limits of the liberal model of society[3]

It is debatable whether this model of state regulation still fits under the circumstances of globalization. Despite liberals' scepticism of a strong state, the liberal model nevertheless assigns regulatory power to the state only. This perspective is problematic in two respects: the limits of formal law and bureaucracy on the one hand and the process of globalization on the other.

First, abstract rules never perfectly fit to all kinds of situations in daily life but need to be adjusted and interpreted constantly. Therefore, in order to implement state-designed rules according to their original purpose, private actors have to consider – like state actors do – how their actions best serve public welfare (see Steinmann and Löhr 1996). Particularly, in the modern society, the state is incapable of recognizing and anticipating all possible conflicts, and by legislation and bureaucracy, coordinating problems that can arise from an increasingly interconnected and highly complex environment. Therefore, social integration cannot be sufficiently achieved by state-designed formal rules only (Stone 1975). In this context, Paine (1994) has pointed out the importance of 'organizational integrity'. She argues that corporations need a comprehensive approach that goes beyond legal compliance because otherwise the organization could be deprived of benefits. Therefore, deficits in regulation have to be managed in self-organizing processes among the parties involved where companies voluntarily abide by self-defined rules. This shows that business ethics are both a necessary and complementary element for regulating the market (Stone 1975; Steinmann and Löhr 1996; Steinmann and Scherer 2000). The commitment to voluntary codes that complement national regulations is, however, only credible if the commitment gets controlled regularly, if the results are transparent and can be verified by an external independent party (Weissbrodt and Kruger 2003).

With globalization, regulatory gaps are increasing (Beck 2000; Giddens 1990; Habermas 2001) and the question arises as to whether the liberal model of society is still the appropriate foundation for explaining the current 'move to law' in international relations. Globalization processes not only increase the complexity of the environment, but also enable economic actors to cross the territory-bound regulation of state agencies (Zürn 1998). Due to technological progress it has become possible for companies to split up their value-chain processes and distribute their production sites worldwide. As a result, companies are no longer subject to the rules defined by the nation state but can choose among alternative regulations according to economic criteria only (Ghemawat 2003; see critically, Scherer 2003, 2004). By doing so, economic actors undermine the internal sovereignty of the nation state, namely the ability of the state 'to independently set rules and limit or regulate any private activity on its territory' (Reinicke and Witte 1999: 345, translation by the authors).

Regarding the obvious limits of positive law and bureaucracy on the one hand and the consequences of globalization on the other, the liberal model of state-regulation has become questionable. International law scholars have also learnt from regional initiatives like the European integration process and they are currently rethinking their definition of sovereignty and starting to develop concepts of multilevel governance (Bernhard 2002).

Interestingly though, many economists do not regard the loss of regulatory capacity of the nation state as a problem for the liberal model of society. Rather, they take the competition between locations and regulations (competition of systems) as an opportunity to limit the influence of the state, to cut back on over-regulation, and to stress market forces, assuming that such a competition of systems results in an optimal level of regulation (see e.g. Marciano and Josselin 2003; Siebert 1998). However, what is neglected in these expectations is that a functioning system of competition requires 'rules of the game' that are enforceable by an arbitrator (see critically, Avi-Yonah 2000). For the competitive markets in goods and services this role has been assigned to the state. For the competition of legal institutions there does not exist a comparable institution at the global level. As a consequence, to attract foreign capital, some states do not protect human rights, rather they, for instance, suppress unions (Chan 2003), only have loose environmental regulation (Greider 1997; Scherer and Smid 2000), or cut taxes and loosen the social safety net (Avi-Yonah 2000) thereby increasing the pressure on other states to do the same. Obviously, we need institutions of global governance that determine which measures are regarded as 'fair-play' in the competition of systems.

Social responsibility of firms in the field of business management

The instrumentalization of corporate social responsibility

Many students of business management deal with these developments in an ambiguous manner. This is particularly true for the research under the labels of 'business and society', 'stakeholder theory' and 'corporate social responsibility' that have gained wide attention. While these theories address the problematic social and environmental consequences of business activities, virtually all these approaches have in common the explicit or at least tacit uncritical acknowledgement of the economic role of the firm. Therefore, these schools of thought are an unstable basis for an extended understanding of the responsibilities of TNCs in a world society (see critically, Margolis and Walsh 2003; Scherer and Kustermann 2004; Scherer and Palazzo (2007); Walsh *et al.* 2003; Walsh 2005).

Carroll (1979, 1991) has come up with a four-dimensional conceptual model of corporate social performance (see also Wartick and Cochran 1985; Wood 1991). The author's definition of CSR addresses 'the entire range of obligations business has to society'. It considers economic, legal, ethical, and discretionary responsibilities and places the priority on the economic role of the firm. In Carroll's model it remains unclear how these different obligations of the firm are interconnected and how tensions between, for instance, the economic and the ethical role of a firm could be resolved. In respect to legal responsibilities, Carroll (1979: 500) states 'society expects business to fulfil its economic mission within the framework of legal requirements', and ignors cases of state failure as discussed in the previous chapter of our paper.

The stakeholder approach was developed by Edward Freeman in the 1980s (Freeman 1984; Freeman and McVea 2001). Freeman pointed out that when managers formulate and implement the company's strategy, they not only have to satisfy the expectations of the shareholders or the clients of the company, but also need to recognize various stakeholder interests. Depending on the amount of pressure a single stakeholder can exert on the company in a conflict, its interests have to be taken into consideration. This highlights that the stakeholder orientation has been instrumentalized for profit maximization (see critically, Scherer and Kustermann 2004; Scherer and Palazzo (2007); Whetten *et al.* 2002). Some authors are now proposing that for the purposes of stakeholder identification not only the power potential, but also the legitimacy and urgency of the stakeholders' claims should be taken into account (Agle *et al.* 1999; Mitchell *et al.* 1997). However, as long as power still dominates the other two factors, as is suggested by Frooman (1999) or Jawahar and McLaughlin (2001), only the stakes of groups will be recognized that are either instrumental for profit-making or able to harm the company economically.

In this perspective, the involvement of TNCs in processes of international legalization is determined by stakeholders. It is the stakeholders' demands and power that are shaping the TNCs' contribution to legalization processes. Since TNCs in this conception are only giving in to stakeholder demands if those can potentially harm their business, TNCs' rule making activities are solely driven by an economic rationale and not by considerations of serving the *res publica*. However, we assume that even though in most cases, scandals have triggered a company's move to self-regulation, some business firms have decided without any pressure from stakeholder groups to commit themselves to a number of principles or join initiatives of self-regulation (Spar and La Mure 2003).

Some scholars of the business and society approach argue that corporate social performance is best monitored through the instruments of public policy and government regulatory agencies (Preston and Post 1975; Buchholz 1992). Likewise, as we have analysed above, scholars in favour of the shareholder value maximization theory rely on the state to design a legal framework (Sundaram and Inkpen 2004). Yet the previous chapter has shown that the effectiveness of national law to regulate economic activities has substantially decreased over time and, therefore, under the circumstances of globalization, such a reference to national law and administration has become problematic.

In sum, business and society as well as the stakeholder approach only offer an insufficient explanation for the involvement of TNCs in processes of international legalization. Both approaches suffer from two major shortcomings. First, some scholars of these approaches still refer to the state when it comes to regulate economic actions and systematically fail to acknowledge the new situation that has evolved through globalization. Second, both approaches remain tightly embedded in the liberal economic model and do not recognize the need for a normative theory to determine the role of the TNC in world society. Reasons for these problems can not only be traced back to the misleading social theory, but also to the problematic positivist research methods that business and society research engages in. Scherer and Kustermann (2004) have demonstrated that the research methodology fundamentally drives the direction of theory-building and can bias results. Therefore, the authors suggest that business and society researchers should critically revise their methods (see also, Scherer and Palazzo 2007).

In light of these problems of existing approaches, alternative conceptions are required. Those have to come up with a well-grounded re-definition of the role of the TNC in the legalization process. In the following parts of the paper, alternative models of the role of the TNC are presented.

From market economics to utopia? – critical management and the ideal discourse coordination

There is one major school of thought in business management, which is highly critical towards the mainstream approaches of business and society, and corporate social responsibility. Critical management studies pick up the 1970s version of Jürgen Habermas's critical theory based on the concept of the 'ideal speech situation' (Habermas 1971). These approaches reject economic ideology and its tendency to support the concerns of powerful actors only. Therefore, critical management studies analyses the conditions of modern organizations and attempts to reveal structures of power and dependency in order to change social conditions (see e.g. Alvesson and Willmott 1992, 1995, 2003). Critical researchers want to give a voice to those whose concerns are systematically suppressed, e.g. low-skilled workers, women, minorities, the poor, etc. The economic constitution of the market as well as the hierarchical structure of modern organizations is conceived of as a measure for systematic suppression and control (see e.g. Boje and Dennehy 1993). Thus, critical management has a tendency to be anti-market and anti-hierarchy. As an alternative mode of coordination, the ideal discourse in the sense of Habermas is suggested. The ideal discourse conditions include freedom of access, participation with equal rights, truthfulness of the participants, and absence of coercion (cf. Habermas 1971: 136ff., 1993: 56). Habermas suggests a form of coordination that is oriented towards mutual understanding and agreement where the participants in discourse coordinate their plans of action consensually. For the business firm the critical management approach

> requires that stakeholders who influence or are influenced by organizations be identified as legitimate participants in the discourse on its strategy. Ideally, organizational goals should be settled discursively, through rational argumentation under undistorted communicative conditions.
>
> (Shrivastava 1986: 373)

This approach is now even acknowledged by stakeholder theorists. In his attempt to fill the normative gap of stakeholder theory, Phillips (2003) suggests designing stakeholder-dialogues according to the Habermasian approach:

While difficult in practice, the implication is that managing for stakeholders would entail duplicating as far as possible the conditions of the ideal speech situation.

However, we think that this approach is not feasible. Rather it appears to be a utopian or at least 'too idealistic' approach to societal coordination which is now even conceded by Habermas (1998: 244) (see also critically, Elster 1986; Scherer and Palazzo 2007; Steinmann and Scherer 2000). From our point of view private economic actors cannot be conceptualized in international legalization processes if market dynamics and hierarchies are abandoned. Rather, a theoretical framework has to be based on the realities of the economic environment. It has to capture the empirical observation that companies have themselves come up with systems of rules that are aimed at disciplining market forces in the global arena. It will require concerted effort and political will of all participants to equip these emerging self-regulatory systems with means that allow for democratic controls (see Scherer and Palazzo 2007). The concept of politics elaborated here is very different from the power politics model underlying economic theory (see, e.g. Keim 2001). Its underpinnings require a renewed picture of the relationship between politics and economics. It has been shown in this chapter that neither the mainstream approaches to CSR with its uncritical acceptance of economic ideology, nor critical management with its insensitivity to the benefits of market coordination and hierarchical control can provide the foundations for a new role of the TNC and its contribution to the legalization of global rules (see Scherer and Palazzo 2007).

Towards a political concept of corporate social responsibility – the contribution of Steinmann et al. and Matten and Crane

In the search of a more suitable foundation of a new theory of the firm, European academics have drafted approaches that are able to take the social responsibility of the firm as a political actor in the world society more seriously. For instance, authors like Horst Steinmann and his colleagues as well as Peter Ulrich and just recently the corporate citizenship approach presented from Dirk Matten and Andrew Crane point into such a new direction. By political we mean activities

> in which people organize collectively to regulate or transform some aspects of their shared social conditions, along with the communicative activities in which they try to persuade one another to join such collective actions or decide what direction they wish to take.
>
> (Young 2004: 377)

The business ethics approach according to the Erlangen conception has a 'supplementing function' in respect to the positive law of the state (Steinmann and Löhr 1994, 1995, 1996; Steinmann and Scherer 2000). This means that ethics in the sense of a self-organizing responsible activity is required whenever there is no other general rule available or when present rules fail to resolve conflicts that result as external effects from business activities. The supplementing function exercised by the corporation results from a republican model of politics. In the republican model, the double role of the corporation as private citizen ('bourgeois') and as citizen of a state ('citoyen') is emphasized (Habermas 1998). It is assumed that the role of the corporation resembles this double role of a citizen in a state.

As 'citoyens', corporations, as much as individual citizens, help to design rules that are of general interest. The 'general interest' is not, as in the liberal model of politics, the result of the aggregation of individual interests, but the result of a communication process through which individuals form or change their preferences over time (Elster 1986). The aim of such an interactive process is to come up with a common understanding of which goals shall be pursued and what rules are required. Only within this collectively defined political order, a domain of freedom is defined where citizens as well as corporations pursue their individual interests in their role as private citizens. In the republican view the citizens define these rules collectively (Steinmann and Scherer 2000). However, the

> state's raison d'être does not lie primarily in the protection of equal individual rights but in the guarantee of an inclusive process of opinion- and will-formation in which free and equal citizens reach an understanding on which goals and norms lie in the equal interest of all. In this way the republican citizen is credited with more than an exclusive concern with his or her private interests.
>
> (Habermas 1998: 241)

By contrast, liberal philosophy, which is part of the economic model of the integration of society, only recognizes citizens as private citizens who always pursue their individual interests, in the market as well as in politics (see Elster 1986; Friedman 1962; see critically, Habermas 1998). Citizen's choices in the market and in politics are an expression of their egoistic motives and therefore politics is in the liberal conception only power politics:

> On the liberal view, politics is essentially a struggle for positions that grant access to administrative power. The political process of opinion- and will-formation in the public sphere and in parliament is shaped by the competition of strategically acting collectives trying to maintain or acquire positions of power. Success is measured by the citizens' approval of persons and programmes, as quantified by votes. In their choices at the polls, voters express their preferences. Their votes have the same structure as the choices of participants in a market, in that their decisions license access to positions of power that political parties fight over with a success-oriented attitude similar to that of players in the market.
>
> (Habermas 1998: 243)

The conception of business ethics by Steinmann *et al.* follows the republican model of politics and regards the corporation as a political actor with rights and duties and by doing so is able to justify why corporations should contribute to the processes of legalization. Matten and Crane (2005) go a step further and do not constrain the role of the TNC on citizen's rights and duties but argue that the corporation holds a 'catalyst function' of citizenship rights.

Then, 'corporate citizenship' refers not only to the citizen-like role of the corporation, but defines corporate citizenship as the 'role of the corporation in administering citizenship rights for individuals' (Matten and Crane 2005: 173). With this conceptualization, Matten and Crane take account of the observation that in times of globalization companies already fulfil the function of protecting, enabling and implementing citizen rights (ibid.). This is particularly true when (1) the state withdraws or has to withdraw, (2) the state has not yet implemented basic rights, or when (3) the state is principally unable to do so. Matten and Crane examine the possible channels of influence for corporations within the framework of corporate citizenship, namely the assistance of corporations in the implementation of private, social, and political rights. This conception provides a major contribution to the discussion of legalization because it highlights the role of the private corporation in the process of designing global rules and implementing citizenship rights. In addition, such a conceptualization of the role of the TNCs also touches upon a realm that in liberal theory has been the sole responsibility of the state.

Regarding those two different perspectives on the political role of TNCs, the question arises of how these concepts of republican business ethics, and Matten and Crane's corporate citizenship approach could be reconciled. We argue that those concepts have a complementary structure. We agree with Matten and Crane that the term 'citizenship' should not be used in a superficial manner when dealing with corporations (see, e.g. Moon *et al.* 2005). Corporations do not have the right to vote, which is essential for the status of a citizen in a democratic state. However, we know that as corporations, business firms are legal persons that bear rights and obligations: corporations can own property, can make contracts, and can be taken to court, their citizen-like role is, however, not restrained to private rights.

Numerous countries have defined such rights and duties of corporations through their constitutions, and even before the European court of human rights, legal persons such as corporations are considered legal entities. The German constitution, for example, points out that all fundamental rights also apply to corporate actors. Due to freedom of association, corporations own in a sense political participation rights. They exert these rights for instance through professional associations that determine the standards of their profession or through committees that determine technical norms, thereby contributing to the legalization of rules. In fact, the exertion of political participatory rights of companies is already included in the corporatist model of the political sciences.

The previous section has shown that corporate citizenship and corporate social responsibility, although sometimes used synonymously, have very different connotations. Corporate citizenship stresses the reciprocal relationships between companies, states and civil society in global governance processes. Whitehouse (2003) elaborates that while CSR on the one hand emphasizes the necessity for corporations to comply with societal norms, corporate citizenship on the other hand stresses the duties and rights that tie corporations to participation in the development, diffusion and execution of various forms of regulatory schemes. We have demonstrated that the corporate citizenship concept of Matten and Crane accounts for the state-like roles of TNCs and thus serves particularly well to theoretically capture the rule-making activities of TNCs. For a re-conceptualization of the societal role of the firm, we therefore suggest further research based on Matten and Crane's definition of corporate citizenship. By going beyond the dominating assumption of a strict division of labour between business and politics, Matten and Crane propose a fruitful theoretical framework for explaining the contributions of TNCs to processes of international legalization.

Legitimacy in question – the politically embedded TNC in a globalized world

In a globalized world we cannot assume that legal and legitimate institutions are already properly in place anywhere in the world. Instead, many developing or emerging countries still have a long way to go towards the rule of law (e.g. see the case of China in Peerenboom 2002). Rather than waiting for governmental agencies starting institutional reform on the national or global level the UN Global Compact asks private business firms to engage in the process of legalization as politically responsible actors.

To date, approximately 2000 companies have followed this call and subscribed to the Global Compact. The motivaton of business frms to take part in this initiative may be mixed ranging from public relations, through instrumental CSR to altruistic behaviour. However, in the course of their membership, business firms get more and more involved in public discourse with civil society groups or governmental agencies on issues of public concern. And even though many business firms are initially pressured by NGOs to engage in CSR projects and react with a strategic attitude (see Spar and La Mure 2003), many of them change their behaviour during an organizational learning process from reactive, instrumental, step-by-step strategies to proactive, responsible, inclusive and open discourse (see e.g. Zadek 2004).

More recently, political scientists have emphasized the role of communication and its binding character in the world wide implementation of human rights. Risse (1999) suggests that initially oppressive political regimes often get into a situation of 'argumentative self-entrapment' when they start dealing with human rights concerns and arguing with human rights activists. Once these communications get under public scrutiny, the behaviour of governments will be critically measured against their own public statements. And they may be motivated to give in the arguments proposed by human rights activists and the world community. The same process may apply to the behaviour of business firms, which often starts as instrumental CSR and sometimes emerges into true socially responsible engagement for public concerns (see Argenti 2004; Zadek 2004).

Through the engagement of business firms in public dialogue on problematic issues they not only apply their own standards, but vis-à-vis the problems and concerns of affected citizens they also assist in interpreting and resolving human rights and social and environmental issues. This process may also help fill the legitimacy gap in global politics (Fung 2003). In addition, if business firms take part in open and public debates, their activities come under the control of a critical public. It is arguable if such discourses can reach the same degree of democratic legitimacy as democratic elections and parliamentary control but it nevertheless shows a route towards greater legitimacy in the process of legalization (see Palazzo and Scherer 2006; Scherer and Palazzo 2007).

In terms of the legal or legitimate 'quality' of rules, one could argue that rules designed and enforced by private actors do not have the same status as rules set by state-actors (Habermas 2004). In this debate, the differentiation between 'rule of law' and 'legal codes' is helpful (see Schachtschneider 2004). While the rule of law describes an ideal situation that has resulted from a deliberate discourse between the citizens (see Habermas 1996); legal codes, which are based on formal rules and institutions are simply an instrument for achieving this ideal. Thus, the legal code is just *one* element of a lawful state and citizens (including TNCs) also need to make a contribution. The quality of rules is then measured by their legitimacy, which in turn is dependent on the aforementioned public discourse and the democratic structures and processes in which public discourses are embedded (Habermas 1996, 1998).

In that context, a debate about 'soft laws' has emerged. Soft laws can be broadly defined as 'rules of conduct which, in principle, have no legally binding force, but which nevertheless may have some practical consequences' (Snyder 1993: 198). In political science, it is mainly discussed whether compliance levels of soft laws are different from compliance levels with hard laws (legal codes). Opinions are mixed but scholars with a narrow legal perspective argue that since soft law lacks the possibility for legal sanctions, compliance levels are lower. For TNCs that are operating in a global arena, however, most rules are 'soft' as neither an individual nation state nor an international organization can in most cases sanction the wrongdoing of companies abroad. Further research should identify the conditions which need to be in place so that companies comply with soft rules. We assume that external as well as internal provisions have to be made (see Weissbrodt and Kruger 2003). Internally, systems and incentives have to be created so that voluntary codes become part of all business decisions and are implemented throughout the company (see e.g. Leisinger 2003; Parker 2002). Externally, the commitment to a code has to be made public and policies have to be made transparent. That enables civil society groups to actively control the activities of TNCs and interact with the company in cases of conflict. Such transparency provisions are thus crucial because in the end, the level of engagement with stakeholders determines whether corporate behaviour is perceived as legitimate or not. Many companies nowadays invite their stakeholders to discuss their corporate policies (e.g. Novartis, Puma, The Gap etc.). Regular dialogue consequently serves the company as well as the stakeholders. Through institutionalized dialogue *fori*, companies can pick up societal opinions and moods, anticipate risks and adjust their policies accordingly. Stakeholders gain a channel through which they can negotiate their positions and hold the company accountable.

Conclusion: problems and unsolved questions of corporate social responsibility

Globalization has consequences for the process of legalization that can no longer be explained through the regulatory power of the nation state alone. On a global scale, rules developed on various levels and were mainly driven by private actors such as International Organizations, NGOs or Transnational Corporations (Günther and Randeria 2001; Teubner 1997). Many TNCs commit themselves to their own 'codes of conduct' that encompass basic standards in the areas of environmental, social, and labour rights. Through the implementation of these standards, TNCs became authentic sources for global rules (Scherer and Baumann 2004).

The rather pragmatic reaction of TNCs to the dynamics of globalization took place long before the theoretical discourse was able to integrate these voluntary initiatives into its analytical framework. Now, as rule-setting activities of private actors are becoming more and more visible in the global arena, a rethinking of the traditional doctrine of sources of law has started and a discourse about the emerging legal pluralism on a global scale is underway.

The argument that TNCs should participate in rule-making mechanisms on the global level provokes several questions and issues. We will concentrate on two major ones: (1) the question of how the problem of a growing democratic deficit of private actor's rule making can be solved; (2) the problem of how the internal organization of TNCs must be changed so that structures and processes allow for engagement in public deliberation to contribute to the legalization of global rules.

(1) Even though the deliberate process advanced in the preceding chapter may lead to higher legitimacy of private engagement in global rule making, the issue is not completely resolved. In a democratic state, citizens collectively form their will. Through elections they decide directly or indirectly under what government and under what rules they want to live together. The political order is therefore based on the agreement of the people and is thus legitimized (Habermas 1998). In the role model of the TNC that we have sketched out in this paper, however, corporations decide on the further development of a global framework and influence its general conditions without having in advance been elected, authorized or controlled democratically (see Palazzo 2002; Scherer and Palazzo 2007). Although political scientists are currently exploring new, pluralistic forms of accountability in global politics (e.g. Benner *et al.* 2004), one could

critically argue that for instance the Global Compact of the United Nations is based on paternalism that blindly trusts on the 'good' corporation, without providing sufficient control mechanisms.

Is corporate citizenship in the end not the solution but the problem itself when corporations exert their power to define global rules in a way that serves their economic interest best (see Shell 2004; Siedel 2002 as recommendations for political lobbying)? How can the democratic deficit in global governance be balanced (Edwards and Zadek 2003; Orts 1995)? Doesn't the new role of the corporation have consequences for the internal constitution of the corporation, the corporate governance? We suggest that to the extent corporations act politically they also have to open up their internal structures and processes for public control, thereby enabling democratic legitimacy. However, the consequences for the corporate governance have to be elaborated in further research (see Driver and Thompson 2002; Parker 2002). Generally though, it has been shown that whether the involvement of private actors in public rule making is seen as a threat or an asset to democracy also heavily depends on the definition and conceptualization of democracy. Frykman and Mörth (2004) discuss three notions of democracy (liberal, republican and deliberative) and conclude that unless democracy is defined merely in terms of representative democracy, there is room for the integration of private actor's rule making activities.

(2) The detailed organizational implementation of a political concept of CSR that is advanced here is beyond the scope of this paper (see Fung 2003; Steinmann and Scherer 2000; Scherer and Palazzo 2007). It will create a number of further questions, including the problem of how the process of strategy development and implementation can be designed concretely in terms of structures, procedures, and personnel in order to take into account the demands for economic success and social responsibility. Considerations already voiced point to a similar structure in the economic and ethical governance process (see Quinn 1996; Simons 1995; Steinmann and Kustermann 1998). This leaves open, however, how the practical limitations of the firm's engagement in public dialogue can be overcome in the context of strategy formulation. To develop answers to this and other questions is the topic of future scholarly effort, at least when it is a question of a socially responsible strategic management that is not only substantiated in theory but can also be implemented practically.

As the previous parts have indicated, in the process of justifying a new role of the TNC many questions remain open. The paper, however, has made clear that the traditional mode of governance with the state as the sole source of rule making is no longer adequate in the light of emerging global governance structures. TNCs as well as other private actors already actively contribute to the protection of human, environmental, and labour rights and thus fulfil state-like functions on a global level. We have shown the different levels to which private actors can be integrated in the theoretical frameworks of economics, business management, and corporate social responsibility. And it has become obvious that social sciences need to cooperate in order to develop an interdisciplinary theoretical framework that is able to explain the role of the TNC in the process of legalization.

Notes

1 Previous drafts of this paper were presented at the International Conference on 'Voluntary Codes of Conduct for Multinational Corporations: Promises and Challenges', NYU, New York City, 12–15 May 2004, and at the EGOS-Workshop 'Corporate Social Responsbility and Business Ethics', 2004 EGOS annual colloquium, Ljubljana (Slovenia), 1–3 July 2004. Some of the arguments proposed in this paper are further developed in Scherer, A.G., Palazzo, G. and Baumann, D. (2006) 'Global Rules and Private Actors: Toward a New Role of the Transnational Corporation in Global Governance', *Business Ethics Quarterly*, 16: 505–532. We thank BEQ editor Gary Weaver and the Philosophical Documentation Center for kind permission to make use of this material in the present paper.

2 In 2004, the UN Global Compact has been supplemented with a tenth principle dealing with the problem of corruption.

3 It is important here to note that our use of the words 'liberal' and 'republican' is drawn from the literature of political philosophy (see Habermas 1998). This may be confusing to readers from the US where bumper-sticker political language has changed the original meaning of these terms.

References

Abbott, K.W. and Snidal, D. (2000) 'Hard and Soft Law in International Governance', in J. Goldstein, M. Kahler, R.O. Keohane and A.-M. Slaughter (eds) *Legalization and World Politics*, Cambridge, MA: MIT Press, 37–72.

Agle, B.R., Mitchell, R.K. and Sonnenfeld, J.A. (1999) 'Who Matters to CEOs? An Investigation of Stakeholder Attributes and Salience, Corporate Performance, and CEO Values', *Academy of Management Journal*, 42: 507–525.

Alvesson, M. and Willmott, H. (eds) (1992) *Critical Management Studies*, London: Sage.

Alvesson, M. and Willmott, H (1995) 'Strategic Management as Domination and Emancipation: From Planning and Process to Communication and Praxis', in P. Shrivastava and C. Stubbart (eds) *Advances in Strategic Management* 12A, Greenwich, Conn.: JAI Press, 85–112.

Alvesson, M. and Willmott, H. (eds) (2003) *Studying Management Critically*, London: Sage.

Annan, K. (1999) 'A Compact for the New Century' [Rede von UN-Generalsekretär Kofi Annan vor dem World Economic Forum in Davos, 31. January 1999], Available at: www.un.org/News/Press/docs/1999/19990201.sgsm6881.html (accessed 8 July 2006).

Argenti, P.A. (2004) 'Collaborating with Activists: How Starbucks Works with NGOs', *California Management Review*, 47, 1: 91–116.

Avi-Yonah, R.S. (2000) 'Globalization, Tax Competition, and the Fiscal Crisis of the Welfare State', *Harvard Law Review*, 113: 1575–1676.

Avi-Yonah, R.S. (2003) 'National Regulation of Multinational Enterprises: An Essay on Comity, Extraterritoriality, and Harmonization', *Columbia Journal of Transnational Law*, 42: 5–34.

Barro, R.J. (1994) 'Democracy: A Receipt for Growth?', *Wall Street Journal*, 1 December 1994.

Barro, R.J. (1997) 'The Interplay Between Economic and Political Development', in R.J. Barro (ed.) *Determinants of Economic Growth*, Cambridge, MA: Cambridge University Press: 49–87.

Beck, U. (2000) *What is Globalization?* Cambridge, UK: Polity Press.

Bernhard, N. (2002) *Multilevel Governance in the European Union*, The Hague: Kluwer International.

Benner, T., Reinicke, W.H. and Witte, J.-M. (2004) *Multisectoral Networks in Global Governance. Towards a Pluralistic System of Accountability.* Available at: www. globalreporting.org/upload/bennerreinickewitte2004.pdf (accessed 15 September 2005).

Berman, S.L., Wicks, A.C., Kotha, S. and Jones, T.M. (1999) 'Does Stakeholder Orientation Matter? The Relationship Between Stakeholder Management Models and Firm Financial Performance', *Academy of Management Journal*, 42: 488–506.

Boje, D.M. and Dennehy, R.F. (1993) *Managing in the Postmodern World: America's Revolution against Exploitation*, Dubuque, IO: Kendall/Hunt.

Braithwaite, J. and Drahos, P. (2000) *Global Business Regulation*, Cambridge: Cambridge University Press.

Breining-Kaufmann, C. (2004) 'The Legal Matrix of Human Rights/Trade Law: State Obligations versus Private Rights/Obligations', discussion paper prepared for the *Third Conference of the ASIL Project on 'International Trade and Human Rights'*, Washington, D.C., 5–6 April 2004.

Brozus, L., Take, I. and Wolf, K.D. (2003) *Vergesellschaftung des Regierens? Der Wandel nationaler und internationaler Politischer Steuerung unter dem Leitbild der nachhaltigen Entwicklung*, Opladen: Leske und Budrich.

Buchholz, R.A. (1992) *Business Environment and Public Policy: Implications for Management and Strategy*, 4th edn, Englewood Cliffs, NJ: Prentice-Hall.

Campbell, T. and Miller, S. (2004) *Human Rights and the Moral Responsibilities of Corporate and Public Sector Organizations*, Dordrecht, Boston and London: Kluwer.

Carroll, A.B. (1979) 'A Three-Dimensional Conceptual Model of Corporate Social Performance', *Academy of Management Review*, 4: 497–505.

Carroll, A.B. (1991) 'The Pyramid of Corporate Social Responsibility: Toward the Moral Management of Organizational Stakeholders', *Business Horizons*, 34: 39–48.

Cavanagh, G.F. (2004) 'Global Business Ethics: Regulation, Codes or Self-Restraint', *Business Ethics Quarterly*, 14: 625–642.

Chan, A. (2003) 'A "Race to the Bottom". Globalisation and China's labor standards', *China Perspective*, 46 (March–April): 41–49.

Christmann, P. (2004) 'Multinational Companies and the National Environment: Determinants of Global Environmental Policy Standardization', *Academy of Management Journal*, 47: 747–760.

Cochran, P. and Wood, R. (1984) 'Corporate Social Responsibility and Financial Performance', *Academy of Management Journal*, 27: 42–56.

Cragg, W. (2005) 'Ethics, Law, Globalization and the Modern Shareholder Owned Multinational Corporation', in W. Cragg (ed.) *Ethics Codes, Corporations and the Challenge of Globalization*, Cheltenham, UK: Edward Elgar, 23–50.

Driver, C. and Thompson, G. (2002) 'Corporate Governance and Democracy: The Stakeholder Debate Revisited', *Journal of Management and Governance*, 6: 111–130.

Edwards, M. and Zadek, S. (2003) 'Governing the Provision of Global Goods: The Role and Legitimacy of Nonstate Actors', in I. Kaul, P. Conceicao, K.L. Goulven and R.U. Mendoza (eds) *Providing Global Public Goods. Managing Globalization*, Oxford: Oxford University Press: 200–224.

Elster, J. (1986) 'The Market and the Forum: Three Varieties of Political Theory', in J. Elster and A. Hylland (eds) *Foundations of Social Choice Theory*, Cambridge: Cambridge University Press, 103–132.

Fort, T.L. and Schipani, C.A. (2002) 'The Role of the Corporation in Fostering Sustainable Peace', *Vanderbilt Journal of Transnational Law*, 35: 389–439.

Freeman, R.E. (1984) *Strategic Management: A Stakeholder Approach*, London/New York: Financial Times/Prentice Hall.

Freeman, R.E. and McVea, J. (2001) 'A Stakeholder Approach to Strategic Management', in M.A. Hill, E. Freeman and J.S. Harrison (eds) *The Blackwell Handbook of Strategic Management*, Oxford: Blackwell, 189–207.

Friedman, M. (1962) *Capitalism and Freedom*, Chicago: Chicago University Press.

Friedman, M. (1970) 'The Social Responsibility of Business is to Increase Its Profits', *New York Times Magazine*, 13 September 1970; reprint in T. Donaldson and P.H. Werhane (eds) *Ethical Issues in Business. A Philosophical Approach*, Englewood Cliffs, N.J.: Prentice Hall, 217–223.

Frooman, J. (1999) 'Stakeholder Influence Strategies', *Academy of Management Review*, 24: 191–205.

Frykman, H. and Mörth, U. (2004) 'Soft Law and Three Notions of Democracy: The Case of the EU', in U. Mörth (ed.) *Soft Law in Governance and Regulation: An Interdisciplinary Analysis*, Cheltenham, UK: Edward Elgar: 155–170.

Fung, A. (2003) 'Deliberative Democracy and International Labor Standards', *Governance*, 16 (January): 51–71.

Ghemawat, P. (2003) 'The Forgotten Strategy', *Harvard Business Review*, 81 (November): 76–84.

Giddens, A. (1990) *Consequences of Modernity*, Cambridge, UK: Polity Press.

Giddens, A. (1998) *The Third Way: The Renewal of Social Democracy*, Cambridge, UK: Polity Press.

Goldstein, J., Kahler, M., Keohane, R.O. and Slaughter A.-M. (eds) (2000) *Legalization and World Politics*, Cambridge, MA: MIT Press.

Greider, W. (1997) *One World, Ready or Not. The Manic Logic of Global Capitalism*, New York: Simon & Schuster.

Grimsey, D. and Lewis, M.K. (2004) Public Private Partnerships: The Worldwide Revolution in Infrastructure Provision and Project Finance, Cheltenham, UK: Edward Elgar.

Günther, K. (2001) 'Rechtspluralismus und Universaler Code der Legalität: Globalisierung als Rechtstheoretisches Problem', in L. Wingert and K. Günther (eds) *Die Öffentliche Vernunft und die Vernunft der Öffentlichkeit: Festschrift für Jürgen Habermas*, Frankfurt, A.M.: Suhrkamp: 539–568.

Günther, K. and Randeria, S. (2001) 'Recht, Kultur und Gesellschaft im Prozess der Globalisierung', Schriftenreihe "Suchprozesse für Innovative Fragestellungen in der Wissenschaft", Werner Reimers Konferenzen, Heft Nr. 4, Bad Homburg.

Habermas, J. (1971) 'Vorbereitende Bemerkungen zu einer Theorie der Kommunikativen Kompetenz', in J. Habermas and N. Luhmann (eds) *Theorie der Gesellschaft oder Sozialtechnologie*, Frankfurt, A.M.: Suhrkamp: 101–141.

Habermas, J. (1993) 'Remarks on Discourse Ethics', in J. Habermas *Justification and Application. Remarks on Discourse Ethics*, Cambridge, MA: MIT Press: 19–111.

Habermas, J. (1996) 'Between Facts and Norms: Contributions to a Discourse Theory of Law and Democracy', Cambridge, MA: MIT Press.

Habermas, J. (1998) 'Three Normative Models of Democracy', in J. Habermas *The Inclusion of the Other. Studies in Political Theory*, Cambridge, MA: MIT Press: 239–252.

Habermas, J. (2001) 'The Postnational Constellation and the Future of Democracy', in J. Habermas *The Postnational Constellation*, Cambridge: Polity Press: 58–112.

Habermas, J. (2004) 'Hat die Konstitutionalisierung des Völkerrechts noch eine Chance?', in J. Habermas *Der Gespaltene Westen*, Frankfurt, a.M.: Suhrkamp.

Hayek, F.V. (1945) 'The Use of Knowledge in Society', *American Economic Review*, 35: 519–530.

Henderson, P.D. (2001) *Misguided Virtue. False Notions of Corporate Social Responsibility*, London: Institute of Economic Affairs.

Hoeckmann, B. and Kostecki, M. (1995) *The Political Economy of the World Trading System. From GATT to WTO*, Oxford, UK: Oxford University Press.

Irwin, D.A. (2002) *Free Trade Under Fire*, Princeton: Princeton University Press.

Jawahar, I.M. and McLaughlin, G.L. (2001) 'Toward a Descriptive Stakeholder Theory: An Organizational Life Cycle Approach', *Academy of Management Review*, 26: 397–414.

Jensen, M. (2002) 'Value Maximization, Stakeholder Theory, and the Corporate Objective Function', *Business Ethics Quarterly*, 12: 235–256.

Jones, T. (1995) 'Instrumental Stakeholder Theory: A Synthesis of Ethics and Economics', *Academy of Management Review*, 20: 404–437.

Keim, G. (2001) 'Business and Public Policy. Competing in the Political Market Place', in M. Hitt, R. Freeman and J. Harrison (eds) *Handbook of Strategic Management*, Oxford: Blackwell: 583–601.

Kingsbury, B. (2003) 'The International Legal Order', in P. Cane and M. Tushnet (eds) *The Oxford Handbook of Legal Studies*, Oxford: Oxford University Press: 271–297.

Kinley, D. and Tadaki, J. (2004) 'From Talk to Walk. The Emergence of Human Rights Responsibilities for Corporations at International Law', *Virginia Journal of International Law*, 44 (4): 932–1022.

Krauss, M. (1997) *How Nations Grow Rich. The Case For Free Trade*, New York: Oxford University Press.

Lal, D. (1998) 'Social Standards and Social Dumping', in H. Giersch (ed.) *Merits and Limits of Markets*, Heidelberg: Springer: 255–274.

Lal, D. (2003) 'Private Morality and Capitalism: Learning from the Past', in J. Dunning (ed.) *Making Globalization Good*, Oxford: Oxford University Press: 41–60.

Lee, E. (1997) 'Globalization and Labor Standards: A Review of Issues', *International Labor Review* 136 (2), Available at: www.ilo.org/public/english/180revue/articles/lee97-2.htm (accessed 6 January 2004).

Leisinger, K.M. (2003) 'Opportunities and Risks of the United Nations Global Compact', *The Journal of Corporate Citizenship*, 11: 113–131.

Marciano, A. and Josselin, J.-M. (eds) (2003) *From Economic to Legal Competition. New Perspectives on Law and Institutions in Europe*, Cheltenham, UK: Edward Elgar.

Margolis, J.D. and Walsh, J.P. (2003) 'Misery Loves Companies: Rethinking Social Initiations by Business', *Administrative Science Quarterly*, 48: 268–305.

Marshall, T.H. (1965) *Class, Citizenship and Social Development*, New York: Anchor Books.

Martinez-Mont, L. (1996) 'Sweatshops are Better Than no Shops', *Wall Street Journal*, 25 June 1996.

Matten, D. and Crane, A. (2005) 'Corporate Citizenship: Toward an Extended Theoretical Conceptualization', *Academy of Management Review*, 29: 166–179.

McWilliams, A. and Siegel, D. (2001) 'Corporate Social Responsibility: A Theory of the Firm Perspective', *Academy of Management Review*, 26: 117–127.

Mitchell, R.K., Agle, B.R. and Wood, D.J. (1997) 'Toward a Theory of Stakeholder Identification and Salience: Defining the Principle of Who and What Really Counts', *Academy of Management Review*, 22: 853–886.

Moon, J., Crane, A. and Matten, D. (2005) 'Can Corporations be Citizens? Corporate Citizenship as a Metaphor for Business Participation in Society', *Business Ethics Quarterly*, 15: 429–454.

Mörth, U. (ed.) (2004) *Soft Law in Governance and Regulation: An Interdisciplinary Analysis*, Cheltenham, UK: Edward Elgar.

Nozick, R. (1975) *Anarchy, State, and Utopia*, New York.

Orts, E.W. (1995) 'The Legitimacy of Multinational Corporations', in L.E. Mitchell (ed.) *Progressive Corporate Law*, Boulder, CO: Westview Press, 247–279.

Paine, L.S. (1994) 'Managing for Organizational Integrity', *Harvard Business Review* (March–April): 106–117.

Palazzo, G. (2002) *Die Mitte der Demokratie. Über die Theorie Deliberativer Demokratie von Jürgen Habermas*, Baden-Baden: Nomos.

Palazzo, G. and Scherer, A.G. (2006) 'Corporate Legitimacy as Deliberation: A Communicative Framework', *Journal of Business Ethics*, 66: 71–88.

Parker, C. (2002) *The Open Corporation*, Cambridge: Cambridge University Press.

Parker, C. and Braithwaite, J. (2003) 'Regulation', in P. Cane and M. Tushnet (eds) *The Oxford Handbook of Legal Studies*, Oxford: Oxford University Press: 119–145.

Peerenboom, R. (2002) *China's Long March Toward Rule of Law*, Cambridge: Cambridge University Press.

Phillips, R. (2003) *Stakeholder Theory and Organizational Ethics*, San Francisco: Berrett-Koehler.

Porter, M.E. and Kramer, M.R. (2002) 'The Competitive Advantage of Corporate Philanthropy', *Harvard Business Review* 80 (December): 57–68.

Preston, L.E. and Post, J.E. (1975) Private Management and Public Policy: The Principle of Public Responsibility. Englewood Cliffs, NJ: Prentice Hall.

Quinn, J.J. (1996) 'The Role of "Good Conversation" in Strategic Control', *Journal of Management Studies*, 33: 381–394.

Reinicke, W.H. and Witte, J.M. (1999) 'Globalisierung, Souveränität und internationale Ordnungspolitik', in A. Busch and T. Plümper (eds) *Nationaler Staat und internationale Wirtschaft. Anmerkungen zum Thema Globalisierung*, Baden-Baden: Nomos, 339–366.

Reinicke, W.H. and Deng, F. with Witte, J.M., Benner, T., Whitaker, B. and Gershman, J. (2000) *Critical Choices. The United Nations, Networks, and the Future of Global Governance*, Ottawa: Int. Development Research Center.

Risse, T. (1999) 'International Norms and Domestic Change: Arguing and Communicative Behaviour in the Human Rights Area', *Politics and Society*, 27: 529–559.

Risse, T. (2002) 'Transnational Actors and World Politics', in W. von Carlsnaes, T. Risse and B. Simmons (eds) *Handbook of International Relations*, London: Sage, 255–274.

Rugman, A. (2000) *The End of Globalization. A New and Radical Analysis of Globalization and What it Means for Business*, London: Random House.

Sahlin-Andersson, K. (2004) 'Emergent Cross-Sectional Soft Regulations: Dynamics at Play in the Global Compact Initiative', in U. Mörth (ed.) *Soft Law in Governance and Regulation: An Interdisciplinary Analysis*, Cheltenham, UK: Edward Elgar, 129–153.

Santoro, M.A. (2000) *Profits and Principles. Global Capitalism and Human Rights in China*, Ithaca, NY: Cornell University Press.

Schachtschneider, K.A. (2004) 'Demokratische und Soziale Defizite der Globalisierung', in H. Neuhaus (ed.) *Der Mensch in der Globalisierten Welt*, Atzelsberger Gespräche, 9–40.

Scherer, A.G. (2003) *Multinationale Unternehmen und Globalisierung*, Heidelberg: Physica.

Scherer, A.G. (2004) 'Schwindende Grenzen zwischen Wirtschaft und Politik. Die neue Verantwortung der Multinationalen Unternehmung und der Beitrag Karl Homanns zu ihrer Bestimmung', *Zeitschrift für Evangelische Ethik*, 48: 107–118.

Scherer, A.G. and Baumann, D. (2004) 'Corporate Citizenship bei der PUMA AG. Der Beitrag der Sportartikelbranche zum institutionellen Wandel in der Weltwirtschaft', in H. Ruh and K.M. Leisinger (eds) *Ethik im Management. Ethik und Erfolg verbinden sich*, Zürich: Orell Füssli, 285–298.

Scherer, A.G. and Kustermann, B. (2004) 'Business & Society-Forschung versus Kritische Strategieforschung – Kritik zweier Ansätze zur Integration von Sozialer Verantwortung und Strategischer Unternehmensführung', *Managementforschung*, 14: 47–77.

Scherer, A.G. and Palazzo, G. (forthcoming) 'Toward a Political Conception of Corporate Responsibility. Business and Society Seen from a Habermasian Perspective', *Academy of Management Review*, 32 (forthcoming).

Scherer, A.G. and Smid, M. (2000) 'The Downward Spiral and the U.S. Model Business Principles. Why MNEs Should Take Responsibility for the Improvement of World-Wide Social and Environmental Conditions', *Management International Review*, 40: 351–371.

Scherer, A.G., Palazzo, G. and Baumann, D. (2006) 'Global Rules and Private Actors. Toward a New Role of the Transnational Corporation in Global Governance', *Business Ethics Quarterly*, 16: 505–532.

Schneider, V. and Ronit, C. (1999) 'Global Governance Through Private Organizations', *Governance*, 12: 243–266.

Sethi, P.S. (2002) 'Standards for Corporate Conduct in the International Arena: Challenges and Opportunities for Multinational Corporations', *Business and Society Review*, 107 (1): 20–40.

Sethi, P.S. (2003) *Setting Global Standards. Guidelines for Creating Codes of Conduct in Multinational Corporations*, Hoboken: John Wiley & Sons.

Sharma, S. and Starik, M. (eds) (2002) *Research in Corporate Sustainability. The Evolving Theory and Practice of Organizations in the Natural Environment*, Cheltenham, UK: Edgar Elgar.

Shell, G.R. (2004) *Make the Rules or your Rivals Will*, New York: Crown Business.

Shelton, D. (2000) 'Law, Non-Law and the Problem of "Soft Law"', in D. Shelton (ed.) *Commitment and Compliance. The Role of Non-Binding Norms in the International Legal System*, Oxford: Oxford University Press, 1–18.

Shrivastava, P. (1986) 'Is Strategic Management Ideological?', *Journal of Management*, 12: 363–377.

Siebert, H. (1998) 'Disziplinierung der nationalen Wirtschaftspolitik durch die Internationale Kapitalmobilität', in D. Duwendag (ed.) *Finanzmärkte im Spannungsfeld von Globalisierung, Regulierung und Geldpolitik*, Berlin: Duncker & Humblot, 41–67.

Siedel, G.J. (2002) *Using the Law for Competitive Advantage*, San Francisco, CA: Jossey-Bass.

Simon, H.A. (1991) 'Organizations and Markets', *Journal of Economic Perspecives*, 5: 25–44.

Simons, R. (1995) *Levers of Control. How Managers Use Innovative Control Systems to Drive Strategic Renewal*, Boston, MA: Harvard Business School Press.

Smith, N.C. (2003) 'Corporate Social Responsibility. Whether or How?', *California Management Review*, 54 (4): 52–76.

Snider, J., Hill, R.P. and Martin, D. (2003) 'Corporate Social Responsibility in the 21st Century: A View from the World's Most Successful Firms', *Journal of Business Ethics*, 48: 175–187.

Snyder, F. (1993) 'Soft Law and Institutional Practice in the European Community', in S. Martin (ed.) *The Construction of Europe – Essays in Honour of Emile Noel*, Kluwer Academic Publishers, 197–225.

Spar, D.L. and La Mure, L.T. (2003) 'The Power of Activism: Assessing the Impact of NGOs on Global Business', *California Management Review*, 45 (3): 78–101.

Steinmann, H. and Kustermann, B. (1998) 'Management Theory on the Way to a New Paradigm? Critical Reflections on the Concept of Robert Simons', in S. Urban (ed.) *From Alliance Practices to Alliance Capitalism*, Wiesbaden: Gabler, 241–274.

Steinmann, H. and Löhr, A. (1994) *Grundlagen der Unternehmensethik*, 2nd edn, Stuttgart: Poeschel.

Steinmann, H. and Löhr, A. (1995) 'Unternehmensethik als Ordnungselement in der Marktwirtschaft', *Zeitschrift für Betriebswirtschaftliche Forschung*, 47: 143–174.

Steinmann, H. and Löhr, A. (1996) 'A Republican Concept of Corporate Ethics', in S. Urban (ed.) *Europe's Challenges. Economic Efficiency and Social Solidarity*, Wiesbaden: Gabler, 21–60.

Steinmann, H. and Scherer, A.G. (2000) 'Corporate Ethics and Management Theory', in P. Koslowski (ed.) *Contemporary Economic Ethics and Business Ethics. Studies in Economic Ethics and Philosophy*, Berlin, Heidelberg and New York: Springer, 148–192.

Stone, C.D. (1975) *Where the Law Ends: The Social Control of Corporate Behavior*, New York: Harper & Row.

Sundaram, A.K. and Inkpen, A.C. (2004) 'The Corporate Objective Revisited', *Organization Science*, 15: 350–363.

Teubner, G. (1997) '"Global Bukowina": Legal Pluralism in the World Society', in G. Teubner (ed.) *Global Law Without A State*, Brookfield: Dartmouth Publishing, 3–30.

Walsh, J.P. (2005) 'Book Review Essay: Taking Stock of Stakeholder Management', *Academy of Management Review*, 30: 426–438.

Walsh, J.P., Weber, K. and Margolis, J.D. (2003) 'Social Issues and Management: Our Lost Cause Found', *Journal of Management*, 29: 859–881.

Wartick, S.L. and Cochran, P.L. (1985) 'The Evolution of the Corporate Social Performance Model', *Academy of Management Review*, 4: 758–769.

Weissbrodt, D. and Kruger, M. (2003) 'Norms on the Responsibilities of Transnational Corporations and Other Business Enterprises with Regard to Human Rights', *The American Journal of International Law*, 97: 901–922.

Whitehouse, L. (2003) 'Corporate Social Responsibility as Citizenship and Compliance: Initiatives on the Domestic, European and Global Level', *Journal of Corporate Citizenship*, 11: 85–98.

Whetten, D.A., Rands, G. and Godfrey, P.O. (2002) 'What are the Responsibilities of Business to Society?', in A. Pettigrew, H. Thomas and R. Whittington (eds) *Handbook of Strategy and Management*, London: Sage, 373–408.

Williams, O.F. (2000) *Global Codes of Conduct. An Idea Whose Time Has Come*, Notre Dame: Notre Dame Press.

Williams, O.F. (2004) 'The UN Global Compact: The Challenge and the Premise', *Business Ethics Quarterly*, 14: 755–774.

Wood, D.J. (1991) 'Corporate Social Performance Revisited', *Academy of Management Review*, 16: 691–718.

Young, I.M. (2004) 'Responsibility and Global Labor Justice', *Journal of Political Philosophy*, 12: 365–388.

Zadek, S. (2004) 'The Path to Corporate Responsibility', *Harvard Business Review*, 82 (December): 125–132.

Zürn, M. (1998) Regieren jenseits des Nationalstaates. Globalisierung und Denationalisierung als Chance, Frankfurt, A.M.: Suhrkamp.

12 Conclusion

Christian Brütsch and Dirk Lehmkuhl

In the introduction to this volume, we suggested thinking of legalization as a series of complex transformations of the structures, institutions and actors that shape international and transnational politics. The emergence of multiple legal and law-like arrangements alters the way in which international affairs are defined, addressed and managed. It modifies interactions among states, their delegated agencies and non-state actors. We also claimed that it would be misleading to think of legalization as a linear development or a general trend. Instead, we argued that research should focus on the elusive and often contradictory conditions, patterns and dynamics that determine the success, scope and reach of emerging legal and law-like arrangements. Indeed, we believe that research on 'complex legalization' should not be expected to provide a parsimonious, robust and reliable interpretation of these transformations. Just like early research on the shift from interdependence to globalization addressed a 'poorly understood but widespread feeling that the very nature of world politics is changing' (Keohane and Nye 2000: 104), studying legalization should enable scholars and practitioners with different disciplinary backgrounds to discuss their findings in order to gain a more systematic and comprehensive outlook on the transformations of world politics.

To capture these transformations, we proposed a common frame of reference that includes the increase in international law-making, the variation among legalized and legalizing regimes, and the differentiation of legal and law-like arrangements. While the theoretical framing of our proposal relies on the existing research about the changing role of law and politics, we believe such a broad frame of reference is necessary to overcome the fragmented views that blur our understanding of the politics of legalization. To test the usefulness and integrative potential of our framework, we invited scholars with different disciplinary backgrounds to address different aspects of legalization in their field of expertise. In the following, we briefly outline some of the main findings of the debate and pinpoint some open questions for future research in the legalization of transnational relations.

Analytical categories and interdisciplinary research

In recent years, a series of legal scholars have offered comprehensive interpretations of the transformation of law that competes with the concept of complex legalization. Weiler proposes interpreting the role of law in terms of an increasingly stratified 'geology of international law', whose first layer consists of bilateral treaties. A second layer adds multilateral treaties, while a third includes customs and general principles of international law. According to Weiler, the key sediments in the (most recent) 'fourth strata' (*sic*) are informal regulatory regimes and self-regulating governance mechanisms (Weiler quoted in Suh 2002: 612). Some of those who are uncomfortable with an excessively static view of additive strata suggest interpreting the transformations of international law in terms of a shifting balance between the different areas of law. Thus, Kirsch and Kingsbury interpret the 'setting or application of rules by bodies that are not legislative or primarily adjudicative in character' (Kirsch and Kingsbury 2006: 3) as administrative acts, which Kingsbury analyses as parts of an evolving global administrative law (Kingsbury and Kirsch 2005).

Although we recognize that such interpretations may provide useful points of reference for legal scholarship, we have opted for a broader approach to capture the political dimension of legalization. Linking research on the changing role of law in international co-operation with research addressing the 'transnationalization' of regulatory activities, we have attempted to bridge the gap between traditional research on international law and international relations (see Goldstein and Kahler 2001; Reus-Smit 2004) and more recent scholarship on 'regulatory fields' (Djelic and Sahlin-Andersson 2006) and the role of private authority in international affairs (Cutler and Haufler 1999; Bruce Hall and Biersteker 2002; Sinclair 2005). We therefore suggested that research on 'complex legalization' should focus on the increase of international law in both breadth and depth, on the variation of international law in terms of a twofold transformation from a law of coexistence to a law of cooperation and from interest-driven to norm-driven justifications of its validity; and, finally, on the differentiation of legal and law-like arrangements driven by the more or less autonomous emergence of law-like regulation in 'new realms', in which states or their delegated agencies are no longer or not necessarily the only actors capable of framing, designing, implementing or monitoring formalized patterns of interaction.

The first findings are encouraging. The contributions in this volume document that legalization cannot be isolated from other 'new' modes to frame, govern, and manage the shift from interdependence to globalization. They show that the shift from regulation to legalization is one but not the only dimension of world politics. They also suggest that efforts aimed at reducing the sensitivity and vulnerability of separate political units co-exist with efforts aimed at facilitating the merging of distinct political spaces. Last but not least, they confirm that the politics of legalization can be analysed in terms of a series of transformations establishing a multitude of overlapping, at times complementary, at times contradictory legal realms, or 'legalities', which alter patterns, institutions and outcomes of international cooperation, and modify how states and non-state actors interact.

However, despite the fact that research in different disciplines may converge on its empirical objects, the volume also documents the challenge of integrating distinct disciplinary perspectives. Even if Arts and Kerwer and Meidinger have a common interest in societal regulation and standards for sustainable forestry, or Wüstemann and Kierzek share Mattli's (Mattli and Büthe 2005) interest in the emergence and development of accounting principles, they pose different questions, apply different methodologies and use distinct terminologies. Some argue that these differences reflect the very nature of scholarly research. That, if we take lawyers and political scientists as examples, and with all due consideration of the limits of such simplifications, lawyers should be expected to analyse the letter and system of law and therefore to focus on the visible outcomes of legalization, while political scientists should focus on processes and factors that led to this outcome and (possibly) analyse its distributional effect (Bank and Lehmkuhl 2005). Others point to the distinct objectives of different disciplines, suggesting that putting a legal lens on legalization clarifies legal doctrine and the formal distribution of rights and responsibilities, whereas the regulatory lens has a stronger empiricist orientation and offers a more instrumental, policy-oriented perspective on law-like arrangements (Parker *et al.* 2004). Lastly, some argue that the differences may be a matter of habits: while lawyers tend to have a positivist-flavoured bias that leads them to privilege norms and rules enacted and enforced by formally institutionalized authorities, usually the state, political scientists dealing with issues in regulation are more at ease with a broader range of intentional efforts to order, influence or control the behaviour of others (Black 2001: 103).

To what extent such assumptions apply is open for debate. However, the contributions in this volume suggest that lawyers will struggle to grasp the significance of legalization if they ignore the politics behind different legal or law-like arrangements. Political scientists will struggle to grasp the impact of legalization if they ignore the letter and system of law. And neither will succeed if they ignore the costs of legalization or the societal acceptance of specific norms and rules. However, the contributions also show that many of these difficulties can be tackled if different perspectives are integrated to question fundamental assumptions in various disciplines. This is particularly evident if we look at how the differentiation of legal and law-like arrangements affects agency in private–public hybrids or global laws 'without the state', or in accounts of legalization in which governance by, with or without government (Rosenau and Czempiel 1992) is clearly at odds with the traditional doctrines of the unity of law.

Assuming that the differentiation of legal and law-like regimes will remain one of the more unpredictable and controversial dimensions of legalization, we believe that more efforts should be made to explain the distinctive and discard inconsistent conceptual toolkits and differences in terminology. Thus, although we are aware that terminologies in this volume vary, we suggest that future research on complex legalization should either treat expressions such as 'standardization', 'regulation', 'regulatory schemes', 'regulatory systems', 'legal or regulatory processes' and 'legalization' as roughly equivalent descriptions of legal and law-like arrangements capable of constituting 'new' actors and realms of interaction – or follow Arts and Kerwer's initiative to work out analytical distinctions that show why this is not the case.

Findings

But this volume is not only about methodology. Its main aim has been to capture different perspectives on the multifaceted phenomena that constitute complex legalization. We asked the contributors 1) to identify legal and law-like arrangements that address specific problems in their areas of expertise; 2) to reconstruct the dynamics leading to the emergence of such arrangements, in particular with regards to the actors and policies that contribute to the framing, implementation and monitoring of these arrangements; and 3) to address issues related to the co-evolution and the interaction among different legal or law-like arrangements. We found that the answers to these questions have to be considered in the context of two common themes.

First, the contributions show that the co-evolution of legal and law-like arrangements advocated by different constellations of state and non-state actors is a frequent (but by no means necessary) element of legalization (for a theoretical discussion see Albert in this volume). The impact of co-evolution varies: as Schanze points out, it can lead to a relatively unproblematic integration of different regulatory approaches. Making use of the 'modularity' of national, international or transnational law, practitioners are able to design and extend legal instruments with a considerable autonomy from traditional law-makers. Schanze confirms that complex legalization is indeed an inherently dynamic process that includes an increase, variation and differentiation of legal and law-like arrangements, and that a wide range of actors and institutions are engaged in designing and operating the multiple layers and fora in which legalization matters.

However, other contributions provide ample evidence of the discontents of co-evolution. Coleman and Reed show that the initiatives of different actors in the same legal space can result in a 'highly complex, sometime contradictory, and often chaotic legalization'. Along the same lines, Cohen argues that legalization can produce a 'much more complex and messy' picture 'than we would expect from the rational–institutional model'. We can therefore confirm Santos's observation that different legal and regulatory initiatives addressing the similar or closely related activities may or may not be synchronic (de Sousa Santos 1995: 473). And we can add that further research on complex legalization should account for the yet underestimated element of contention. Further research will also have to show whether complex legalization has a systemic impact on structures of political contention and, therefore, on the relationships between different actors or types of actors.

The second common theme that emerges from the contributions concerns the dynamics of complex legalization at work. We observe a tension between more complementary and more competitive elements in many of the initiatives aimed at designing or implementing legal and law-like arrangements. In the legalization of the international financial markets, complementary patterns seem to dominate. Arts and Kerwer show that the new standards for the risk management of banks are the result of a complex but relatively seamless process involving a small club of states, private entrepreneurs and state regulators. The standards adopted by the Basle Committee for Banking Supervision had been established by rating agencies, and their implementation and enforcement has been delegated to national banking regulators even if they are not members of the Basle banking club. Others found the endorsement of private standards by public authorities more controversial. Wüstemann and Kierzek lucidly elaborate on how the frustration about the failure to harmonize company law led European policy-makers to endorse privately set standards for accounting and reporting. They also recall, however, that the establishment of private authority has been the result of an initiative of the British government at the time the UK entered the European Economic Community.

Although in economic terms, the impact of forest certification is dwarfed by the impact reporting and disclosure standards have on business financing, Meidinger's discussion of certification programmes provides a further important insight into the significance of complementary strategies used by advocacy groups and government officials. Meidinger shows that activist-driven certification schemes benefit from governmental support which in turn benefit from the added societal legitimacy that certification programmes such as the Forest Stewardship Council can confer to national laws and international treaties – even if they are only mentioned in their bylaws. The importance of governmental support for private initiatives is confirmed by Pieth's illustration of the obstacles private initiatives against money-laundering and corruption face as long as their objectives are not endorsed by governments and international organizations.

But Meidinger's contribution is also intriguing because it challenges the notion of complementarity among different forms of legalization. However, rather than emphasizing the dynamics of contention that conditions the legalization of a specific issue area, Meidinger focuses on competitive forms of legalization. The notion of 'competitive regulation' substantiates legal pluralism by extending the analysis to capture constellations that are affected by multiple initiatives to advance legalization in order to govern or control the behaviour of different actors within an issue area. In the case of forest management, Meidinger identifies not only a series of industry-driven programmes, but also an attempt of the International Organization for Standardization to compete with the Forest Stewardship Council in order to determine how sustainable forest management is defined and implemented. Coleman and Reed identify similar patterns in the area of organic food certification, and highlight some of the methodological problems they pose for research on complex legalization: even though they are able to document the broad cooperation between public and private actors across different geographical areas, they struggle to assess the impact competition or cooperation have on individual standards or approaches to certification. Wüstemann and Kierzek fare batter in identifying the considerable consequences of 'competitive' legalization: caught in the struggle between the European Commission and the US Securities and Exchange Commission, companies listed at both European and US stock markets are faced with two different sets of accounting and disclosure standards.

Questions for further research

The notion of contentious or competitive legalization should encourage scholars to re-frame research on the politics of legalization. In fact, research focused on regulatory instruments risks conceiving legalization as an excessively or exclusively technical matter. Arts and Kerwer's choice to spotlight the key role of expertise – and leave interests in the dark – in order to explain the emergence and spread of particular standards rather than others is a case in point. In their view, the relative success of the Forest Stewardship Council's efforts to define criteria to guarantee sustainable forest management on the one hand, and the risk management criteria developed by rating agencies on the other hand, ultimately depends on the credibility the stakeholders assign to the experts that designed the standards.

While expertise and credibility no doubt matter, Meidinger's account of forest certification suggests that it does not determine the outcomes – at least not as long as there are clear and diverging interests favouring both the standards and arrangements most likely serve their cause. Similarly, Wüstemann and Kierzek show that cultural differences or different national regulatory philosophies do matter, but may well be trumped by the power (in this case: the influence and the material resources) of those that back different approaches to legalization. This is confirmed by Cohen, who reminds us that:

> In the process of legalization, power relationships and differentials are enacted through, and must be understood within, the contest over the norms and principles that inform institutions. . . . Legalization projects almost always combine considerations of power, interests, and normative vision; states and private interests must articulate their goals in terms of legal-normative projects, and legal norm entrepreneurs and advocacy networks must link their goals to the power and/or interest agendas of other actors.

The case of secured transactions is a good illustration: it shows that transnational legalization may have domestic roots. However, it also shows that the domestic roots per se do not matter much. What matters is that the domestic roots are in the US, i.e. in a country which occupies a dominant – if not hegemonic – position in the global financial markets. Quite tellingly, Cohen recalls that a successful reform of the US American Uniform Commercial Code served as a model for the 'transformation of the world of international commercial law-making' as an 'unanticipated effect' of the reform.

While this may well be the case in this context, it would be naive to underestimate the systemic impact US American interests have on complex legalization. There is considerable evidence that the model character of US American solutions in policy or regulatory transfers does not necessarily reflect their superior design or effectiveness. Rather, the spread of US 'endorsed' patterns of legalization benefits from the natural gravity of its huge domestic market and the clear political will of most parts of the US administration to extend its rules and institutions beyond that market. As Coleman and Reed show, this is exactly what happened in the certification of organic foodstuffs, when the US Department of Agriculture delegated the competence to control product and production standards compliance outside the US to 'foreign accredited certifying agents'. Needless to say, export of US American rules has been contested both within and outside the US, and only recently the former chairman of the Security and Exchange Commission described the Sarbanes–Oxley Act as an 'unhealthy export' and an 'embodiment of American geocentrism' (Pitt 2006). Yet, such exports do occur, suggesting that in certain circumstances, agency may be just as decisive in determining the success or spread of different approaches to legalization as the social or economic structures in which they are designed to operate. Also, it would be misleading to believe that the US administration is the only actor that matters for legalization. Taking into account structural constraints and diffuse interests, individual actors can and do play a significant role in framing, designing, implementing and monitoring the many moves to law that constitute complex legalization. Not surprisingly, their composition and their techniques vary. Cohen documents the importance of professional networks and coalitions that participate in the formulation of the principles and rules for secured transactions. They have a similar role in the case of accounting standards. However, Wüstemann and Kierzek show that accountants do not only define standards, but also advise decision-makers at the European Union. Yet, the cooperation among different actors is not always that smooth. Pieth illustrates some of the difficulties actors face in forming coalitions, and thereby highlights that, irrespective of the presumed odds, accident or coincidence does play an important role in deciding whether contentious coalitions emerge, and – we suspect – whether they succeed in diffusing specific legal or law-like arrangements.

A second incentive to reframe research on the politics of legalization is rooted in the tension between the globalization of specific legal and law-like arrangements and the harmonization of their domestic counterparts. Cohen shows that globalization must not be confused with harmonization. Competing interests attempt and often succeed in bending territorially bound arrangements to fit their needs. Thus, although the Canadian Personal Property Security Act and the model law of the European Bank of Reconstruction and Security incorporate key elements of the US American model, they were adapted and ultimately produced a new generation of competing models. The case of accounting standards shows other similarities. Although most market participants would benefit from a unique set of generally accepted accounting standards, Wüstemann and Kierzek notice that the persistence of specific national provisions, different practices of enforcement and variations among national regulatory approaches obstruct a harmonization at both the European and the international level.

The effects of a proliferation of competing legal or law-like arrangements become obvious if we look at the certification of organic food. In addition to the diffusion of national provisions in the international markets, by 1999 there were already two competing sets of global standards: a private standard set by the International Federation of Organic Agriculture Movement and the multilateral Codex Alimentarius. In an attempt to explain the dynamics behind the proliferation of competing standards, Meidinger emphasizes the importance of the time factor, arguing that 'creation of one certification scheme typically provokes the establishment of at least one other'. However, Meidinger also identifies the potential for convergence of NGO-driven, industry-supported and government-made certification programmes, arguing that in certain conditions, stakeholders expect to be able to achieve some of their objectives through the initiatives of their competitors. But even though such developments provide some room to establish coherent and complimentary arrangements, Meidinger cautions us against all-too-optimistic expectations about a generalized convergence of standards and approaches.

Which brings us back to methodological considerations: the question of coherence or convergence affects not only how legalization affects world politics. It is also a key problem in the study of the patterns, dynamics, institutions and structures that inform both complex legalization and transnational relations. Throughout the contributions to this volume, the unity of law is either questioned or challenged. Yet, the consequences of the loss of integrity, consistency and coherence of norms and rules in constellations in which competing legalities may govern the same or similar issues remains largely unexplored. At the same time, the empirical cases provide bits and pieces that may eventually help in explaining why complex legalization works – and when it does not. Coleman and Reed interpret equivalent technical regulations as a means to reconcile differences (see also Nicolaidis and Shaffer 2005). Meidinger's analysis suggests that communication tames excesses of competitive legalization. Cohen emphasizes the importance of the socialization of principles and rules within communities transgressing borders and promoting specific models.

The last significant question we believe would benefit from future research on complex legalization concerns its political desirability. Again, there is some information spread across the different contributions. There is Meidinger's reference to the way in which a private scheme adds societal acceptance and legitimacy to national and international provisions by explicitly referring to them or the – complementary – observation that governmental support can add legitimacy to private solutions. At a more basic level, Scherer and Baumann argue that profit-oriented private actors have an obligation, rather than an opportunity to engage in the development and spread of norms and rules in international and only partially legalized markets. However, Scherer and Baumann also remind us of the reluctance of mainstream economic scholarship to engage in normative discussion of the role and responsibility of firms. While most economists are quite happy to accept decentralized efforts to define and implement norms and rules expected to improve market efficiency, they shy from addressing the externalities of economic effectiveness and avoid questioning the legitimacy of the market-driven pluralization of legal orders.

To conclude, the contributions to this volume illustrate that the increase in international law-making, the variation among legalized regimes, and the differentiation of legal and law-like arrangements transforms international and transnational affairs. They show that legalization is complex and multi-layered and that it involves a wide range of actors that may cooperate or compete with each other. They provide ample evidence that complex legalization is one of the consequences (and possibly triggers) of the disaggregation of governance at the domestic level, that multiple moves to law reflect the multiplication of non-state actors in the international arena, and that the constitution of multiple legalities modifies the terms of engagement of non-state actors in transnational affairs, including changes in the interaction between governments, civil society and firms. Last but not least, they show that further research is needed to deepen our understanding of the political, social and economic conditions, causes and consequences of legalization.

References

Bank, R. and D. Lehmkuhl (2005) Law and Politics and Migration Research: On the Potential and Limits of Interdisciplinarity, *International Migration Research. Constructions, Omissions and the Promises of Interdisciplinarity*. M. Bommes and E. Morawska (eds) Aldershot: Ashgate, 155–178.

Black, J. (2001) Decentring Regulation: the Role of Regulation and Self-Regulation in a 'Post Regulatory' World, *Current Legal Problems*, 54: 103–146.

Bruce Hall, R. and T.J. Biersteker (eds) (2002) *The Emergence of Private Authority in Global Governance*. Cambridge: Cambridge University Press.

Cutler, A.C. and V. Haufler (eds) (1999) *Private Authority and International Affairs*. New York: State University of New York.

Djelic, M.-L. and K. Sahlin-Andersson (2006) *Transnational Governance in the Making – Regulatory Fields and their Dynamics*. Cambridge: Cambridge University Press.

Goldstein, J. and M. Kahler (eds) (2001) *Legalization and World Politics*. Cambridge, MA/London: The MIT Press.

Keohane, R.O. and J.S. Nye (2000) Globalization: What's New? What's Not? (And So What?), *Foreign Policy*, 104–119.

Kingsbury, B. and N. Kirsch (2005) The Emergence of Global Administrative Law, *Law and Contemporary Problems*, 68: 15–61.

Kirsch, N. and B. Kingsbury (2006) Introduction: Global Governance and Global Administrative Law in the International Legal Order, *The European Journal of International Law*, 17(1): 1–13.

Mattli, W. and T. Büthe (2005) Accountability in Accounting? The Politics of Private Rule-Making in the Public Interest, *Governance*, 18(3): 399–429.

Nicolaidis, K. and G. Shaffer (2005) Transnational Mutual Recognition Regimes: Governance without Global Government, *Law and Contemporary Problems*, 68(3–4): 263–318.

Parker, C., C. Scott, *et al.* (2004) *Regulating Law*. Oxford: Oxford University Press.

Pitt, H. (2006) Sarbanes-Oxley is an unhealthy export. *Financial Times*. London: 21 June, p. 17.

Reus-Smit, C. (ed.) (2004) *The Politics of International Law*. Cambridge: Cambridge University Press.

Rosenau, J.N. and E.-O. Czempiel (eds) (1992) *Governance without Government: Order and Change in World Politics*. Cambridge: Cambridge University Press.

de Sousa Santos, B. (1995) *Toward a New Common Sense. Law, Science and Politics in Paradigmatic Transition*. New York/ London: Routledge.

Sinclair, T.J. (2005) *The New Masters of Capital: American Bond Rating Agencies and the Politics of Creditworthiness*. Ithaca, NY/London: Cornell University Press.

Suh, D. (2002) Situating Liberalism In Transnational Legal Space, *Duke Journal of Comparative & International Law*, 12(1): 605–630.

Index

For Product Safety Concerns and Information please contact our EU
representative GPSR@taylorandfrancis.com
Taylor & Francis Verlag GmbH, Kaufingerstraße 24, 80331 München, Germany

www.ingramcontent.com/pod-product-compliance
Lightning Source LLC
Chambersburg PA
CBHW072121270326
41931CB00010B/1628

* 9 7 8 0 4 1 5 5 9 9 6 8 9 *